cut here

Test Your Own Potential

On a scale of one to ten (ten being highest), evaluate your strengths and weaknesses regarding these entrepreneurial characteristics.

Characteristic	Score
Capacity for work	_____
Goal-oriented	_____
A self-starter	_____
Good judgment	_____
Self-confidence	_____
Honesty	_____
Persistence	_____
A problem-solver	_____
Ability to take a risk	_____
People-oriented	_____
Profit-oriented	_____
Flexibility and adaptability	_____
Accountability	_____
Desire to win	_____
Innovative	_____
Total	_____

The value of this rating depends on the answer you have to one characteristic: honesty. If you haven't been totally honest with yourself in evaluating these factors, you should adjust the results accordingly. It is wiser to evaluate yourself too low than too high.

- ➤ If your score was between 120 and 150, you have a strong entrepreneurial personality and will probably do very well as the boss of a new business.
- ➤ If you scored between 100 and 120, you probably have enough of the right stuff to be successful if you make the effort to bolster your skills in the weaker areas.
- ➤ If you scored between 80 and 100, you probably shouldn't try to shoulder a new business on your own. Look for partners or reliable employees who can strengthen the firm in the areas where you are weak.
- ➤ If you scored less than 80, you'll be happier and more successful as a manager in someone else's company than in a business of your own.

Reprinted with permission of the author, Roger Fritz, from his book Nobody Gets Rich Working for Somebody Else: An Entrepreneur's Guide. *Dr. Fritz is president of Organization Development Consultants in Naperville, Illinois.*

alpha books

Business Plan Outline

Executive Summary

Write this section last, so you can give a good 1–2 page overview of the plan as a whole.

Industry Analysis

Assume the banker or investor reading this plan knows nothing about your industry and try to give him a mini-education in this section: what the opportunities are, what's going on in the market, who the big players are, and how they have succeeded.

Market Analysis

After giving a macro view of your industry, talk specifically about what's happening in your geographic market: what the opportunities are, who the competition is, how you can differentiate yourself from them, and how you will succeed, given market demands and trends.

Business Description

Describe your business: how long it has been in operation, what the legal structure is, who the owners are, what your short-term and long-term goals are, and why you need money now—is it for expansion, marketing, equipment purchase, or debt reduction?

Competitive Advantage

In order to convince potential investors to put money in your business, you need to clearly explain how your business is better than the competition and why it will succeed.

Marketing Plan

Explain who your current customers are, who you would like to have as customers, why they would be interested in buying from you, what your pricing strategy is, how you distribute your product, and how you promote your business.

Organization

After describing how your business operates, describe who is responsible for making it work. Write a brief paragraph about each of your top managers, detailing their expertise and background. Convince the investors that these are the people most capable of making your business a success. Include an organization chart and describe your plans for adding or subtracting staff members.

Operations

This section is most important in manufacturing operations, which have many different pieces of equipment and operational processes that need to be described. For service businesses, describe how your business is being run, what the departments are within the business, and how you will be able to expand (by hiring, buying equipment, moving to a new location, outsourcing production, and so on).

Funding Needs

Explain the total amount of money needed, how it will be used (such as for marketing materials, working capital, hiring, equipment purchase), and why that is the right way to spend it.

Financial Statements

This is where you place the past three years' balance sheets and income statements. In addition, include five years of projections: balance sheets, income statements, and a five-year cash flow with monthly projections for the first three years and quarterly projections thereafter.

Appendix

This section should be used for important reference information that needs not appear in the body of the plan. For instance, include a summary of a recent contract you won, a map of planned sites, résumés of key managers, or marketing literature.

The COMPLETE IDIOT'S GUIDE TO Starting Your Own Business

by Ed Paulson

with Marcia Layton

alpha books

A Division of Macmillan Publishing
A Simon & Schuster Macmillan Company
1633 Broadway, New York, NY 10023

To my parents, John and Jean Paulson, for their continued support of me and my writing.

International Standard Book Number: 1-56761-529-5

Library of Congress Catalog Card Number: 94-72723

97 8 7 6 5 4

Interpretation of the printing code: the rightmost number of the first series of numbers is the year of the book's printing; the rightmost number of the second series of numbers is the number of the book's printing. For example, a printing code of 95-1 shows that the first printing of the book occurred in 1995.

Screen reproductions in this book were created by means of the program Collage Complete from Inner Media, Inc., Hollis, NH.

Printed in the United States of America

Publisher
Alan Oakes

Vice President and Publisher
Theresa H. Murtha

Editorial Services Director
Elizabeth Keaffaber

Publishing Manager
Lisa Bucki

Managing Editor
Michael Cunningham

Development Editor
Melanie Palaisa

Technical Editor
William H. Black

Production Editor
Mark Enochs

Copy Editor
San Dee Phillips

Cover Designer
Karen Ruggles

Designer
Kim Scott

Illustrations
Judd Winick

Indexer
Kathy Venable

Production Team
Angela D. Bannan, Anne Dickerson,
Amy Gornik, Dennis Clay Hager,
Daryl Kessler, Bob LaRoche,
Bobbi Satterfield, Kris Simmons,
Michael Thomas, Tina Trettin
Scott Tullis, Jody York

Contents at a Glance

Contents

Foreword

Twenty thousand businesses were started this week! Like you, most of these new entrepreneurs who started these businesses possess the lifelong dream of being their own boss. Like you, they believe they have a great idea for a product or service that is desperately needed in the marketplace. Like you, they don't have an extensive or sophisticated business background. And, like you, they are both thrilled and terrified about the possibilities.

Most of these businesses will never make the headlines, but in a basement home office, the next Liz Claiborne and her team are designing clothing we will all want to wear. In some garage, the next Steve Jobs and Steve Wozniak are building the Apple Computer of the future. In an airport bar, the next Ray Kroc is closing a deal to expand a little-known restaurant concept, like McDonald's, worldwide. And, around the kitchen table, the next Anita and Gordon Roddick are not only creating new products but also developing innovative business practices, as in the Body Shop. If you read about the early days of these now well-known companies, you'll be surprised to discover that the people behind each of these companies got their start just like many of you. So much for the myth of the entrepreneurial genius. You don't have to be a superstar to become a successful entrepreneur. However, you *do* have to be dedicated, focused, and willing to learn.

The Complete Idiot's Guide to Starting Your Own Business is a practical, informative how-to guide for anyone who is thinking about getting into business for themselves. Ed Paulson and Marcia Layton speak from their experience as entrepreneurs and as consultants to entrepreneurial firms. They demystify the entrepreneurial process with their systematic description of the critical elements of business development and business planning. If you follow their advice, you will be able to overcome or avoid some of the typical obstacles encountered by first-time entrepreneurs.

This is not a textbook. As an advisor to hundreds of owner/managers and senior executives of small- and mid-sized, rapidly growing firms, I know that the personal stories and vignettes in this book describe the common problems new business owners face. Most textbooks won't talk honestly about the harsh toll that a new business has on the entrepreneur's personal life and family; this book does. And, who would expect that a founder with too many new ideas would become a management problem? You'll learn why here. Most gurus won't caution you about the hazards of success. Ed Paulson and Marcia Layton understand the psyche of the would-be entrepreneur and the roller coaster ride of starting a new business. Their insights about the quirks of human nature and their suggestions for modifying your behavior can make or break your business.

Although this book offers a personalized approach, don't think that it's short on substance. If you take this book seriously, you will work hard, you will ask yourself tough questions, and you should be surprised by your answers. The exercises, tables, and charts are easy to understand and apply to your own situation. Business novices will get a crash course in the basic language of business. The simple analytical tools like break-even and cash flow analysis will help you evaluate your business idea to determine if it is a good investment of your time, energy, reputation, and money. Your customers, suppliers, investors, and employees will expect you to have this information. If you don't do your homework, your competitors will. If you do your homework, you can't avoid the fears, but you can prevent some nightmares.

As I read this book, I was reminded of some of the pointers I include in my presentations to business executives and classroom lectures to graduate MBA students:

- Forget the myth of the Genius Entrepreneur. Entrepreneurship can be learned.
- Be sure that starting your own business is the right thing to do at this time.
- Build a business with forgiving gross margins to cover the tuition for the lessons you will learn and the mistakes that you will make along the way.
- If you think you have a good idea, ask someone to pay for it! Without customers and sales, you have no business.
- You can't stay in business if you don't manage cash.
- Love your competitors. They are one of your best sources of Research & Development.
- Find good advisors and listen to them.
- Be sure to start a 1990s business. With computers, software, fax machines, e-mail, and online services, a small business can have the capabilities and resources of a much larger organization.

The Complete Idiot's Guide to Starting Your Own Business will help you get your business off the ground. If you are thinking about starting your own buiness, remember that there are millions of people who share your dream and countless others who are willing to be of assistance. You are not alone. Indeed, you are part of a national and international trend. Given the current era of corporate downsizing, outsourcing, and vast workplace change, launching an entrepreneurial venture has become a viable career alternative. And, it is important to remember the advice of Thomas Edison, an habitual entrepreneur who started five businesses in addition to his countless inventions, "Genius is 1 percent inspiration and 99 percent perspiration."

Jennifer A. Starr
President, UptoData Group
Hollis, New Hampshire

Jennifer A. Starr has more than 15 years' experience in consulting, teaching, and research in new business development. Her consulting firm specializes in growth strategies for small- and mid-sized, rapidly growing, owner-managed firms, including two INC500 companies. Among other courses, she has taught Entrepreneurship and New Ventures and Managing Growing Businesses; she has taught at the Wharton School (from which she earned a Ph.D.), Babson College, and Boston University, among others. She has published articles on new venture management and has been cited in the business press, including the *Wall St. Journal, Financial Times, Inc. Magazine,* and others.

Introduction

You have an idea. You have a vision. You are willing to put your butt on the line to make it happen. Your family is starting to wonder if you have a chemical imbalance in your brain and the word is out that zeal has entered your life. OK, but you don't know where to begin and feel like a complete idiot.

Here you are taking your personal time to cruise the bookstore looking for a guide to the business creation process. The publisher and I think that people in your situation present an excellent business opportunity, which is why this book now exists.

Starting your own business is a lot more complicated than any of us initially realize. It helps to know that you are not alone in your thoughts, desires, fears, and ecstasy. This book is written with the intention of guiding you through the pitfalls and sharing in your successes. Great pains were taken to distill the "mumbo-jumbo" of business down to the basic ingredients that everyone can understand. No critical information was left out.

In this book, I start with you and your motivations. You are the key ingredient in any successful startup, scary as that may sound. You are your most valuable asset. Who else will work evenings, weekends, and holidays for free? The more you know about you and your motivations, the more likely you are to create a successful business venture.

I have been part of several startup companies, including a few of my own. There is nothing more exciting than seeing your idea become a thriving reality… and there are few things more painful than letting it die. Lots of real-world lessons have been learned along the way. You don't have to go through a windshield to learn to wear a seatbelt. I've already been through several of these business "windshields" and hope to pass on the thoughts and ideas that will be your seatbelt. Take them to heart and apply them where appropriate to your situation.

In short, this book will not only lead you through the business plan creation process, but it will also be your mentor as your business comes to life. You will probably keep this book in your desk, near the throne, or on a nightstand as a cure for insomnia.

Creation is a uniquely human trait and is not limited to the fine arts. I had an artist in one of my seminars apologize for her narrow-minded view of business. She thought of art as creative, and business as very uncreative. After the seminar, she realized that a new business creates job opportunities that didn't exist. It creates new products and services that perform useful functions. It fulfills dreams for those involved in its success, and each business is a unique reflection of the owner, just like fine art.

You are on the verge of a wonderful roller coaster ride where you decide the direction of the track and the speed of the cart. Use this book to pick the optimal track layout, and then apply our management philosophy to successfully steer the cart.

I want you to be successful in your new venture. It breaks my heart to talk with entrepreneurs who took the risk, put it all on the line, and lost. If I can talk you out of starting your company in a few chapters, then you really didn't want it badly enough. If you get through the first few chapters and still want to be a business owner, then finish the rest of the book and make your business idea happen! You clearly have strong entrepreneurial tendencies.

If you knew everything that would happen in the future, you probably wouldn't do anything. You will certainly feel more of yourself come to life as your idea unfolds, and if you are *really* lucky, you will never have to worry about financial freedom again. It will be yours in abundance and well deserved. Is that wonderful, or what? All of a sudden, you don't feel like such an idiot, do you?

From one idiot to another, it is a privilege to be invited along with you on your ride. Bon voyage!

How to Use This Book

The book is divided into several parts. The sequence is designed to lead you through the business plan creation and startup management process.

Part 1: Starting with You and the Business Plan asks you to take a hard look at you, your motivations, and personal situation. Are you ready to pay the price needed to get your business up and running? Is your family ready? If the answer is still yes, then get into the big and small picture of things by comparing short-term gains with long-term wins. Finally, a business plan is outlined with references to a sample business plan included in the Appendix.

After finishing Part 1, you will either believe that starting your business is the right thing to do or will realize that you aren't ready yet. Either way is fine, but you will know what awaits you if you decide to take the plunge. You'll also understand the basic components of the business plan. The chapters in this part provide the details needed for completing the business plan sections.

Part 2: Establishing the Framework of the Business presents the legal aspects of business formation. This part introduces various legal business forms with special emphasis on corporations. It's kind of dry, but critically important. Take the time to read this part since it truly lays the foundation upon which everything else is built.

Part 3: Making Marketing and Sales Work for You talks about pricing, advertising, competition, and sales. These three chapters are a lot of fun and a welcome relief from the legal stuff in Part 2. Anyone who is thinking of giving you money will study the information you develop from these three chapters. Living here for awhile is time well spent. Wear shorts. This topic area can be pretty hot!

Part 4: Dealing with the Financial Aspects, or delving into the structured mind of the accountant, presents the essence of financial management. These chapters introduce accounting and financial terminology in an understandable way (a really tough thing to do… trust me!) while making you credible in your presentation to bankers and other financial people. These chapters deal with banks, cash flow management, credit card sales, credit-oriented transactions, and avoiding payment delinquency with your clients.

Part 5: Additional Topics of Importance covers stuff you will need when you are really up and running. When you add people to the organization, all kinds of things change. Reading these chapters will prepare you for the major crisis points. Reading Part 5 today may seem a little premature, but not really. The problems covered are those that any successful business encounters. In short, you want to have these problems, or you are probably not as successful as you would like. Read Part 5 today and create the vision of your business running at a level where this information is applicable. For sure, read chapters 15 and 16 before hiring employees.

The Appendix contains a complete business plan that I wrote but never used because it didn't meet my personal objectives. It is a real plan that some of you may choose to try. Go ahead! It would be great to see it making someone money. It just wasn't for me. Most importantly, it presents you with a concrete starting point for your plan.

Some Extras to Get You Through

To help guide you through the minefields of starting your own business, this book also provides some additional tips and bits of information from those who have been there. You'll find words of wisdom, cautions, and helpful tips in these boxes:

This box gives you some perspective from business people who have gone through the same painful decision-making process you're going through now.

This box adds interesting information, shortcuts, and helpful advice.

This box provides warnings to let you know about pitfalls along the way.

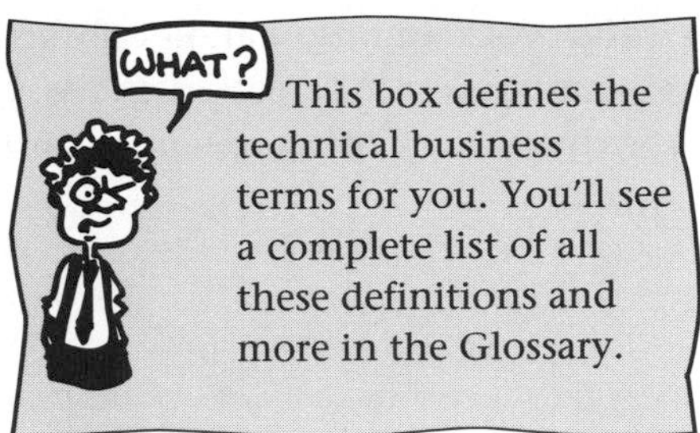

Acknowledgments

There are numerous people to acknowledge and thank for their contributions to this book. Here is a partial listing of people who provided vision, commitment, inspiration, talent, and information that made this book more than it would have been.

Thank you, Marie Butler-Knight, for the business commitment to extend the series to noncomputer topics. Thank you, Tom Godfrey, for your continued product vision, prodding, and support. Thank you, Marcia Layton, for enhancing my original manuscript. Thank you to Melanie Palaisa, the tech editors, and the other members of the production staff for adding the final touches that make this product special.

There is a lifetime of experience and thank-yous that go out to everyone whom I have worked with over the years. Here are several people who contributed to this work in specific ways: Frank Warner for being the incurable entrepreneur that he is; Dick Holmes (alias "Wilson") for general business; Raymond Luckie for accounting; Dave Stanfield for marketing and sales; Jeff Fuller for a banker's perspective; Gerry Tucker for legal; Mark Fern for sports retail; and Jeannie Letteff for restaurant retail. War stories were provided by Jim Cameron, Bill Cartmill, Dave Kalstrom, Jeff Kolling, Jim Herlinger, Ted Keane, and Dr. An Wang.

How-to-do, and not-do, insight was provided by various people from GenRad, Plantronics, Seagate, NuTech Testing Services, DAVID Systems (DSI ExpressNet), Telenova, IBM, Wang Laboratories, AT&T, and others. If you are not mentioned here, please accept my apologies along with a thank-you for the contribution you know that you made.

My sincere personal appreciation is given to Ruth Rinehart for running things while I wrote, Loree Plourde for nonstop support, Jan Gillespie for initial insights, Dan McManus for being an idea sounding board, my brother John Paulson for his continued interest, and Kathy Wright for being "the warden" who kept me on schedule.

A final thank you goes to you, the reader. Without your ambition and desire to excel, books like this would not be needed. I salute your passion for creation and your desire for something better. You keep me in touch with my own entrepreneurial spirit, and I hope this book returns some of that enthusiasm to you.

Author Biographies

Ed Paulson

Ed Paulson is the Executive Director of Applied Concepts, an Austin, Texas-based technology training and consulting company. He is the author of numerous software training books, a telecommunications textbook titled *The Complete Communications Handbook*, and numerous technological/business-related articles.

Mr. Paulson is a registered Texas professional engineer. He holds an M.B.A. from the University of Texas at Austin's executive program along with graduate degrees in engineering from the University of Illinois. He has taught at the university level for both St. Edward's University and the University of Dallas Graduate School of Management. He is also a frequent lecturer at Austin Community College and guest speaker on both business- and technology-related topics.

His professional background includes working with, for, and sometimes against such notable companies as IBM, Wang Laboratories, Seagate Technology, Plantronics and DSI ExpressNet (formerly DAVID Systems). He was nominated for 1994 Austin Entrepreneur of the Year and is included in the 1993 *Worldwide Who's Who Platinum Edition*.

He is also the founder of New Venture, a now defunct startup company, that created the 1993 introduction of the Snit McPherson's Original Punk Rock product. That's right: a rock with a mohawk haircut, wrap around sunglasses, and a discipline manual. It may be hard to believe, but he sold 25,000 of them in the U.S., Canada, and the Far East. At one time, he had 14 people making "rocks," received national coverage of the product from NBC News and ABC News, and had special write-ups in *Seventeen*, the *LA Times*, and the *Boston Globe*. It just goes to prove that complete idiots come in all shapes and sizes.

He can be reached at Technology and Communications, Inc., 7701 North Lamar Blvd., Suite 501, Austin, Texas, 78752, (512) 458-9700/458-9794 (fax), CompuServe 74201,2664.

Marcia Layton

Marcia Layton, president of Layton & Co., has several years of experience in helping companies get started and grow. Through her business planning and marketing consulting firm, Layton & Co., Layton works with small and mid-sized clients worldwide. She is currently an assistant system operator in CompuServe's Entrepreneur Forum where she answers questions and provides advice on the business start-up process.

Formerly a Marketing Communications Director at Eastman Kodak Company, Ms. Layton worked with several of the Kodak venture firms, Image Acquisition Products Division, and the Office Imaging division. Her most recent projects included creating and managing a new corporate magazine for Kodak, as well as establishing a communications research function to support the department.

Before Kodak, Ms. Layton was associated with the University Consulting Group, acting as the Vice President of Administration and Project Manager for this Ann Arbor-based management consulting firm. Her responsibilities there included preparing business plans for smaller businesses in the Ann Arbor and Detroit areas.

Active in several Rochester-area and national organizations, Ms. Layton is on the Board of Directors of the National Association of Women Business Owners and is a member of the Small Business Council, the National Association for Female Executives, the Rochester Ad Council, the Rochester Women's Network, and the American Woman's Economic Development Corp.

Ms. Layton was a featured speaker on the topic of starting your own business at the 1993 Entrepreneur Expo in New York, which was sponsored by *Entrepreneur Magazine*. She has also delivered seminars on marketing and public relations to the American Women's Economic Development Corporation and locally at the Arts for Greater Rochester Media Workshop.

Ms. Layton received an M.B.A. from the University of Michigan Business School and a B.A. with Honors in Sociology from Wellesley College. Ms. Layton can be reached at Layton & Co., 304 Newbury Street, Suite 338, Boston, MA, 02115 or on CompuServe at 71045,2627.

Trademarks

Part 1
Starting with You and the Business Plan

So you think you can be a successful entrepreneur? Well, you can. Yes, you read that right, I'm agreeing with you. You can be successful at starting your own business if you take the time upfront to do some very important things.

One of those things is choosing the right kind of business to start. Each of us has different skills, interests, and abilities. To give yourself a fighting chance, you need to do some honest self-analysis to determine what kind of business would be best for you. Once you know what kind of business you'd like to start, you need to figure out whether you can make money in this business of yours. You also need to create a plan for starting and running it.

Sounds like a lot of stuff to do, doesn't it? Well, don't worry, this first section is going to help you with all of it.

Chapter 1

So, Why Go into Business in the First Place?

In This Chapter

- Why start your own business?
- A look at your personal goals
- A look at your financial goals
- Your family and spiritual motivations

Bill and his friend were walking through a mall doing some last minute Christmas shopping. In one store, on the second shelf in the back, Bill saw the dual-pronged, slotted trammel-widget-thingy that he had drawn on a bar napkin at a company party three years ago. Everyone had agreed that it was a great idea and that Bill should "make it happen."

"I had that idea years ago," said Bill. "I can't believe that somebody is going to make a fortune from my idea. I'll never forgive myself if this thing turns out to make him a million dollars. I should sue him for stealing my idea."

"Why didn't you pursue the idea back when you had it?" asked his friend supportively, but knowing that he was on dangerous ground.

"I had just gotten married and had just received my promotion at work. There was just so much going on back then that I never took the time to make it happen. I still have the napkin in my desk drawer at work. Now look at this. Someone is going to make a fortune off my *idea. This will never happen to me again. The next idea I have, I am going to make it happen. After all, I am in my forties. If not now, then when?"*

Have you had this experience? Did it suggest to you that you should rush into self-employment as quickly as possible before missing out on other opportunities?

While many people have done just that—rushed into entrepreneurship—I hope that perhaps you'll put off that decision for a short while, until after you've done an analysis of your own situation and goals to determine whether that's really the smartest move. Maybe now is the time for you… or maybe not. Hold off from making any quick decisions one way or another for a few more pages. Okay, if you can't wait until after you read this book, at least wait until after Chapter 3.

Journeys always start at the beginning, which is why we start our discussion with you: your interests, your motivations, and your goals. You must understand your own motivations first in order to decide whether starting your own business will bring you happiness or grief. Believe it or not, not everyone is meant to be an entrepreneur. There are plenty of people who prefer working for someone else.

Next, looking at your skills and experience will help you choose what kind of business you should start. And finally, taking into consideration what people want and need will help you decide what kind of business can make money. (I'm making a big assumption here that you *do* want to make lots of money.)

You'll quickly learn that it's extremely easy to start a business. All you have to do is fill out some forms and you're set. However, starting a business that makes money is much more difficult, and you will need help to make decisions that will be both fulfilling and profitable.

Masochism or Passion: Investigate Your Motivations

Just as there is a thin line between love and hate, there is a thin line between masochism and tenacity. If you're having trouble distinguishing between the two, you may want to have a chat with your therapist.

The following sections discuss several of the common situations that lead people to start their own businesses. Think about whether any are similar to your own situation. If you're in the game for the right reasons, you will have one of the most exciting rides of your life. If you are in it for the wrong reasons, you will probably not succeed, and even if you do succeed, it will probably be a hollow victory. Brutal honesty with yourself is the key here as you decide whether this is really for you. Only you know when you are being honest with yourself, and nobody has more to gain from your honesty at this stage than you.

Situational factors such as the amount of money you have, the contacts that you've made, and your expertise in a particular industry are all important to success. But their importance dwarfs in comparison to the burning desire that you *must* have to make your business venture succeed. You can always make changes to your business once you start it, but you can't buy burning desire. It has to be there from the start. Otherwise, you're at a severe disadvantage.

> **Brutal honesty**
> Saying all of those things to yourself that you would hate someone else to say to you. You will thank yourself later for the candor.
>
> WHAT?

If you're considering starting a business because you've had difficulty finding a full-time job that interests you or meets your financial goals, DON'T. Starting a business is not the same thing as creating a job for yourself. Starting a business means that you're ready to give up that regular paycheck, benefits, regular working hours, bureaucracy, clueless co-workers, and policies that make no sense. But I digress....

A business is much more than a job; it's a serious commitment to your customers who will rely on you and to your employees who depend on you to provide their pay-checks. Your success or failure doesn't just affect you and your family; many others will feel it too.

If you're currently employed and thinking about quitting to start a business, don't give up the stability of your day job until you feel confident you'll be able to replace that income in the near future. Starting a business while you're still employed is an excellent way to "test the waters." Once you jump in, you have to be ready to work hard to keep your head above water. Be sure you have the interest and the stamina.

Personal Motivations and Goals

Running your own small business is tougher work than anything you have tried before, but it also offers rewards that are generally greater than your current employer can give you. Here is a partial list of common reasons why people decide to start their own businesses:

- **Creativity** I have a great idea for a new product (or for a new service) that no one is currently offering.
- **Competition** I can do what my current company does but for less money.
- **Control** I want to be my own boss and make my own decisions for the company.

- **Flexibility** I want a schedule that allows me to spend time with my kids and work when I want to.
- **Finances** I'm not paid what I'm worth in my current job, but if I worked on my own, I'd make more money.

Are these valid motivations? Yes. We each have reasons we do things to fulfill our own needs. It is often as simple as, "This is just something that I have to do."

The need to exercise your own judgment, take your own risks, and create something from nothing can be profound. You may want financial independence to provide the freedom to do things with your life that you couldn't do otherwise. You may have an idea that nobody at work supports or thinks is a good idea. If you believe in the idea strongly enough, you have to try it yourself or you will always wonder how it would have turned out.

When I decided that I wanted to write business plans for smaller companies in need of financing, I spent some time talking with local business people to see what they thought of the idea. No one liked it. They all had reasons why I wouldn't succeed, such as, "Entrepreneurs don't have money to spend on a business plan," or "They can do it themselves by reading a book; why would they hire you?" and on and on.

The more people I asked, the more I heard about the lack of business available, but I disagreed with them and went ahead by starting the business. They were wrong, or at least, they've been wrong so far. The business is growing at a double-digit pace with more clients signing on each week. The lesson in this is: If you are convinced your idea will work, you may be right even if no one else agrees.

Be clear that while you may not report to a supervisor, you will still be working for someone else: your clients and customers. But you will also be working to achieve your own dreams, not your employer's. You provide the energy, vision, and sustenance that keeps the dream alive and strong. You also need determination and dedication to keep going when the going gets tough.

I started my business ventures simply because the thought of continuing to work for someone else looked a lot like going to prison. I needed to exercise my creative and technical sides in ways that were just not possible in the professional positions I held. I possessed all the classic symptoms of an entrepreneur. I had to do something about it!

Entrepreneurs are a strange breed. They will give up almost anything to have the right to make their own choices, decisions, opportunities, and mistakes—even when they know that many of those choices and decisions may turn out to be bad ones. Hey, at least they had the power to make them!

Entrepreneur An individual who starts and runs his or her own business, rather than remain an employee of someone else's company.

When an entrepreneur starts to talk seriously about getting a job working for someone else, things must be pretty bad. All business owners fantasize about giving up the administrative hassles of running a business at some point or another—I'll even admit to fantasizing about a mindless job ringing up food at the grocery store every once in awhile—but the ones committed to reaching their goals don't throw in the towel so easily. What often happens at those low points is that entrepreneurs come up with a really creative solution that helps turn things around.

A few years ago when things were on a downturn with my business, I was talking with a fellow entrepreneur. She asked, "How are things going?" I replied, "They are pretty bad right now, and I think some radical changes are due." She thought for a moment and asked, "Are you thinking of getting a job?" I smiled and said, "No," to which she replied, "Then things aren't that bad."

If you don't feel that level of passion about your venture, then you should re-evaluate your plans to become a business owner. If you have doubts about your motivations, then this is probably not your time to take the plunge. Wait until the need to work on your own becomes unbearable; then you know you're ready for entrepreneurship.

Financial Motivations and Goals

How much money do you *want* to make, and how much money do you *need* to make? Understand that these two dollar amounts are not the same. I've never met anyone who made as much money as they wanted, but most people make as much money as they need.

Wealth is a relative term. If you make $100,000 per year and spend $110,000, you are living beyond your means and are poor. If you make $65,000 and spend $50,000, then you're saving or investing $15,000 a year. In short, calculate how much money you need to earn to cover all your living expenses. Don't forget to account for federal taxes, state taxes, and other additional expenses such as health insurance, life insurance, tuition assistance programs, and such. You have to make at least this amount of money or one of three things must happen:

Wealth
Consistently having money left over after you pay all your bills.

1. You must decrease your expenses.
2. Figure out a way to make more money from your venture.
3. Stay with your current job until your finances are in order.

Look at your finances both on a short-term (12 months) and long-term (2–5 years) basis. You first need to get through the short term to make it to the long term. If you do not have the money to support yourself for at least 12 months (and some people think 18–24 months), then you should hold off starting your venture until you have the needed savings. Or you can look for outside sources to provide the money you need, such as family members, friends, or banks and government agencies. You need to be able to support yourself during those initial lean months when your business probably will not be making enough to pay your rent or your mortgage. So start saving those pennies now.

Most people dream of running their own businesses because they believe that it is the only way they'll become wealthy. For some, this is true. Most of the extremely wealthy members of our society obtained their money by owning a business, either one they started or were given. In many cases, they saw an opportunity to introduce a new product or service to the market and jumped in quickly. Some have succeeded and made millions, even billions. How about Bill Gates of Microsoft, Debbie Fields of Mrs. Fields' cookies, or even Henry Ford?

Not everyone who starts a business becomes wealthy. Statistics show that only 20 percent of all new businesses will be around in five years. Generally, when a business fails, the owner doesn't make a lot of money on the deal. The average business owner makes somewhere around $30,000–40,000 a year in salary. That may not sound bad to some of you, but just keep in mind the number of hours entrepreneurs have to put in to make that money. It's hard work!

Of course, as you're starting your business, aim high. Set financial goals beyond what you are making now, but also set limits for the amount of money you will invest in the business and the length of time you will go without taking a salary. If you reach that point and still can't afford to pay yourself a reasonable wage, it's time to decide whether this particular business is right for you.

Family Motivations and Goals

If you are the type of person who cannot leave your family alone for the evening or weekend without intense feelings of guilt, then you should examine your intentions and your family's needs before you begin a new business venture. Your family needs to support you in your venture, or they might undermine your success. There will be times when you will need to work at night, on weekends, and on holidays. At these times, you will have to choose between family involvement and business commitments. Your family needs to accept your commitment to your business without being hurt or mad.

Communicate openly with your spouse, children, parents, or friends about what you want to do and what kind of a time and energy commitment it will take. It is a good idea to prepare them in advance for some of the sacrifices that you and they may have to make. And make sure they're willing to make those sacrifices!

If you sense from initial discussions that your family may resent your directing attention away from them and toward a business, think about ways that you can involve them in the company. Instead of thinking that you have to choose between business and family, talk with them about what you can all do together to run a business.

I recently saw a friend who has a company that makes metal stamps. He travels around the country selling the copper stamps used for imprinting on wax or a conventional ink stamp pad. It was the Christmas rush, and he had been working a steady 7 a.m. to 11 p.m. day since before Thanksgiving. In fact, his final sale day was Christmas Eve at 11 p.m. His wife was attending the craft shows with him, and the children often came along for the ride. His father had even come over from England to work in the shop making the stamps. In short, the entire family was pulling for the success of the business. He looked vibrant, healthy, and happy. So did his wife.

Imagine how different this scenario would be if the family waited at home grumbling about how their Christmas was being disrupted by dad's obsession. Many divorces have resulted from the feeling that the business is more important than everything else in the business owner's life. Be sure your family knows that this is not the case. Typically, just telling them won't do it; you have to show them by setting aside time to be with them.

Spend the time to get your family involved from the beginning. Set their expectations properly to best avoid having recurring, ugly scenes later. The family can become a source of strength if they understand the importance of their support in your and the business's success. Nobody is an island, and you may end up alone on your island if you don't handle the family situation with respect.

What Are Your Spiritual Goals?

Spirituality has more to do with what makes us feel good as human beings than with formal religion. For some of us, a business helps us achieve spiritual goals through the belief that providing a valued service to our clients improves their lives at some level. Spiritual goals can also be reached by creating an organization to perform social service work such as a food kitchen or a halfway house. Some entrepreneurs want to create an organization where their employees can experience an environment in which they can realize their full potential.

One of my clients is determined to start her own business, but not for any of the reasons we've discussed so far. She has enough money to support herself and has started businesses before, but she now wants to start one to bring new attention to the plight of people in recovery for alcohol or substance abuse. Her feeling is that by creating products to better meet the needs of this population, she can draw attention to them and help support them, donating the bulk of the profits to related charities and human service agencies. Like many other entrepreneurs, she is dedicated to her business idea; she just happens to be doing it for spiritual reasons.

If you are someone who believes making money is bad, then there is a strong chance you won't make any and your business will fail. If you believe that computer automation is the root of all evil, then you should probably avoid becoming a personal computer dealer. However, if you believe that training people is the most important way to contribute to the quality of their lives, then starting a training business would be a viable option.

In essence, don't neglect the nonbusiness side of your soul when deciding to start your own business.

What Is Your Ultimate Motivation?

Ultimately, it all comes down to you. What do you want and why do you want it? Do you think that running your own business will give you the fulfillment that's been missing in your current job? Are you willing to earn less money for awhile as you try to establish your company? How far are you willing to go to make your business work?

If you feel that you were born to be an entrepreneur and are willing to do just about anything to succeed, you have the energy and the drive typical of entrepreneurs. However, if you like the stability of working 9–5, wake up! Owning your own business means that you don't have set hours because you'll be working close to 24 hours a day to get things going. If this paragraph alone is enough to talk you out of pursuing your own business, then send me a thank-you card. You are not ready yet to make that kind of commitment. It doesn't mean that you never will, just that right now is not your time.

The Least You Need to Know

If, after reading this chapter, you feel that starting your own business is still the right thing to do, then congratulations! I am privileged to be your tour guide through this maze of business planning, legal structuring, and daily management. I hope my insights keep you from bloodying your nose in the same places I did, and I look forward to hearing about your successes.

- ➤ Understanding your personal goals before you go into the venture is critical to later success.
- ➤ Setting a limit on your losses and time investment is a valuable step going into the venture.
- ➤ Getting your family's support and acceptance for starting a business is a necessary step, or you may find yourself choosing between the two.

Chapter 2

What Kind of Business Should I Start?

In This Chapter

- Consider what you like to do
- Assess what you are good at
- Where are the opportunities?
- Can you make money?

Have you always wanted to own your own business? There are many people who have had the urge to be on their own since young adulthood. Often this is due to their upbringing; mom or dad may have been self-employed, serving as entrepreneurial role models. Some of the most successful entrepreneurs started their first business before age 30. Of course, that doesn't mean that the first business did well, just that they started trying to make a go of it early in life. Successful entrepreneurs often start and fail at several businesses before hitting on the one that makes them millionaires.

If you're past the age of 30, don't worry. The extra experience you've gained by working several years in your profession may make you more qualified to start your own business than some young whippersnapper. Perhaps you've realized that your job or your career just isn't satisfying anymore and you want to start fresh with a new idea. Or maybe you've thought of a revolutionary product idea you want to introduce to the market.

All of these are valid reasons to start your own business. Now you just have to figure out what kind of business is best for you. There are literally thousands, maybe even millions, of different types of businesses you could start. Just skim through a magazine, such as *Entrepreneur, Business Start-Ups*, or *Home Office Computing*, to see the range of business ideas that are out there.

You'll find familiar types of businesses, such as franchises for fast-food restaurants, quick oil-change garages, and maid services, all available to you. You'll also see some businesses that have cropped up in response to changes in the way we live and work, such as meal delivery services to help time-starved families, child chauffeur services, and recycled products for our homes and offices. In with the familiar and new types of businesses, you'll find some innovative and sometimes bizarre ideas. One that I was rather intrigued by was a dog doo clean-up service. Yes, for a weekly fee, an enterprising business owner will visit your yard and clean up your pet's little leave-behinds!

Don't feel that you have to come up with a totally new or unique business idea in order to succeed. Most new businesses are similar to existing companies or are even carbon copies. What will make your business successful are the individual talents and experience that you have.

Developing Your Business Idea

Even though you may have decided that you want to own your own business, it's very possible that you have no idea what type of business to start. There is probably no single answer to this question, because it really depends on a number of different things. These include the following:

- Your interests
- Your experience
- Your abilities
- How much money you have to invest
- What else you could be doing to make money

You must have a clear picture of what you will sell in order to make money. This can be either a product or a service. In many cases, people stick with what they know; they will choose to sell products they are familiar with, such as computers, flowers, or kitchen appliances, or to offer services they are already trained to offer, such as accounting, plumbing, or repairing cars.

The following questionnaire should help you brainstorm some potential businesses to start. Take your time. Jot down your answer to each question in the questionnaire and complete the lists and exercises provided in the next few sections of this chapter. Be honest; these exercises will provide you insight into what kind of business you will most likely succeed at.

Questions to Ask Yourself in Choosing a Business

1. BASED ON YOUR EDUCATION, YOUR CURRENT OR PAST JOBS, AND ANY SPECIAL INTERESTS AND HOBBIES, WHAT THREE THINGS DO YOU KNOW THE MOST ABOUT? This expertise could be the basis for a business.
2. WHAT OTHER EXPERIENCES IN YOUR BACKGROUND COULD YOU DRAW UPON FOR A BUSINESS?
3. WHAT DO PEOPLE TELL YOU THAT YOU DO WELL? THINK ABOUT THE TIMES YOU'VE HEARD SOMEONE SAY, "YOU KNOW, YOU REALLY OUGHT TO START A SUCH-AND-SUCH, YOU'RE SO GOOD AT THAT." Maybe they're right. And maybe they would be your first customer.
4. WHAT THINGS DO YOU LIKE DOING MOST? THINK, FOR EXAMPLE, ABOUT THESE QUESTIONS:
   WHAT DO YOU LIKE TO DO ON YOUR DAY OFF?
   WHAT KINDS OF THINGS DO YOU LEAP OUT OF BED FOR?
   WHAT MAGAZINES, NEWSLETTERS, AND BOOKS DO YOU ENJOY READING?
   WHAT HEADLINES CATCH YOUR EYE?
   WHAT THINGS DID YOU LOVE DOING MOST WHEN YOU WERE A CHILD?
   WHAT IS IT YOU'VE ALWAYS SAID YOU WERE GOING TO DO SOMEDAY?
   IF THIS WERE THE LAST DAY OF YOUR LIFE, AS YOU LOOKED BACK ON YOUR LIFE, WHAT WOULD YOU SAY YOU WISHED YOU HAD DONE?
5. HOW MUCH DO YOU WANT TO BE INVOLVED WITH PEOPLE? All the time? Sometimes? From a distance? Not at all? The answers can help you rule in or out businesses that have a lot of or very little people contact.
6. HOW MANY HOURS A WEEK ARE YOU WILLING TO INVEST IN YOUR BUSINESS? Do you want a full-time or a part-time business? Be realistic about this. The amount of time you're willing to invest is what separates full time from part time and profits from losses.
7. HOW MUCH MONEY DO YOU NEED TO MAKE? How much money do you want to make? Each week? Each month? Each year? You'll notice that some of the businesses can charge considerably more than others, so choose a business that will produce the income you want and need.
8. WHAT RESOURCES DO YOU HAVE AVAILABLE TO YOU IN TERMS OF PROPERTY, EQUIPMENT, AND KNOW-HOW? These resources could become the basis of a business. If you look around your home, you may have many untapped resources right under your nose such as a personal computer, a van, a spare room, an automobile, a camcorder, your kitchen stove, vacuum sweeper, backyard, or mailbox.
9. DO YOU WANT TO START A BUSINESS FROM SCRATCH, OR WOULD YOU PREFER A FRANCHISE OR DIRECT-SELLING ORGANIZATION SUCH AS AMWAY OR AVON THAT WILL TRAIN YOU IN WHAT TO DO?

The information above is taken directly from Paul and Sarah Edwards' book, The Best Home Businesses for the 90s, *Second Edition, 1994, Jeremy P. Tarcher/Putnam Books, ISBN: 0-87477-784-4, Page 20.*

Using Your Hobbies and Interests as a Springboard

Taking a long look at how you like to spend your free time is a good place to start in trying to decide what kind of business is right for you. One of your reasons for starting your own business may be to escape dissatisfaction or boredom with your current job. For this reason alone, make sure that you aren't jumping out of the frying pan and into the fire. Nothing could be worse than quitting a stable job you hate for a more stressful job with longer hours, less pay, and no guarantee that you'll like it anymore than the job you just quit.

Make sure that the type of business you start will give you *more* satisfaction and joy than your current job. By doing this, it is more likely that you'll stay in business, because you'll be committed to doing what you love.

To begin compiling a list of potential types of businesses you might like to run, make a list below of all the things you like to do in your spare time. Include formal hobbies, such as drawing or stamp collecting, as well as informal activities, such as reading, running, or cooking.

HOBBIES AND INTERESTS

Apply Your Job Training to Your Own Company

If you've been working the last few years as a dedicated employee somewhere, you've obviously been doing something right to still be on the payroll. During that time, you've been able to improve the quality of your work as you've gained experience. You've probably also developed new skills, as a result of training or exposure to different aspects of the company's operations. Maybe you've even been offered jobs at other companies as word has gotten out about your talents. Although you may have turned down those opportunities, now may be the time to "go out on your own" and offer others the same services and know-how you've been giving your employer.

That may sound great to some of you, who may be thinking, "I can do what I do now, but I won't have to deal with my boss, the jerk. And I can pick and choose what work I take." But the reality is that you first need to determine exactly what you would offer clients.

To begin figuring out what kinds of services you might offer or types of products you could sell, make a list of your major responsibilities at your current job. Think about what you do on a daily basis and also what big projects you have worked on recently. Are there types of activities you enjoy most? What kinds of things do people ask you to do most often?

JOB RESPONSIBILITIES

ition to thinking about what you do in your current job, also think back to u've held, what you did there, and what you enjoyed most about those dd these responsibilities to your list.

What Are Your Strengths?

This may sound silly at this point, but of all the activities and interests you've listed so far, which ones are you good at? No, really. Which ones do you really excel at? There may be things you like to do in your spare time but that you know could never be the basis of a business, and there may be other interests where you have an in-depth knowledge of the subject that you could apply to a business.

For instance, you may enjoy painting watercolors in your spare time, but you know that in comparing your work to professional artist's, people would laugh at your creations. If that's the case, don't try your luck as an artist. However, if you have studied art, spend a lot of time in museums and galleries, and know the local art scene, how about starting an art gallery? I know, I know, it's not as simple as that, but you can see my train of thought here.

Gather all of your completed questionnaires and read them through again. What kinds of activities come up repeatedly? Are there some types of things you like doing more than others? Do you see similarities across some of your abilities, skills, and interests? Could they be combined as the basis for a business? This is the process you'll need to go through in reading and re-reading the forms you've filled out.

Look at what you're good at and what you enjoy, and try to combine them into a kind of business you could start. It can be a service-related business, based on your past experience as a secretary, medical transcriptionist, or chef.

If you start a product-related business, what kinds of things can you see yourself selling? Based on your interests and experiences, you can think about selling anything from cars to cosmetics to computers to plants. Try to make connections between your background and the businesses you might like to run. Keep looking over your lists for new ideas or confirmation that you're on the right track.

Look at what you like, compare it to what you're really good at, and think about related businesses you could run. Here are some simple, yet effective, exercises to go through to determine where you may have the greatest success.

Step 1 Take out a piece of paper (yes, you have to write these things down!) and number it from 1–15 on the left side of the page. Now, write down a minimum of 10 and a maximum of 15 accomplishments. These events can be from your recent professional past or from your childhood. Typical events include "Made the varsity basketball team as a freshman," "Raised three children while working full time," and "Improved sales revenue in my territory over 300 percent in 12 months."

Step 2 Take out 10–15 sheets of paper (depending on how many accomplishments you listed) and write an accomplishment from step 1 at the top of each sheet and divide the rest of the sheet into two vertical columns. Mark the left column "Successful Skills Applied" and mark the right column "Successful Personal Attributes Applied." You should have a separate sheet completed for each successful project or event you listed in step 1. Do not worry about redundancies between the events. These will be taken into account later in the process.

Step 3 Now, take out two other sheets of paper and rewrite all of the "Successful Skills" on one sheet and the "Success Personal Attributes" on another. Cross out items that are on the lists more than once, and mark the number of times a skill or attribute appeared (on your sheets in step 2) next to each skill or attribute. Reorganize the lists in decreasing order from most to least frequent. Some items may appear on both the attributes and skills lists; that's okay. At this stage, you should have a pretty good idea of what makes you tick when you are successful.

Step 4 Try to group the skills and attributes into clusters that describe a general characteristic associated with the similar skills in the cluster. For example, typing, filing, and detail work may be grouped under Administrative Skills.

Step 5 Put these clusters into your perceived order of importance from most important to least important.

Step 6 Write a sentence that describes your top skills and attributes so that someone reading it would clearly understand what type of environment you'll work best in.

The exercise above is adapted from Job and Career Building, *Chapter 4, Setting Objectives, Richard Germann and Peter Arnold, 1980, 10 Speed Press, ISBN: 0-89815-048-5.*

There you have it. You should now have a clearer idea of the type of job, work, and business environment in which you stand the best chance of success.

Your Personality and Abilities

In addition to your interests and experiences, your personality and abilities also play an important role in determining what kind of business is best for you.

Take a look at the following list of activities, and circle the ones that you like to do. Focusing on what you're capable of can help lead you toward a certain type of business.

Information-Oriented	People-Oriented	Thing-Oriented
Working with words	Advising	Cleaning
Working with numbers	Caring	Making
Analyzing	Communicating	Organizing
Compiling	Helping	Repairing
Creating	Informing	Working with animals
Evaluating	Organizing	Working with food
Finding	Negotiating	Working with plants
Keyboarding	Performing	Working with tools
Organizing	Persuading	
Synthesizing	Planning events	
	Teaching	

The information above is taken directly from Paul and Sarah Edwards' book, The Best Home Businesses for the 90s, *Second Edition, 1994, Jeremy P. Tarcher/Putnam Books, ISBN: 0-87477-784-4, Page 21.*

What Are the Results Telling You?

The questionnaire, exercises, and forms in this chapter were designed to help you find the business that's right for you. Look at each of the forms you've completed and try and find the commonalities. What types of activities keep coming up over and over? Can you envision certain kinds of businesses that you would like to start? Are there others you now know are of absolutely no interest to you? Keep coming up with new ideas and refining them according to some other factors we'll go over in a minute.

What Does the Market Need Now and in the Future?

Up until this point, we've been focused solely on you: what you like to do, what kind of work experience you've had, and what types of products or services you could offer clients. Now we need to consider whether there is demand for what you have to offer in the way of products and services. This is a crucial consideration, because it really doesn't matter what you are good at if no one is willing to pay you for your products or services. I might have the best recipe for chocolate-covered grasshoppers, but if there are only a handful of people in my town who would consider eating one of my creations, there really isn't a business opportunity here.

It may be easiest to start this process by looking at recent trends in the market to give you some ideas for where you should focus your attention. To figure that out, you'll need to do some research. This doesn't have to be the typical, tedious, lengthy process you may be used to; it can be done in short spurts over time.

> Not everyone is a potential entrepreneur. Some like stability, routine, and a regular paycheck from someone else. If this is you, you'll be unhappy in the always changing, stressful life of a business owner. If you're really not excited by working long hours and relying on customers, rather than an employer, for your rent and food money, maybe you should put this book aside for awhile.

Researching Different Opportunities

The best way to learn about what consumers and businesses need is to turn to the media. Newspapers, magazines, reports, and radio and television stations reflect all of our interests and concerns. By studying what kinds of things they've been writing about or talking about, you'll learn a great deal about products and services that everyone needs.

The best way to undertake this research process is to read the following:

- National and trade business magazines.
- Local newspapers (and watch local news programs).
- Publications in subject-areas in which you have an interest.
- National news and business publications.

Keep an eye and ear open for topics that everyone seems to be interested in or that everyone is talking about. Barney is the first example that comes to mind, though I'm ashamed to admit it. Although the purple dinosaur has fallen from favor these days, for several months, all I ever heard about was Barney this and Barney that. The same is true for the O.J. Simpson trial, which occupied our lives for many months as well. Are there related products or services you can imagine that would tie into events such as these? That's how you have to start thinking.

Pick up a copy of *American Demographics*, whose sole purpose is to monitor trends as a result of changes in population.

If you already know what you want to sell but don't know whether people will pay you for it, narrow the focus of your research to similar businesses in your area. Study them, read all the recent articles about them in your local library's clipping files, talk to the owners about how their business is going. If you find that local companies are unwilling to share their secrets, try calling a similar business owner in another town or state. Since you're unlikely to be a competitor, they may be willing to talk with you about what they've done that has worked… and not worked.

In your conversations with business owners and people you know, ask them what they would be willing to pay for the product or service you intend to sell. Keep track of what price they tell you is reasonable. After several conversations asking questions about reasonable prices, you should have a pretty good idea of what people want and what they'd be willing to pay.

Your Employer Could Also Be Your First Customer

One of the first questions to ask yourself is: Do you currently do something for an employer that other individuals or businesses may also need? You've probably heard about the new trend toward *outsourcing*, which is pushing companies to keep their full-time staff small and pay others to handle short-term projects or work unrelated to the company's main business. Outsourcing may provide opportunities for you to secure some new clients.

Outsourcing
Corporate-speak for hiring outside consultants, free-lancers, or companies to provide services that in the past have been provided by employees.

What outsourcing can mean for you is the chance to continue doing what you do for your employer, but as an outside *consultant* or *free-lancer*. When companies lay workers off, typically they don't eliminate the work that person was doing, they just shift the burden to someone else. That can work in the short term, but after awhile, employees get overburdened and downright irritable at having to do everyone else's work in addition to their own.

A potential solution for many companies is to hire people on a per-project basis when the workload is too great, or to turn over responsibility for a particular type of activity to an outside company that specializes in that area. Larger corporations started this trend several years ago as they sought ways to cut costs by cutting back on the number of employees on their payroll. Eastman Kodak, for instance, turned over responsibility for maintaining corporate computers to an outside company that specialized in computers. Kodak wanted to focus its attention on its own products, not on keeping everyone's computers running properly.

To determine whether your current employer might consider paying you as an independent contractor, free-lancer, or consultant to do what you do now, consider your boss' point of view. What are the advantages for your employer?

- As an independent contractor, you do not have to be paid benefits or have taxes taken out of your pay.
- In some cases, you may be able to work on individual projects and be paid a flat fee for that work, rather than an hourly wage, potentially saving the company money.
- You don't need an office or work space at the company. Equipment such as a computer, telephone, copier, and fax machine will not be provided.

If you have a good relationship with your boss and your employer and you believe that there would be a way for you to continue to do work for your employer if you were self-employed, it may make sense to suggest that your employer become a client. I'd suggest having this discussion with your boss when you are sure that you want to leave and are ready to start your business. The reason for this is that if your employer becomes angry that you want to leave, you may find yourself on your own faster than you expected. However, if you perform a service that your employer needs and could be completed from a location outside of their offices, it's worth it to see if they will work with you.

Think of your former employer as a potential client, just like anyone else who has a need for your product or service. Don't just assume that your boss will want to hire you as a free-lancer (he or she may not). Don't rely on your old company to be one of your first clients. You may be seriously disappointed.

> WHAT?
>
> **Free-lancer** An individual who works for several different companies at once, helping out on specific projects. Free-lancers are like consultants and are paid a set rate for their services but given no benefits, sick pay, or vacation allowance.
>
> **Independent contractor** Another word that the IRS uses for a free-lancer. It means that the company you're doing work for is not your employer. You have the freedom to decide when, where, and how you will get the work done that your client has given you. You pay your own taxes and benefits, but you can also deduct expenses associated with getting your work done, such as for a business phone line, travel, and supplies.

> BANKRUPT
>
> If your client begins requiring you to work certain hours and to complete your work in a certain way, you're being treated more like an employee, and your tax status may be affected, so be careful.

Will Your Business Idea Make Money?

Before jumping in with both feet, wouldn't it be nice if you could get a better idea of whether your business will succeed? Yes, I've heard that fortune tellers can be helpful, but how about some basic financial analyses? Don't worry, you don't have to be an accountant to do this stuff.

How Much Are You Able to Invest to Start the Business?

You don't have to have millions of dollars to start a business—far from it. Many people start small, often on a part-time basis, spreading their money between living expenses and business startup costs. Other business owners get loans for thousands and thousands of dollars. For example, some fast-food franchises cost more than $100,000 just to open.

You have to decide for yourself how much money you are willing and able to set aside to start your business. It may be less than a thousand dollars, or it may be much more. Everyone's situation is different. Just be aware that the type or size of business you start may be somewhat limited by the amount of money you have available. Don't expect to start a restaurant with just a couple thousand dollars, for example; it's highly unlikely that you could afford to pay for everything you'll need. Even if you were able to squeak by the first month, you may be jeopardizing your future by not having enough money to fall back on.

It All Comes Down to the Numbers

Only by estimating how much money you can make, and how much it will cost to run your business, will you know whether you should continue to pursue your dream. If there is no money to be made by starting the business, then you should drop the idea. While there are probably several reasons why you want to start your own business, the first and foremost must be that you expect to make money at it.

When trying to calculate how much money you need to start your business, you must include the cost of your living expenses during the startup phase. Don't assume you can live on bread and water until the business hits. You will start to resent the business if you find yourself lacking a decent meal several nights in a row. This can cloud your judgment and significantly dampen your enthusiasm.

To estimate the total startup costs of your company, determine how much money you need to start the business and how much money you need to pay yourself during that time in order to cover your basic living expenses. For example, if the business requires $50,000 to start and you will need $48,000 to cover your personal living expenses until the company is on its feet, then the initial investment required is $98,000, not $50,000. Don't try and scale your living expenses to the bone when you estimate these costs because, if for some reason, sales are slower to appear than anticipated, you don't want to be out of business just as things start to pick up. If no additional money is available, then the initial $98,000 could be lost just as the company is getting off the ground. Once you've already received one loan to get the company started, it will be even tougher to go back to your investors and ask for just a little more to keep you going. Make sure you can cover your living expenses for several months, and give yourself some leeway.

Startup Costs

Equipment to be purchased	$________
Office rental	$________
Inventory	$________
Renovations	$________
Supplies	$________
Marketing	$________
Utilities	$________
________	$________
________	$________
________	$________
________	$________
________	$________

Living Expenses

Rent or mortgage	$________
Food	$________
Car payment	$________
Utilities	$________
Insurance	$________
School tuition	$________
Credit card	$________
________	$________
________	$________
________	$________
________	$________
________	$________ per month x 6 months
	= $________

Note: Assume you'll need to cover at least six months of living expenses before the company becomes profitable. It may take years, but use six months as an absolute minimum.

It is either your money or your investor's money that funds the business. It will definitely be your time, and time is also worth money. Professional investors require a formal business plan before they will invest. Even if you don't need outside financing because you have the cash to invest yourself, be as serious about evaluating the opportunity as an investor would be (check out Chapter 4 to learn more about creating a business

Opportunity cost The profit that you could have gained by pursuing another investment instead of the one you currently have. For example, if you go out on a date with one person, you lose the potentially good time you could have had with someone else. Sound familiar? That is opportunity cost.

plan). Make sure that this is an investment you believe is going to pay off for you.

What else could you be doing with your money? How could it be spent if not working to start your business? All those other ways that you could have spent your money is the *opportunity cost* of starting your business. Investors frequently look at situations in terms of opportunity cost: what other investment options are they giving up by investing their money here, rather than there? If the return from your business idea is lower than their next-best option, then they will not give you the money.

How Much Do You Give Up to Start and When Will You Make It Back?

There are worse fates than having a business fail miserably. One of them is having it fail gradually so that it slowly bleeds your reserve funds and energy. It never really takes off, but it never really is bad enough to just close the doors. Beware, because the steady drip-drip-drip of cash leaving the company on a monthly basis will keep you around while draining your finances. When this happens, you find yourself digging into your personal savings each month to keep the company afloat. The problem is that both you and the company may now go bankrupt.

For this reason, I suggest that you set some guidelines for when you will evaluate your company's performance. These milestones should include desired, or even required, levels of personal income and time investment required to keep the business running. If you have exceeded these goals, then you and your business are successful. If you are below those goals, then you need to make some goal adjustments or business management adjustments. At that time, you can choose to either recommit to the venture or decide that it's time to call the idea a bad one, and move on by either closing, selling, or restructuring the business to meet your desired goals.

Get your family involved in this goal-setting process. It is important that they know the sacrifices on their part are only in place for a set period of time, after which things will be re-evaluated. If the business does well, you'll all benefit, but if it just never takes off, your family can take comfort in knowing you'll shut it down after a certain period of time and try something else.

The hardest question to answer is, "How long do I keep investing in the company before I can expect a profit?" This is a tough question, but you can expect to lose some money for at least 18–24 months and should be making a decent living at between 36–48 months. (These are simply rules of thumb based on discussions with other business owners and do not represent scientific findings.)

A Break-Even Analysis Is a Good Test

One way to get a rough idea of whether your business can make any money is to do a *break-even analysis*. In a nutshell, a break-even analysis tells you how much you have to make in dollars or products sold in order to cover all your costs. Obviously, your goal is to do much better than that, but let's start first with ensuring you can at least pay for the products or services to be produced.

A break-even analysis takes into consideration three pieces of information:

- The average price of what you sell, which can be for products or services. Just estimate how much your typical sale will be.
- The average cost of what you sell, or how much it costs to produce your typical sale.
- Your total fixed costs per year, which would be your total expenses for the year that you have to pay no matter how much you sold. This includes things like rent, employee salaries, and utilities.

> WHAT?
>
> **Break-even analysis** A calculation of how much money you need to make to cover your basic costs of doing business. Above that, you're profitable.

Your break-even price in dollars is calculated by dividing

Fixed costs/(1 - average cost of products/average price of products)

So, for example, if I have annual fixed costs of $30,000 and sell software programs that are priced at an average of $100 and cost me $20, my break-even in dollars is $37,500.

$30,000/(1 - 20/100) = $30,000/.8 = $37,500

This means that I have to have sales of $37,500 a year just for my business to break even. To calculate the number of software programs I have to sell, I just divide $37,500 by the price of the program, which is $100.

$37,500/100 = 37.5 or 38 units

These numbers by themselves may mean nothing to you, but if you put in some estimates of your average sales price, cost, and total fixed costs, you'll see what you can expect. Once you figure out the break-even in dollars and units, think about whether those figures seem high, low, or reasonable.

When you do this calculation, be sure to divide the average cost by the average price *first*, before subtracting the number from 1. (Remember that old math rule about doing the work within the parentheses first, and that division should be done before subtraction, and so on, in order to get the right answer.)

For those of you starting a service business who think there's no way to figure out an average sale price, here are some pointers. Keep in mind that calculating your break-even point isn't supposed to be exact at the moment. You're just trying to get a rough idea of whether you can ever sell enough of your product or service to pay all of your expenses and make some money.

If you're not selling a product, there are other ways of estimating your break-even point. If you were thinking of becoming a consultant, for instance, you would determine your hourly rate and divide your fixed costs by your hourly rate. That will tell you the minimum number of hours you need to bill each month to break even. If you come up with 10 or 11 hours a week, or 40 a month, you're doing well. The average number of hours a consultant bills weekly is 14. If you're having trouble choosing an hourly rate, call some of your competitors and ask what their rate is; that will be a guide for what local clients are willing to pay.

Even if you are selling a product and you can't figure out the average price, just take the prices of all or most of your products and calculate an average. If you own a restaurant, you can estimate the average meal price by taking the average price of an appetizer and adding it to the average entrée price and drink price. Taking that number, which could run anywhere from $5.00 at McDonald's to over $50 at an upscale eatery, and dividing your costs by it will tell you how many people you need to feed each month. Does it look feasible given the number of hours you'll be open? These are the types of questions you're trying to answer with this exercise.

If you come up with a number that is much higher than you think you could ever achieve, your business may have serious problems. Are there ways you can reduce your fixed costs, such as by setting up a home-based office or not hiring employees right away? Those are the kinds of decisions you'll need to make in order to create a successful business. However, if your break-even appears well within reason in terms of sales, look again at your numbers to be sure you haven't forgotten to take something into consideration.

One Last Look at All Your Options

Now that you've done some initial research into the kind of business you want to have and what it might cost to make it a reality, step back and consider what else you could do with your time, energy, and money over the next few years. If you weren't starting a business, what would you do? Would you stay with your current employer? Find a new job? Chuck it all and move to the Caribbean? These are all valid options that you need to re-evaluate before committing all your resources to starting a business.

Starting a business is exciting, exhausting, and expensive (the three Es). If, at this point, you're questioning whether you're ready to take the plunge, consider some of these options to hold you over until you're ready:

- Ask for a transfer to another division of your current employer to learn some parts of the business that you know nothing about.
- Apply for a job at another company.
- Sign up for some training or course work to teach you the skills you need to get a different kind of job.

The same is true if you start a business and it doesn't succeed immediately; you always have other options:

- You can shut the business down and get a job working for someone else again.
- You could apply for a loan to invest more in the business to help it grow faster.
- You could look for a partner who has business skills you've discovered you don't have.

The list goes on and on, but the point is that you always have options. Make sure that starting a business is your best option, and if so, go for it!

The Least You Need to Know

You can significantly increase your odds of starting a successful business by taking several factors into account, namely, your personal interests, experience, qualifications, and financial resources. Carefully considering each aspect of your personality and situation will improve the quality of choice you ultimately make.

Just because someone else is making gobs of money with a particular type of business does *not* mean that you should try and do the same thing. For example, coffee houses have become very popular and are springing up around the country. Many entrepreneurs are jumping on the bandwagon by purchasing franchise rights or starting their own from scratch. While I see the potential for profit, I would never try to start a coffee house myself. The reason? I hate coffee. This would make it kinda difficult to advise sophisticated customers about the newest flavors and selections or to know when I received a bad shipment of coffee beans.

- ➤ The best business for you combines your interests, abilities, and experience with a market need.
- ➤ The amount of money you have to invest in a new business may be a limiting factor in the kind you can afford to start.
- ➤ If no one is interested in buying the products or services you want to sell, you have no business.
- ➤ Financial tools such as break-even analyses can help you determine whether your business has potential.

Chapter 3

Plan to Win the War

In This Chapter:

- The difference between strategy and tactics
- Creating your own business strategy
- Ensuring that your personal goals further those of your company
- Taking action to achieve goals

"Why the special staff meeting?" asked Jake, the VP of Sales and Marketing. "Not sure," was the reply from his colleague.

The company had introduced two new lines of frozen fast-food items that were now making their way through the established distribution channels. The response had been tepid at first, but the distributors were now more willing to take a chance due to the strong retail response. The company's main beverage product line was doing well and supporting the new ventures, but Jake had reservations about how long it could last without the new lines carrying their respective part of the profits. It seemed a good time to maintain the status quo, but the president liked new projects. Jake didn't think the company could stand another introduction so soon after the frozen-food lines' near fiasco.

"Thanks for coming," said the president and company founder. "Now that I have more free time, I have been experimenting with new methods of food preparation. I think the American people will pay for fresh, vegetable-based foods that taste good and are easy to prepare. As a result, I want to introduce three new, fresh vegetable side dish lines that will open up new markets for the company and take us into new retail outlets. I expect the full support of management in taking these products to market."

Jake mustered up his courage and asked, "Sir, don't you think we should wait a little while before moving into new markets? Our frozen foods line is just now being accepted, and I have a concern that diffusing our efforts with fresh vegetable lines may be too much for us now. Why don't you take some time and perfect the recipes and give our distribution channel a chance to settle down?"

As the president and founder, what would you do? Would you fire Jake for not supporting your plan? Would you listen to him and take his advice? Would you thank him for his input and do what you want anyway? How you respond to questions like these will determine how your company grows, and whether it grows in the right direction.

In this chapter, we'll talk about the importance of *strategic* and *tactical planning* when starting a new business. You are the leader of your own company and need to set a course your company will follow. Like the president in our example, at some point, you will probably face a decision whether to take the advice of a trusted employee or ignore it completely and do what you want to do. While you may believe strongly that you know more than your employees, sometimes it pays to listen to their ideas. Heck, sometimes they may even have a good one!

The topic of strategy is presented early in this book to help you set short-term goals that result in sales now, while also leading to sales in the future. Success is always a balance between today's activities and tomorrow's promise.

Comparing Strategic and Tactical Actions

Don't let the terminology scare you. Strategic and tactical planning are a part of everyday life, though you may not think of every decision you make as *strategic* or *tactical*. For instance, have you ever said:

"She won the battle, but lost the war."

"Don't throw out the baby with the bathwater."

"He can't see the forest through the trees."

Each of these quotes refers to a short-term event or situation and its effect on the overall results of something else. Each quote suggests that by focusing too much on the short-term (the battle), or on what's right in front of us, we lose sight of the bigger picture (the war). This is the essence of strategic and tactical planning.

> WHAT?
>
> **Strategy** A careful plan or method; the art of devising or employing plans toward a goal.
>
> **Tactical** Relating to small-scale actions serving a larger purpose such as a strategy.

A strategic plan is made up of many tactics, or short-term actions, that together help you reach your goal. For example, winning the battle may have been a tactical success, but if it contributed to losing the war, then it was a strategic mistake. Introducing a new advertising program is a tactic you might use to increase sales, but if your products aren't manufactured yet, you'll wind up with irritated customers who may not want to buy from you even when the products arrive. That would be a strategic mistake. Your efforts to bring in immediate sales caused more harm than good because your company simply wasn't ready to handle the sales.

Every decision you make in your company either moves you closer to or further away from reaching a strategic goal. It is the responsibility of the company's management (you) to determine the strategic direction for the company and to ensure that all employees know what to do to achieve those corporate strategic goals.

Taking the time to create an overall strategy is time well spent since it provides a road map for future decisions.

Business Requires the Ideal Blend of Short-Term and Long-Term Planning

Nothing happens in the long term without short-term actions that move you toward your desired outcome. Short-term actions cannot help achieve any particular goal if no goals have been set or no plan has been developed. You have to know where you're going before you can figure out a route to get there, right?

Taking the time to determine your own goals and your company's long-term mission and objectives will guide your daily actions. Without this framework, you and your employees may be busy, but the business will not move forward since everyone is pulling in separate directions. Making sure everyone knows and understands the goals and objectives of the company will make life a lot easier—for you *and* your employees. Defining the company's goals will minimize employee frustration because they will know what they're working toward. You can minimize confusion by identifying and eliminating activities that don't directly support the goals of the company.

It all starts with you. Take the time to learn more about yourself, your personal motivations, and your long-term goals, to ensure that you take the company in the proper direction. For example, if you like the idea of working alone from a home office, make sure that you're not setting your business up to grow to a point where you have to hire employees or get an office outside your home. If something like this happens, where your business starts to grow in a direction or at a speed that makes you uncomfortable, you may start to resent the business and eventually unravel what is otherwise a good thing. You can avoid this by simply deciding up front what kind of business you want to have, both short term and long term. Once you decide, you can move ahead to make it happen.

You Are an Integral Part of the Strategy

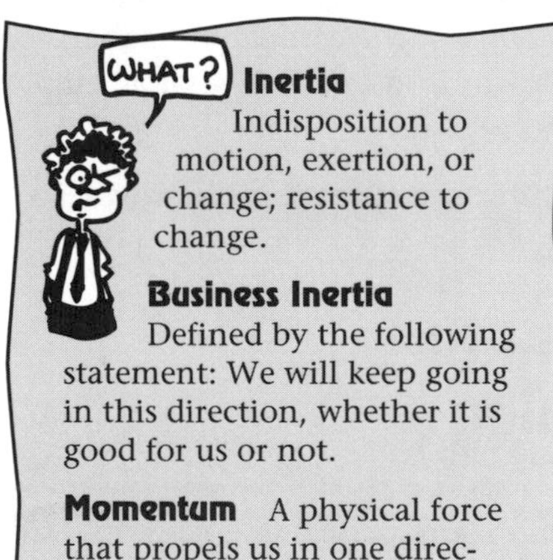

Inertia Indisposition to motion, exertion, or change; resistance to change.

Business Inertia Defined by the following statement: We will keep going in this direction, whether it is good for us or not.

Momentum A physical force that propels us in one direction and makes it difficult to change course or stop.

Businesses, like people, develop *momentum*. Once they get moving in a particular direction, it is difficult to re-orient the people and procedures to a new way of thinking and doing business. Businesses also develop inertia, or resistance to change. The larger the organization, the longer it takes for change to occur, even with total support from top management.

Beware. You, the owner, also have momentum and inertia that may take you and your business in directions you may not have intended. The rallying cry "We can do anything!" may be true, but on limited resources, you can get yourself and the company in a lot of trouble. Be careful not to try to do too much too quickly. Like the food and beverage company example in the beginning of the chapter, you have to pick your battles and fight them well, or your company can become spread so thin that it loses its focus and competitive advantage. You must keep your own inclinations in check, trust your instincts, and keep the company on its chosen strategic track. This is the essential value of strategic planning and goal setting.

Synchronize Your Goals with Those of the Company

Here's an interesting question: Do you work for the company or does the company work for you? After all, you pay the bills, you sign the checks. You provide the overall direction and determine whether someone has performed effectively. You do the hiring and firing. Shouldn't the company dance to your tune? Yes and no.

A part of your job is to ensure the company's survival. If the company goes under, so does your dream of independence and all of your hard work. There go the paychecks for all of your employees. Away go the services you provide your clients that they have come to depend upon. So who works for whom? Do you work for the company and its clients or does the company work for you? In the final analysis, it's really a balancing act.

> BANKRUPT
>
> Don't assume that what brought you success in the past will be enough in the future. Stay informed about what's going on in your market so you can adjust your strategy if neccessary.

Take it from Tuco in the movie *The Good, The Bad and the Ugly*, "There are two types of people in this world, my friend. Those with the gun and those who dig." The one with the gun sets the overall direction, and the one who digs gets the job done on a day-to-day basis. The one with the gun is the leader and probably has more of a startup temperament. The workers have more of a maintenance temperament.

If you are the type of person who enjoys the startup phase of business, then the daily routine of running the business will probably bore you to tears after awhile. You will probably, unconsciously, create change within the organization just so you can experience the excitement of solving real-time problems. Or you may come up with endless ideas for new products and services, new markets to go into, new distribution channels to conquer. Anything to bring back the excitement of a new venture. Unfortunately, change and new directions may not be what your company needs.

> WHAT?
>
> **Start-up temperament** Someone who thrives on new and exciting projects and challenges.
>
> **Maintenance temperament** Someone who enjoys keeping established systems running like a well-oiled machine.

If you are a person who dislikes change, who prefers routine, you will go to extremes, once again unconsciously, to avoid disrupting the status quo. This is also not the best situation since business life is never static, no matter how much you may want it to be, and treating it as such is a guaranteed death knell. Ignoring opportunities for expansion or product improvements that everyone is clamoring for is very dangerous.

A blending of the two types of temperaments is required for success, and the first step is knowing where you sit on the mayhem-to-routine continuum. Surround yourself with people who have different temperaments than the one you have. If you have a maintenance temperament, make sure you have startup people around to keep you from becoming static. If you have a startup temperament, make sure you have maintenance temperament people around to keep you from creating chaos and driving people crazy. In both cases, creating balance in your organization will help keep the business from going under.

"I don't want any yes-men around me. I want everyone to tell me the truth—even though it may cost him his job." Samuel Goldwyn, 1939

Know that you, the boss, set the course for the organization. You set the strategic direction for the company. The more aware you are of your own inclinations, the more likely you will be to steer the company in its best direction, instead of the one most in accord with your personality. Look for the ideal where the company's goals and your goals are in sync and have the best of both worlds.

Planning to Grow Beyond Your Own Capabilities

With success comes a new challenge: What do you do when your own limitations are holding your company back? This is often a crisis point for small business people because they have to learn to delegate in order to grow.

They now need to turn over their favorite accounts and routine activities to somebody else. This relinquishing of control is often done ineffectively, and the business eventually stagnates because as the manager/owner, you just can't let go. The employees become frustrated since they think you don't trust them. The clients become frustrated because they are no longer getting the level of service they expect from your company simply because you are so busy that you cannot respond to their needs in a timely manner. You are frustrated because you are paying your employees to work for you so you can improve the quality of your life, and here you are working 60 hours per week when they only work 40–50. What are you paying them for, anyway?

This is a common situation and one that has strangled more than one small company. The need for more people is a sign that you are doing something right. Trusting your employees enough to delegate responsibility to them, while continuing to keep a close eye on the important things, can make or break your company.

Plan from the beginning to grow beyond your own abilities, or know that you will always need to live within the resources you alone provide. Plan to grow not only in the day-to-day *logistics* area, but also in the strategic areas. Adding people to your company in either an employee or partnership capacity opens up new marketing avenues that were previously not available due to your limited expertise. That's right! You can't do everything, even though you think you can. Let go of the things that do not make the best use of your time and give them to people who want to do them well. Spend your time doing what you do well, and use your team to balance the other areas.

> WHAT?
>
> **Logistics** The set of activities that deals with making the daily routine effective. You will probably need clerical help, once you become succesful, to hand off the daily routine paperwork so you can have time for other activities.

On the other side of that coin, don't give away everything you like to do, or you could find yourself in a job you would never have taken with another company at any price. It is still your company and you have the expertise that made it successful. Apply that expertise as appropriate, add other people as applicable, and delegate the items that make minimal use of your specific talents. In this way, you lay the groundwork for yourself, your employees, your client relationships, and the company to grow beyond your limitations.

Determine a Strategic Direction: Defining Your Mission Statement

If this next section turns you on, check out the book, *The Essence of Small Business,* by Colin Barrow. Before you can even begin creating your business plan, which outlines how you will run your business on a daily basis, you must identify the strategic direction of

> WHAT? **Mission statement** A mission statement is a written document that explains why you're in business. Usually only a few paragraphs long, it explains to employees and customers what values the company has, such as excellent customer service, the lowest prices, and a fun place to work.

the business you're about to create. You need to define the overall company direction in a *mission statement*. This simple statement covers, in just a few sentences, the reason for your company's existence. It provides the overall umbrella under which all other goals and actions fall. It says what your company does and who it does it for.

A typical mission statement for a clothing designer might be:

"To provide colorful, trendy, and form-fitting clothing to health-conscious women between the ages of 18 and 35. We will provide these clothes at reasonable prices in an environment where buying is fun and an integral part of the overall experience."

Notice the mission statement is brief and to the point, determining the overall direction of the company. It also sets limits. Should someone want to provide men's clothing in one of the stores, they would clearly be in violation of the mission statement. Either the company's prescribed mission statement needs to be changed or the idea to add men's clothing needs to be dropped so the company can stay focused on its core mission.

When you create your company's mission statement, consider the following:

- What you plan to do, such as sell office equipment or provide marketing consulting.
- Who you plan to do it for, such as businesses, nonprofit groups, or men over age 60.
- Time frames within which it will be done, such as within the next 18 months or next 5 years.
- How your company will deal with changes in the marketplace, such as technology advancement, new competition, or by investing in new equipment or hiring more staff.

- What the *benefits*, not the *features*, are of your product or service that are the reason someone would buy from you.
- How following the mission statement will contribute to the company's short- and long-term success, such as by keeping the company focused on a high-growth market or keeping expenses down.

It may take you days to write these simple sentences.

After defining your company's mission statement, you can now define the company's overall *objectives*, or *goals*. These are larger scope projects that have specific time frames and measurable results. A typical objective may be to "add 10 new products to the line over the next 12 months."

You can then break this goal down into individual *tasks* that you assign to individuals for completion within specified time frames. These tasks all contribute to the completion of a particular objective. A task in our scenario may be "review the product lines for 15 potential vendors within the next six months."

Tasks give rise to *action plans* that literally define who is doing what on which day. For example, "Visit XYZ Dress Company on Tuesday from 1–3 p.m.," would be a typical action item that helps complete a particular task. Completing the task moves the company closer to achieving its objectives and continues to support its mission.

Features The different characteristics of a product or service. For example, the features of a drill bit may include its size, length, and the type of material it is made of.

Benefits What the customer gains by using your product or service. The benefits of the drill bit are that it makes holes.

Beware of being too specific in defining your mission statement. Consider the *benefits* of your product or service more than the features, so that you express the true value of your product to the customer. Taking the drill bit example further, the company's mission statement might focus on improving technology for the creation of holes, rather than for making improved drill bits.

Action plans, tasks, and objectives are related to each other in the same way that tactics and strategies are. Action plans make up tasks which make up objectives, just as tactics are components of a strategic plan. Different words, same idea.

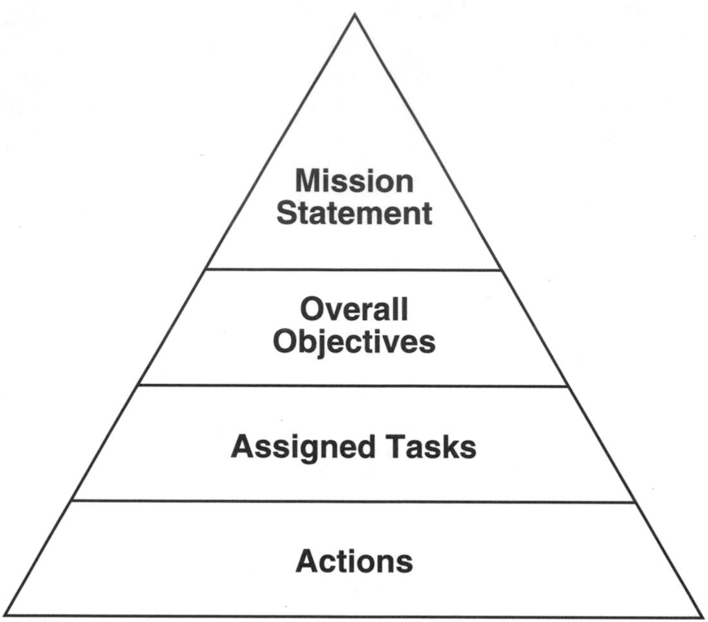

The mission statement identifies the strategic direction of the company; action plans, specific tasks, and objectives accomplish that mission.

The above section was taken from* The Essence of Small Business*, by Colin Barrow, Prentice Hall, 1993, ISBN: 013285-362-0.

Think Strategically While Making Today Happen

So here is the challenge (like you needed another one at this point): keep one eye on the long-term opportunity while taking care of today. This is where focusing on your goals is so incredibly valuable. The daily "fires" that erupt can look critically important when, in fact, they are irrelevant to the long-term objective. Actually, some of those fires can be left alone to burn themselves out while you focus on those objectives that lead to your desired strategic goal.

Hopefully, at this point, you are starting to understand the difference between strategic and tactical planning. Do things today that make tomorrow's goals a reality.

Actions Without Direction Lead Nowhere

Ever said this? "I was busy all day, but when I walked out the door, I didn't really remember what I did or feel like I accomplished anything."

This is a classic action-without-direction statement. You may have dealt with many small issues that appeared important at the time but which did not contribute to achieving your objectives.

If you find yourself in a high-stress, high-activity, and low-sense-of-accomplishment mode, time management techniques are available to help keep you on track. The essence of most techniques is simply teaching yourself to focus on the important things and allowing the less critical things to take a back seat. You can also hand off tasks to a person (if you are at that stage) who can take care of them for you. Prioritizing the most important tasks helps ensure that you'll spend time on those activities that will make a difference, and you will move closer to achieving your goals. Ask around for recommendations on an effective time management class and carve out the time to take it.

WHAT?

Action plans The detailed activities you do to help the company achieve its goals. These actions include meetings, proposals, visits, or creating something.

Tasks The individual assignments given to people to help the company reach its objective. Each task is broken down into action plans.

Objectives Large projects that affect your company involving several people. Objectives helps the company grow and become more successful, which means they are usually rather involved and may take several months to reach.

You'll Never Have All the Information You Need

Doing a lot but accomplishing nothing is "analysis paralysis." In this mode, you never know enough to make a decision or take any action and, consequently, nothing gets done. You keep trying to gather more information before you make a decision. If you have meetings to schedule your next meeting, you are in real trouble. Take your staff out for a meeting and say good-bye, because this is a surefire way to kill any startup company.

You'll never have all the information you need; so in many cases, you have to just make a "best guess" and proceed. At first, this will be extremely nerve-racking, but once you see that one bad decision won't make or break your company, you'll become better at moving ahead.

You have to do something, or nothing will get done. Don't be too afraid to make a mistake, or you will get too bogged down trying to make a perfect decision and you will accomplish nothing. You can analyze a problem to death, and if this happens often enough, it will kill your business and dreams along with it.

Setting Deadlines for Your Goals

Remember from earlier in the chapter that the mission statement is at the top of the stack, but it translates into specific actions that make the company's mission become a reality. Deadlines and time-frame commitments drive action. If you do not have a time frame attached to an action, objective, or task, you will probably never achieve it. If your objective or task is important enough to track as a project, then it is important enough to have a time frame attached.

Risk and Reward Go Together: Take Smart Risks

Don't create a task, objective, or goal without a time frame attached or you will never accomplish the actions needed to make it happen. Train yourself to look for items without time frames like a hawk looks for a field mouse. They are the items that will drag down your financial and energy reserves.

"If it sounds too good to be true, it probably is." Few people would argue with the wisdom of this statement, and I want to take a few moments to investigate why we know this to be so. We all know that few valuable things come without risk. If someone offers you something of value with no risk, you immediately get suspicious, or you question whether it has any value at all.

Know that you will be making risky decisions as you move your business along. The risk is created from not knowing what will happen as a result of the decision you made yesterday or the one you're making today. You will never know everything there is to know about a decision before you make it. Some people think if you knew everything, you wouldn't do anything since the eventual outcomes are rarely what we thought they would be initially. Accept the fact that you will need to make risky decisions with incomplete information, and do everything you can to minimize the uncertainties.

Managing your business in a constant state of high risk creates a high-stress environment that will eventually undermine morale, enthusiasm, and customer service. Be prepared to take risks, but choose your risks properly to ensure that you use your company resources to their best advantage.

Small Tactical Wins Lead to Major Strategic Victories

Many of your projects and objectives may take months to complete. The middle of a project often looks like the inside of a tunnel with darkness behind and in front of you. At times like this, like the middle chapters of a long book, you simply need to keep moving forward until the light at the end appears. (Hopefully, you're not feeling that way about *this* book.)

Keep yourself going by creating a set of "small wins." These are the interim milestones you use to pat yourself on the back for a job well done. For example, I may treat myself to an expensive sundae when I hit specific milestones such as making a certain number of sales calls. On occasion, I will throw an unexpected office party for my staff to let them know I appreciate their accomplishing a particularly important project.

Add up enough small wins and the strategic objective is met, which is what you ultimately want to happen. There is nothing like winning, and the small-wins technique leads to the big wins that really count.

Lee Iacocca was once asked what he did to become successful. "I waited 62 years," was his response. This funny statement belies the underlying philosophy that he later expressed when asked how to become successful. "Get an education, learn as much as you can about your field, and for God's sake, do something!"

The Least You Need to Know

You have to learn to manage yourself before you can effectively manage the rest of your business. Managing yourself requires insight, honesty, and discipline and is often the undoing of most businesses or careers. The success of your company and your own personal success have a much better chance of occurring if you take the time to ensure that the goals for both complement each other. Good luck on this part of your journey.

- Plan short-term tactics in support of your long-term strategies.
- Your goals and those of the company should be in sync, or trouble may later arise.
- Thinking is good, but taking action is what makes things happen.
- Give all action items a time frame for completion or drop them from your list. Nothing happens on its own without a pending completion date.
- Managing means getting things done through others. Even one-person businesses need to manage their clients and suppliers.

Chapter 4

Preparing Your Business Plan

In This Chapter

- Why write a business plan?
- How to find the information needed for your business plan
- Identifying the contents of a business plan
- How to use your plan
- What to do if your plan is not financially feasible

A group of holy men on a religious pilgrimage stopped for the night at the edge of a large stretch of sand. As the younger members of the group tended the animals, the elders gathered around the fire to discuss the day's events and the finer points of life. The setting sun stimulated a religious discussion, and all heads reverently turned to the wise leader who asked, "Where is the next town?" One of the disciples eagerly offered, "It is a small town on the edge of a river just a short distance from the holy rock." "It is good," the leader somberly replied. All heads nodded in agreement and a tranquillity settled over the group. The serenity was interrupted by Abdul who impertinently asked, "What is good about it, great leader?" The leader wisely smiled and responded, "It is good to know where we are going."

A good business plan cannot guarantee success, but you can bet that not having one will increase your chances of failing. If you do not know where you're going, you probably won't ever get there.

While everyone knows that a business plan is a good idea, I have to be honest and tell you that not many businesses actually have one. According to an AT&T survey, only 42 percent of all businesses have a written business plan. Maybe this explains why only 20 percent of all new businesses will be around after five years! Do you want to risk being part of the 80 percent that won't be around? I didn't think so.

Most people plan more extensively for a trip to another country than they do when starting their own business. Big mistake! Don't quit your day job until you have researched the type of business you want to start and feel confident that you can succeed. Unless you are pretty sure that over time you can earn a better salary with your business than you can if you stayed at your current job, why risk what you have? However, if you take the time to plan all the steps involved in starting and running your new business, you'll be on your way to success.

In the previous chapters, you learned the importance of understanding your motivations for starting your own business; the need to evaluate your business idea (whether it is sound); and the importance of planning a strategic direction for your company to ensure that you reach your goals. This chapter shows you how to turn all that initial thinking into a written report, called a *business plan*, which clearly explains just what you intend to do, and how you intend to do it. You can do this; it only takes a little discipline, research, and clear thinking to put your ideas into a typical business plan format.

In short, a business plan is a document about 25–40 pages long that outlines your plans and intentions for running your business. Some sections of the plan may remain confidential (such as financial information, new technology overviews, or client data); you won't share them with outsiders. However, you should assume that most of the plan will become public because you'll be sharing it with many different audiences. Those less-sensitive sections may include personnel, existing products and services, industry analyses, and any other company background information that would normally appear in marketing literature.

About the Kwik Chek Business Plan

Almost anything is easier to do when you have a picture of how it is supposed to look when it's done. It's kind of like trying to assemble a model or toy without the picture of what it's supposed to look like all put together. It is one thing to read about how a business plan is created and something completely different to see or read an actual plan.

For this reason, I have included a business plan (see the Appendix at the end of the book) I wrote for a used car evaluation service business I called Kwik Chek. When I wrote this business plan many years ago, I did it so that I could find out whether the idea would fly, or whether I should go back to the drawing board. My original intent was to franchise the business nationwide, and I created the plan in order to meet that goal.

You might want to take this opportunity to read through the Kwik Chek plan because I will frequently refer to it throughout this chapter. The Kwik Chek plan will give you concrete examples of how a plan can help you start and manage your business better. Although the format I used in preparing the Kwik Check plan is not the only one that works, it provides a starting place and a guide for you to follow when you start to write your own plan. You thought you were going to be able to get away with just reading business plans, didn't you? Wrong! You'll be writing yours soon enough.

REALLY!?

The Kwik Chek business plan didn't work for me, since I wanted to be an absentee owner and franchise the concept, but it would work for someone who wants to be an owner-operator. This was not of interest to me, and I decided to drop the idea for personal reasons. Should you decide to pursue the idea using this business plan, good luck! If you succeed with the idea, please let me know; send me a dozen free car inspection certificates, and buy me dinner sometime when you're passing through Austin.

Why Prepare a Business Plan?

While you may have heard that you only need a business plan if you are trying to get financing to start a company, this is not true. Besides using a business plan to secure funding, there are several other reasons you should write a business plan. These include:

- Putting your goals and ideas down on paper helps to organize your thinking.
- Writing down your plans and goals demonstrates your commitment to your business, which will impress potential investors, suppliers, and employees.
- Once you have your plan down on paper, you have a guide to achieving your goals that you can refer to regularly.
- Not only do you have a guide that will help keep *you* on track, it will also ensure that all your employees understand where you plan to take the business.
- Your plan will help focus your organization on its mission, reducing the chance that the business will become sidetracked by other less important activities.

Let's face it: others do not believe in your idea like you do. Part of the reason is that they probably don't know as much about your business, your product, and your plans as you do. In order for everyone else to believe in your idea, they'll need to see what you intend to do. There will probably be many different people who will want to see your business plan, each for different reasons, including some of the following:

- Banks and other funding sources will use your plan to determine whether you are capable of starting and running the business.
- The Small Business Administration (SBA) will review your plan to make sure it will be profitable so that you won't have any problem repaying their guaranteed loan.
- Employees will want to see sections of the business plan to understand whether the company has long-term career opportunities for them.
- Strategic partners or joint venture participants will want to read your plan to determine whether your overall direction is in alignment with their plans and their mission.

Be Honest with Yourself and Your Potential Investors

If you plan to show your business plan to potential investors, include the assumptions you made when writing the plan, potential risks and rewards, and important milestones to ensure the investor understands the whole picture. Trying to make your situation appear too "rosy" will make investors skeptical, while making it appear too risky may scare them off. By simply being honest about what you see as the strengths and weaknesses of your situation, you allow investors to make up their own minds based on as much information as you have.

Experienced investors know that things can go "off-plan" as a project unfolds. They simply want to minimize the likelihood of losing their investment due to mistakes or poor management on your part. The business plan provides a framework for working out the details of your relationship with investors.

Being up front with potential investors will help you avoid problems down the road if things don't go as well as you planned. Given the right opportunity, you can lead professional investors into a minefield, as long as you first tell them that there *is* a minefield. Investors bring resources to the table that can keep you from getting into big trouble if and when it arises. However, if they feel you have misrepresented your company and the potential rewards they can expect, your may seriously damage your working relationship.

Finding the Information

God bless the Dewey Decimal System and the librarians who use it. Virtually all the information you'll ever need is out there. You just have to know where to look to find it.

Before you can begin to write your business plan, you must first learn more about your business: the market you're working in, the type of products or services you'll be offering, and the needs of your customers (check out Chapter 2 for more about developing your business idea). Although you may have years of experience in the type of business that you want to start (perhaps you've been working in your family's printing shop for decades), investors want to feel confident that your instincts are correct. To show them that your ideas are on target, you have to give them proof in the form of reliable, published articles, reports, and other statistics. Saying that you know the market for printing is growing exponentially each year is nice, but being able to back that statement up with a report from the Department of Commerce that says essentially the same thing gives you a lot more credibility—and that's what you need at this point. To accomplish this, all you need to do is visit the library.

If you're lucky, you may find that more information exists than you could ever use in your business plan. Chances are good that somebody, somewhere has compiled exactly the information you want. The challenge becomes finding it. Once you find it, you may need help getting it in the form you want. (I know a guy who studies the sex life of fire ants! Go figure! The point: Somebody, somewhere, is working to find an answer to your questions.)

Public and university libraries contain a gold mine of information. General information is available from books, and more up-to-date information is found in magazines, newspapers, and industry newsletters. Using the *Reader's Guide to Periodicals* or the online search services in the library, you can get your hands on articles that relate exactly to what you're interested in. I'll talk more about the online services available to you for your research in Chapter 18.

> **REALLY!?**
> Talk nicely, and softly, to your librarian; he may be willing to do a lot of the work for you.

It is unlikely that you'll find all the information you need in a single article. You may need to piece together information from several sources to get a complete picture of the market or industry you're working in.

Subscribe to industry-specific publications and trade groups. They offer support and research that may not be available to the general public. Find a Federal Repository, frequently located at a local university, that contains all of the latest government document information. You already paid for the research with your tax dollars, so you may as well use it. A listing of documents is also available from the Government Printing Office. In Chicago, call 312-353-5113; nationally, call 202-512-0000.

Using the Kwik Chek business plan as an example, assume your product relates to used cars and that you need to know the number of used cars in service today, along with the expected growth in used-car ownership over the next five years. In one article, you may find the percentage of households in the U.S. that own used cars, and another may contain the growth rate expected, by household, in ownership of used cars over the next five years.

Census data can tell you the total number of households in the U.S., and with some simple math, you can calculate the number of used cars and the expected increase over the next five years. You now have the total available market information needed to estimate market size and potential sales revenues. For example, the market demand evaluation data found in the Scarborough Report (see the "Market Analysis" section of the Kwik Check Plan) shows that 14 percent of car buyers in Austin, Texas plan to buy used cars.

SCORE Big with Free Business Plan Help

You are not alone when preparing your plan, even though it often feels that way. There are organizations out there that have a vested interest in helping you succeed at starting your own business. These include the local Chamber of Commerce, entrepreneur associations, and the Federal government. That's right! The Small Business Administration (SBA) sponsors a business support group to assist businesses just like yours to create a business plan and acquire funding. They are a group of retired executives who call themselves SCORE (Service Corps Of Retired Executives). These are people who have already been where you plan to go; they can help you assemble the plan and guide you through the creation and management process. Better yet, their services are free! They are volunteers, and you already pay for SBA coordination with your tax dollars.

Make maximum use of available resources, especially when those resources are free. You can only do so much on your own; you need help to make it all come together in a successful way. SCORE is a good place to start to gain insight from mentors.

Simply contact your local SBA office (get the local number from the phone book) and ask for the phone number of the local SCORE office. They will tell you where to go from there. Why not spend the time with these people and save yourself the aggravation of writing your plan several times without guidance. (You'll probably go through many drafts anyway.)

Small Business Development Centers (SBDCs), which are collaborative efforts between the SBA and local colleges and universities, also provide free counseling help to people trying to start a business. There are more than 750 SBDC locations across the country to assist you. You can find a local office by calling 202-205-6766.

The Basic Components of the Business Plan

Effective business planning is a lot like assembling a jigsaw puzzle. You have all of these stray pieces that need to be put together in a logical order for the puzzle to work. As you become more familiar with the pieces, the proper fit reveals itself, and there is only one way to assemble the puzzle that makes any sense.

> REALLY!?
>
> You will learn more about your business idea, as a result of the planning process, than you ever thought possible. Treat it as a learning experience, and watch where it takes you.

The more complicated the puzzle, the longer it takes to put it together. Most people start with the border and work their way to the center. Establishing this reference point helps identify where the other pieces should fall and simplifies puzzle assembly.

The puzzle analogy carries over directly to business plan preparation. You need to arrange the various pieces of business information you've collected and organize it so that it tells a story. Once you've developed an outline of the major pieces of information about the business you want to communicate, you can start to write, fitting all the bits of information together.

The business plan is essentially a document that is broken into related subsections. Each subsection deals with an important part of the way you will manage the business.

> One of my early sales managers described an effective sales presentation in this way: First, tell them what you are going to tell them (Executive Summary), tell them what you want to tell them (the detail sections), then tell them what you told them (Summary and Conclusions). A business plan is ultimately a sales document that explains your business idea.

Your business plan should contain the following basic elements:

I. Table of Contents
II. Executive Summary
III. Description of Your Product or Service
IV. Market and Industry Analysis
V. The Competition
VI. The Management Team
VII. Operations Plan
VIII. Marketing Strategy
IX. Financial Analysis
X. Conclusion
XI. Appendices or Supplementary Materials

Let's take a look at each of these sections in detail.

Table of Contents

The Table of Contents is not a major element of your business plan, but it will help show the reader what information they will find in the coming pages. Since Tables of Contents are generally found in well-organized documents, you can make a good impression by including one at the front of your plan.

The Executive Summary

Although this section is the first in the business plan, it will be much easier if you write it after you write all the other sections. Write up one paragraph to describe each section of the plan. Finish the Executive Summary by listing the amount of money required, the projected return on investment, and the major advantages your company will have over the competition.

The Executive Summary should be one to two pages long and is often the only section a potential investor will read. Based on those few paragraphs, he will decide whether to continue to read the rest of the plan. If he doesn't proceed to read your plan, you've just lost a potential investor. For this reason, your summary needs to catch and hold the reader's attention.

Take a look at the Executive Summary provided in the sample plan at the end of this book. It is short and concise and describes the Kwik Chek concept and the amount of investment required for the business to make a profit, explains the potential market penetration, and includes a brief explanation of why and how it will be a successful business.

Description of Your Product or Service

This part of the plan explains your product or service idea and how it meets the needs of your market. Describe exactly what it is you will be selling and why people, or businesses, will buy it. How is it different from similar items already on the market? If it is a revolutionary concept, try and explain why the world needs this new breakthrough.

In this section, describe what your product or service is. For instance, is it a new kind of car, a tasty new type of cookie, or a better house-cleaning service? Explain what the product or service does for the user; what the benefits are and why they would buy it. If there are similar products or services already on the market, briefly compare them to what you are offering and explain how yours is better. If your new product or service is unlike anything currently available, convince the reader of why it is needed.

> Make sure that "Company Confidential Information" is marked on every page of the plan (header or footer), including the Executive Summary. This will alert readers that the information should not be shared with outsiders.

Take a look at the idea described in the Kwik Chek plan in the "Business Description" section. For this business concept, you will see a real-world scenario that explains how the Kwik Chek service would benefit a customer. It provides a clear description of all the areas of the car that the service would check, the average amount of time it would take to perform the service, and how the service will be performed (the Kwik Chek van comes to the customer). It also explains the benefits to the customer; this is the difference between Kwik Chek and the competition.

Market and Industry Analysis

The Market and Industry Analysis section presents information describing the market need for your product or service. This is where you detail all the information you gathered at the library regarding the size of your market, the number of potential customers for your product or service, and the growth rate for your market or for the industry as a whole (which usually means worldwide). This section not only relies heavily on the

Market penetration A measure of the percentage of total customers that have bought from you. If there are 1 million people in your market and 500,000 have bought your product, you have captured 50 percent of the market.

Market opportunity An estimate of the number of customers who'd be interested in buying from you. If there are only 100 people in your town who might be interested in your new service, the market opportunity (also called potential market) is not very big.

Potential sales revenue The dollar value of sales if everyone who is a potential customer bought from you. If each of those 100 potential customers bought one of your \$500,000 custom-built homes, your potential sales revenue would be \$50 million (100 customers × \$500,000).

results of your research, but also on your ability to compile the information into a simple, concise, and easy-to-read format. See Chapter 7 for details regarding creating market estimates.

You will have to make a number of assumptions when completing your market analysis. For example, the percentage of available customers that you expect would pay for your product or service, called *market penetration*, is a key estimate in determining your *potential sales revenue*. You can find these numbers through information from other companies who did what you plan to do, or from "guesstimates" from people experienced in the field. No one expects you to know exactly how many sales you will make during the first year, or even the first two years, but you can provide fairly accurate estimates by making some educated assumptions.

Looking at the "Market Analysis" section in the Kwik Chek plan, you'll notice immediately how I have used facts and figures to support my belief that there was a market opportunity. These facts were summarized from all the information I gathered when I researched my business concept.

The Competition

Who are the established companies already selling products and services similar to yours? How will they react to your company? Depending upon your idea and how long your product or service has been available, your competition may consist of other new and aggressive companies just like yours or established companies from whom you intend to take business. Anyone who believes that they have no competition is in for a rude awakening, even if you have a totally revolutionary product. Remember the introduction of the facsimile machine just a few short years ago? The fax machine replaced services such as overnight mail and TELEX that already existed.

There is no reason to be afraid of competition. Take every opportunity to learn from them. What are they doing right, and what can you do better? It is okay to copy things that work and to learn from their mistakes. They may hate you for it, but who cares? Tell them that imitation is the highest form of flattery. I'll tell you more about dealing with the competition in Chapter 9.

In this section, it's a good idea to provide a list of the other major players in the marketplace to show that you know exactly who your competition is. You should also indicate your impression of their strengths, weaknesses, and overall success in the market. By learning about your competition, the reader of your plan can better understand how you will succeed: either by going after a market opportunity that no existing competitor is addressing or by doing what everyone else is doing, but with a different twist.

> We all think our idea is unique, but the customer may truly think it's just like dozens of others. Beware of your ego at this stage. Bravado can quickly lead to failure if you are not careful. Try to rely more on the market data you've collected rather than your opinion as a guide to whether there is a similar idea already in existence.

The competition for the Kwik Chek concept is defined in the plan under the "Market Analysis" and the "Competitive Advantage" sections. There is a clear description of what each competitor offers the customer, the price of their service, and additional information about each business, which will give investors an honest picture of how your idea stands up to the businesses already out there making money.

Marketing Strategy

If nobody buys your product or service, you're out of business. Period! Nothing ends a business faster than no customers. In this section, you need to explain to the reader what you intend to do to get customers.

As part of your marketing strategy, you should describe how you intend to let the public know that you're open, such as through a number of marketing methods that I'll go through, and explain what your sales approach is, such as selling by direct sales representatives, a mail-order catalog, or through a retail storefront. You'll find a detailed discussion of all the different ways you can market your business later in the book, but start to think about how you'll describe your plans to the reader of your business plan.

> The sales targets you set now can be used later to evaluate how well you're doing. Make sure you are willing to live up to your projections and that you can make them a reality. Otherwise, the targets are useless.

In the Kwik Chek plan, I have outlined the major approaches I will take for getting word to my target audience about the benefits of the Kwik Chek service. Notice that to effectively bring in customers, several methods are used to increase public awareness of Kwik Chek.

The Management Team

One of the most important elements of your business plan is the section telling the reader why you and your partners are the most qualified group to start and run this business. Investors want to feel confident that you have experience in the type of business you're starting, and that other members of your management team complement your skills. That means that if you hate numbers and love marketing, it would be smart to hire someone who loves numbers, so that they can handle the financial and accounting aspects of the business.

Assuming that you intend to grow, you'll also want to describe the types of people you'll need to hire in the first year. You don't have to have a particular person in mind for each position to be filled; you just have to know that you need someone to do a certain job. If you end up with more than five people on your staff in the first year, draw up a simple organizational chart to explain what each person is responsible for and who they report to. Of course, if you are president, secretary, and janitor all rolled into one, skip the chart.

In this section, you need to briefly describe the backgrounds and experience of your management team to show the reader that you know what you're doing. If you have a woman with 25 years of experience in the business who's going to be working with you, be sure and mention it; it makes your company much more credible.

Define each of the major jobs that will be held by the people who will be working with you. So if you have three people who'll be working for you at the start, describe what their titles are, what their responsibilities will be, and why they are qualified to have this job. You're going to put their résumés in the Appendix at the back of the plan (in case anyone wants to read the specifics), but also write a paragraph or two about each person in this section, nothing too lengthy.

If you have advisors or consultants who have been working with you and giving you advice, mention them if they are fairly well-known or if they have a lot of experience. If you've set up a board of directors, briefly mention people who are members of your board. The point of mentioning other people here is to show the reader that you're not trying to do everything yourself and that you recognize you don't know everything and will rely on professionals in those instances. Many business owners think they know everything and don't need advice from other people. These are usually the ones who don't last very long either.

The "Management and Staffing" section in the Kwik Chek plan describes a very small management team consisting of two people. One person will provide the marketing and technical expertise for the company; the other person will be the bookkeeper and office manager of the company.

Operations Plan

This section describes operational procedures, manufacturing equipment, the level of production required, locations, international arrangements, licensing arrangements, and any other aspects related to providing the product or service defined in the idea section.

For those of you who are starting service businesses, this section may be very short, because service providers such as management consultants, accountants, and attorneys sell their time and experience. They don't use big machines to crank out words of wisdom, so production capacity is less of an issue. Assumptions should still be outlined to explain how many hours per month you expect to spend on client-related work that you'll be paid for.

Check out the Operational Plan and the assumptions outlined in the financial statements in the Kwik Chek plan for one way to address operational issues for a service business.

Financial Analysis

Now, down to the bottom line. Everything else, up to this point, was presented as the foundation for the financial analysis. This section spells out the actual investment required and when and how the business will make enough money to pay it back. You define the amount of initial investment and how much you will need in the future based on certain sales and operations projections. The investor really wants to know how much money will be invested, how much they can expect to make, and in what time frame. Everything else is simply a teaser to whet their appetite for the financial feast that follows. You should also include a *break-even analysis* that covers the volume required to push the company from a deficit to a profitable operation.

You should include an *income statement, balance sheet,* and *cash flow analysis* that projects the first 12 months of operations. This is sometimes called a *pro-forma* income statement. A pro-forma balance sheet for the next three years is also

> WHAT?
>
> **Break-even** The point where you are making just enough money to cover your expenses. You are living at a subsistence level, paying the rent, and putting food on the table with no extra money for movies and popcorn.

a necessary component. Pro-forma just means that the numbers are projections, or estimates, of future sales and expenses.

Your income statement summarizes how much money you made and how much money you spent for a specified period of time, which is typically one year. It allows you to look at the big picture of how much money you expect to make.

Use a balance sheet to determine the value of what you own (your assets) and what you owe (your liabilities) at a particular point in time, which is usually the last day of the year. Bankers are interested in this statement because it gives them an idea of what your business is worth and whether you can pay off your loan by selling all your assets.

A projected balance sheet shows what your assets and liabilities are expected to be at the end of your first year in business.

Now for the clincher. Estimate and show your actual cash needs for the first 12 months, broken out by month, and then for years 2 and 3 on an annual basis. The key here is figuring out exactly when you will receive payment for your sales, keeping in mind that if you do not receive payment when you sell your product, such as in a fast-food restaurant, you will always be waiting for some customers to pay their bill. There is sometimes a time-lag between when you make a sale and when you get paid that you have to account for. Putting together a cash flow statement will assure that you are always ahead of your expenses so you won't run out of cash to pay your bills. (Generally, that's called bankruptcy.)

It's also a great idea to show the investors when they can expect to get their money back and how that is supposed to happen. Spell it out, along with your assumptions, in great detail.

The initial capital required to start the business, the funding sources, and how it will be spent is summarized in the "Funds Needed and Their Uses" section.

A set of financial statements has been completed to show investors, expenses, revenue, cash flow, and asset and liability projections for the Kwik Chek operation.

Conclusion

This section is optional and summarizes all the presented information in the plan and provides recommended actions on the part of the reader's investor. This section must directly complement the recommendations made in the Executive Summary but can include more detail.

The Kwik Chek plan does not include a conclusion.

SAMPLE PROJECTED INCOME STATEMENT	1995
Revenues	
Products	120,000
Services	57,555
Net Revenues	**$177,555**
Cost of Sales	
Products	42,000
Services	16,593
Total COGS	**$58,593**
Gross Profit	**$118,962**
Expenses	
Salaries and wages	34,500
Benefits	6,210
Payroll taxes	5,175
Rent	0
Insurance	1,290
Utilities	4,800
Office supplies	4,500
Postage	3,000
Advertising and marketing	12,000
Entertainment	1,440
State sales tax	14,204
Bad debt	5,327
Total Operating Expenses	**$92,446**
Net Income (Loss) before Taxes	**$26,516**
Taxes paid	**$9,281**
Net Income (Loss)	**$17,236**

A projected income statement shows how much your sales and expenses are expected to be for the next year. The difference between your sales and your expenses is your net income.

SAMPLE		
PROJECTED BALANCE SHEET	**For the Year Ending December 31, 1995**	
ASSETS		
Current Assets		
Cash	2,000	
Accounts receivable	10,000	
Inventory	5,000	
Prepaid expenses	500	
Total Current Assets	**17,500**	
Property and Equipment		
Building and land	0	
Equipment	25,000	
Furniture	18,000	
Vehicle	25,000	
Less:		
Accumulated Depreciation	13,600	
Total Property and Equipment	**54,400**	
TOTAL ASSETS		**$71,900**
LIABILITIES		
Current Liabilities		
Accounts payable	9,400	
Taxes payable	730	
Current Portion of L/T Debt	0	
Short-term notes payable	5,000	
Total Current Liabilities	**15,130**	
Long-Term Liabilities		
Long-term notes payable	20,000	
Total Long-term Liabilities	**20,000**	
Equity		
Shareholders equity	36,770	
Retained earnings	0	
Total equity	36,770	
TOTAL LIABILITIES AND EQUITY		**$71,900**

A projected balance sheet shows what your assets and liabilities are expected to be at the end of your first year in business.

Sample
PROJECTED CASH FLOW

	January	February	March	April	May	June	July	August	September	October	November	December	1995
Cash On Hand	$20,000	$97,154	$102,547	$110,921	$121,154	$132,728	$140,062	$143,562	$146,843	$155,463	$166,954	$179,454	
REVENUES	16,920	20,160	23,140	25,000	26,340	22,100	19,000	18,780	24,120	26,990	28,000	31,000	180,000
Total Inflows	36,920	117,314	125,687	135,921	147,494	154,828	159,062	162,342	170,963	182,453	194,954	210,454	
EXPENSES													
Cost of Goods Sold	8,500	8,500	8,500	8,500	8,500	8,500	8,500	8,500	8,500	8,500	8,500	8,500	102,000
Advertising	333	333	333	333	333	333	333	333	333	333	333	333	4,000
Bad debts	200	200	200	200	200	200	200	200	200	200	200	200	2,400
Car and truck expenses	192	192	192	192	192	192	192	192	192	192	192	192	2,300
Insurance	217	217	217	217	217	217	217	217	217	217	217	217	2,600
Interest expense	389	389	389	389	389	389	389	389	389	389	389	389	4,664
Legal and professional services	23	23	23	23	23	23	23	23	23	23	23	23	272
Salaries	2,533	2,533	2,533	2,533	2,533	2,533	2,533	2,533	2,533	2,533	2,533	2,533	30,400
Benefits	1,000	1,000	1,000	1,000	1,000	1,000	1,733	1,733	1,733	1,733	1,733	1,733	16,398
Office expense/mortgage	200	200	200	200	200	200	200	200	200	200	200	200	2,400
Repairs and maintenance	267	267	267	267	267	267	267	267	267	267	267	267	3,200
Taxes	482	482	482	482	482	482	482	482	482	482	482	482	5,784
Travel	117	117	117	117	117	117	117	117	117	117	117	117	1,400
Utilities	200	200	200	200	200	200	200	200	200	200	200	200	2,400
Publications	16	16	16	16	16	16	16	16	16	16	16	16	190
Memberships	42	42	42	42	42	42	42	42	42	42	42	42	500
Contributions	25	25	25	25	25	25	25	25	25	25	25	25	300
Bank charges	32	32	32	32	32	32	32	32	32	32	32	32	387
Total Expenses	14,766	14,766	14,766	14,766	14,766	14,766	15,499	15,499	15,499	15,499	15,499	15,499	181,595
Total Outflow	14,766	14,766	14,766	14,766	14,766	14,766	15,499	15,499	15,499	15,499	15,499	15,499	181,595
Net Cash	22,154	102,547	110,921	121,154	132,728	140,062	143,562	146,843	155,463	166,954	179,454	194,955	
Bank Loan	75,000	0	0	0	0	0	0	0	0	0	0	0	75,000
Cash at End of Period	$97,154	$102,547	$110,921	$121,154	$132,728	$140,062	$143,562	$146,843	$155,463	$166,954	$179,454	$194,955	

A projected cash flow analysis shows, month-by-month, what you expect to make in sales and what you expect to pay out for expenses. Since sales figures vary monthly, you need to keep careful watch of your cash flow to ensure that you always have enough money to cover your expenses.

Appendix

Most of the work that goes into building a house doesn't show, such as the foundation and the walls. However, without these "invisible" ingredients, the house wouldn't stand up on its own. The appendices and supplementary materials are similar in that you refer to them often throughout the plan, but they appear as detailed references at the end. Included are the charts, graphs, extrapolations, résumés, and literature pieces needed to convince the investor that you have done your homework.

Your Business Plan: Length Is Not the Only Criteria

It's not what you have, but how you use it. This statement applies to many important aspects of life and is particularly true when creating a business plan. A small plan that clearly and concisely addresses all the major points of interest will be better received than a lengthy one that drones on about irrelevant information for pages and pages. You don't get bonus points for the weight of your plan.

Busy people, which includes most investors, won't take the time to read a plan that is much longer than 40 or 50 pages. They also won't try and figure out what you're talking about if you haven't been crystal clear. You need to do the work for them; spell it out for them, in plain English. Lead your readers through the plan, step-by-step, explaining your idea and how you intend to make money doing it. Present the information succinctly to that end, and keep the following in mind:

- Don't present an opinion as fact without any supporting information. Investors want to hear facts, not your personal beliefs.
- Don't present droves of information. (Just because you walked ten miles through the snow doesn't mean someone else has to. Take the time to make the important points easily understood.) Create a financial section to organize the detailed financial charts and tables and other supporting information.
- Summarize the implications associated with the information presented. Don't just present facts and figures without explaining why investors should care. (Investors can easily miss the point if left to draw their own conclusions.)
- Don't present conflicting information. (Analysts will eat you alive if you present inconsistent information.)
- Don't trivialize the competition. (They are already there. Where are you?)
- Don't use obsolete data while analyzing a rapidly changing marketplace. (You may not have a choice if new information isn't available, but avoid this one if possible.)
- Don't lose focus midstream and meander your way to the end without direction. (This may work at parties, but not with business plans. Stay on target.)

- Don't use a lot of technical jargon; keep it simple.
- Don't assume that customers will buy simply because it's your idea. (Get real! Your ego will not sell product! It is price, quality, availability, and competitive positioning that will close the deal. Concentrate on these areas and leave your ego at home.)
- Don't assume everyone who said they would work with you will actually work with you when the chips are down. As a former IBM employee was told when he went out on his own looking for business as a consultant," Oh, you no longer work for IBM? Sorry."

Keep the Plan Alive!

Congratulations! You've finished your business plan. Take your family out to dinner at a nice restaurant and gloat on your recent triumph. Enjoy the moment while you can because you now have to make it work according to your estimates.

Don't throw away the business plan now that it's done or leave it on the shelf to accumulate dust. It is a working document that outlines your best guess on how to create a successful business. In a lot of ways, it becomes a friend who reminds you of what was important to you when you were just starting out. Use it as a barometer for determining your performance as compared to estimates (sometimes called *performance to plan*). Know that your investors will be checking your performance against the business plan on a regular basis since that is the set of specifications against which they made their investment. A well-executed business plan provides milestones for determining whether your initial estimates and assumptions were accurate, which allows for midcourse corrections if needed.

Performance to plan A comparison of how well you thought you'd do (financially and otherwise) with how you actually did.

It is a good idea to allocate time at the end of each year to track your performance to date and to budget for the next year. This exercise allows you to make corrections in anticipation for the upcoming year and minimizes the likelihood that mistakes from the prior year are carried over to the next. Use it wisely as a reference point to obtain the best return on your initially invested time and money.

Don't Get Discouraged—Try a New Perspective

What a drag! You perform the entire analysis to discover the idea does not hold financial water. Now what? Be thankful! You have just saved yourself a nasty experience.

If you find that the business just won't work, then your original assumptions were not valid. If you had pursued the venture based on those assumptions, you would be either personally bankrupt after investing all your hard-earned savings or apologizing to your angry investors. Take heart! A negative outcome on this round does not negate the entire venture. You can now consider a different, potentially more successful approach.

Take a look at your approach to the business to see if modifying it can provide a better, and more profitable, strategy:

- Is the problem with the idea itself or simply how it is being presented?
- Are you the right person to shepherd the idea to success, or should you be looking for others to round out other critical positions? Should you look at merging your talents with another more established firm?
- Do you need more money to buy you more time to achieve the needed market recognition?
- Should you initially offer a product or service that is more readily acceptable and then convert your customers over to your new product/service line once they are already familiar with you and your company?
- Are your sales estimates too low? What could you do to increase the sales faster, and what would be the additional cost?
- Are there things you can do to minimize the level of perceived risk?

Keep your chin up and remember: creating a successful business plan is a lot like solving a mystery. You have many stray facts that need to fit properly before the venture makes sense on all levels. Take the time to learn the facts.

Using Business Planning Software

Automation is a wonderful thing for performing routine tasks such as extensive number crunching and the creation of standard text. Business plans contain the same basic information, and the overall structure is fairly well defined. For this reason, you may find that business planning software can help you start writing your plan. There are a number of business planning software packages on the market designed to ask you questions to "fill-in-the-blanks." Your responses are then entered into the appropriate plan sections and the plan contents are automatically created.

That is the good news. The bad news is that no automated business planning computer software can add your personality and style to the plan, and your personality is crucial to the success of your venture. In addition, nobody can predict all of the special situations that apply to your business idea. As a result, some topics won't be addressed and unnecessary topics may be included. Also, investors don't always like to see the "plan-in-a-can" format that results from using one of these packages.

Computers perform routine tasks in a highly efficient manner, but they have zero capability to create something new. The creative aspects of the plan are in your hands. Using an automated business planning software package is worth a try because it will force you to organize your thoughts and give you a place to start. If you are really lucky, it will create a plan that is adequate for your needs. To make sure, run the plan past a colleague or "friendly" investor for preliminary feedback. I'll talk about the basic use of this software and other business software in Chapter 18.

> **REALLY!?**
>
> Two of the more popular business planning applications you can pick up at your local computer store are Biz Plan Builder ($129) and MultiMedia MBA ($99.95). For more information on Biz Plan Builder, call 1-800-346-5426; for MultiMedia MBA, call 1-800-228-5609.

The Least You Need to Know

Just as our friends in the desert felt better once they knew where they were going, you'll feel better once you understand all the details associated with running your prospective business. Uncertainty is difficult to accept, and the greater the risk, the more you need to minimize that uncertainty. Using the planning process to develop your personal and business goals will quickly increase your chances for success.

- Use your business plan as a sales document to convince someone to give you money.
- Your business plan is also a valuable management tool that can help you make decisions for your business.
- Going through the process of writing a business plan will help you determine if the business is worth starting. You may find that your original idea can't make money.
- A business plan is a requirement in today's business climate, and if you cooperate with the process instead of fighting it, you will learn a lot about your proposed business idea and yourself.

Part 2
Establishing the Framework of the Business

Now that you have a plan for what you want to accomplish with your business, you need to make some decisions about whether to incorporate or not. Some people start a business and never incorporate. Others incorporate as the first order of business. And people starting partnerships often write up some sort of agreement, whether they file the paperwork to that effect or not.

The reason that people approach the process of incorporating very differently is there are lots of things to consider. From taxes to liability (if something goes wrong), to taxes, to raising money, to taxes... there are many things to think about. In this section, you can figure out what kind of corporate structure may be best for you, and you will receive some tips on setting up a corporation.

Chapter 5

Which Business Form Should You Choose?

In This Chapter

- Consider the various legal business forms
- Review the legal implications of each type of business structure
- An overview of the tax impact of each form

Bill shouted, "What do you mean I could lose everything I own? I didn't even know Ted bought that equipment for the company."

"The problem is you never incorporated like you planned, and the law treats the two of you as a partnership," replied the attorney. "Under the law, you are responsible for the company obligations whether you agreed to them or not."

"No way," shouted Bill. "I'm not going to pay. Let them go after Ted first."

"The equipment company will first go after the business, and then you and Ted at the same time. As far as the law is concerned, you and Ted are the same and both equally liable for paying off the debt. Sorry, but you have no choice. Next time, pick your partners more carefully and consider incorporating to avoid this situation again."

Bill didn't like it, but he accepted what he heard as the truth. How could his life's savings and a thriving company take a dive so quickly based on the irresponsible actions of one person? What could he have done differently? How could he have known?

What Are the Various Business Structures?

Just as one house style will not meet the living requirements of all families, no single business form meets everyone's business needs. Depending on your current situation and future business aspirations, one business form may meet those needs better than another. Take the time to determine where you want the company to go using the information provided in Chapter 3. This long-term perspective will suggest the best business form for your specific situation.

There are three basic business organizational forms: *sole proprietorship*, *partnership*, and *corporation*. Under each category are subclasses that apply to specific situations.

A *sole proprietorship* is the most common and easiest type of business to create. Anyone who performs any services of any kind, such as a gardener, caterer, or even baby-sitter, is, by default, a sole proprietor unless they specifically set it up otherwise. A small company with only one employee is often kept as a sole proprietorship, but there are no restrictions on how big a sole proprietorship can become. It depends exclusively on the desires of the owner, or proprietor.

> WHAT?
>
> **Sole proprietorship** You transact business without the legal "safety net" associated with a corporation. You are personally responsible for all of the business' obligations, such as debt, even though the business may have a different name than yours. Essentially, you and the business are one and the same in this instance.

A *partnership* is formed whenever two or more people decide to enter into a for-profit business venture. Each partner owns an equal portion of the company's profits and debts. You do not need to file any special paperwork to form a partnership, but you should make sure you and your partner sign an agreement to minimize misunderstandings regarding each person's rights and liabilities. If you do not have an agreement signed by both parties, then any partnership-related disputes will be handled under statutes based on the Uniform Partnership Act (UPA) used in most states.

A partnership agreement states the terms and conditions of the partnership. However, the UPA defines generally accepted standards on items not covered in the agreement. It is essentially a "gap filler." Any law library will have detailed information on the UPA, but the best way to avoid UPA issues is to work with a complete partnership agreement from the beginning.

For many people, forming a corporation is a sign of how serious you are about your business, because it is more involved and more expensive to set up a corporation than to set up a sole proprietorship or partnership.

When you form a corporation, you are actually establishing a separate organization; separate and distinct from you personally. Some of you may be asking why that's such a big deal—what's the advantage? The advantage is that if the corporation is sued, you are not personally responsible for any damages that may be awarded (unless, of course, you are also named in the suit). Paperwork and record-keeping is also more involved with a corporation, which is why some people decide it's not worth the hassles. There are other ways besides incorporating to protect yourself personally from liability.

Many corporations are formed in the state of Delaware because its unrestrictive incorporation laws make it attractive as a corporation state of origin. Delaware was one of the early states to allow you to incorporate in their state while carrying out business and keeping the headquarters in another state. Most other states now allow the same procedure. It is generally easier to form a small or *close* corporation in the state where the principle shareholders reside and work. Since state tax laws vary, be sure to check with an accountant before making this decision. A close corporation consists of an owner or owners who are active in managing the business on a day-to-day basis, with no public investors.

Select the business form that is right for you based on where you are today and where you want to wind up down the road. Consider the advantages and disadvantages of each business structure before making a decision. Liability issues can also be addressed through insurance, so while limited liability is one reason to choose a corporate form of organization, check with knowledgable advisors before making a final decision.

WHAT?

Partnership
Where you and one or more people form a business marriage legally linking your debts and assets from the start. Any partner can make a commitment for the business, which also commits the other partners. Unless there is a specific agreement to the contrary, each partner owns an equal portion of the company's profits, assets, and debts.

WHAT?

Corporation A separate legal entity that is created through the state in which the business is to be incorporated. A corporation has owners who purchase shares in the corporation. The percentage ownership is based on the number or shares owned as compared with the total number of shares sold. A properly organized corporation bears all legal and fiscal liability, shielding shareholders (owners) from personal risk (unless they are also sued personally or guarantee corporate obligations).

Sole Proprietorship: Going It Alone

Judy woke up this morning and decided to begin selling those little wooden dolls she gives away every Christmas. She just became the head of a *sole proprietorship*.

Once you begin providing products or services with the intention of making money from these activities, you become a sole proprietor. Your business expenses are deductible, all income is taxable, and you assume the liabilities of the business. (More on the tax implications later.)

Notice that Judy did not have to come up with a separate name to start her business. She simply started her business and began selling her product, using her own name. This is why the sole proprietorship is such a popular business form.

However, should Judy want to call her business **Dolls and Such**, she must file a *Doing Business As* (DBA) form with the local authorities, usually the county clerk's office in which she plans to do business. The DBA filing is sometimes called a *fictitious name statement*. If no one else is using the name she has chosen, after filing her DBA form, Judy can transact business as Dolls and Such. Filing the DBA gives her legal rights to the name within the jurisdiction of the governing body, which is typically the county. If someone else uses the name within the county, Judy can ask the courts to order that person to cease operations under the name she legally owns. The other business would then be forced to rename itself.

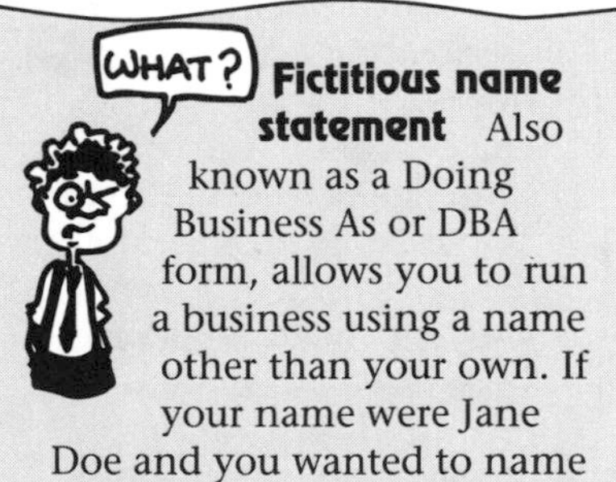

Fictitious name statement Also known as a Doing Business As or DBA form, allows you to run a business using a name other than your own. If your name were Jane Doe and you wanted to name your business anything other than Jane Doe, you'd have to file a fictitious name statement to that effect.

A sole proprietorship is easy and inexpensive to create, and all profits go directly to the owner. The major disadvantage is that all legal and financial obligations incurred by the company are also passed directly to the owner. That means that if the company were sued for any reason, such as if a child ate one of Judy's dolls and was hospitalized, Judy is personally responsible for answering that lawsuit. The owner could lose everything she personally owns if the business-related lawsuit is lost and the damages are high. For this liability reason alone, many people choose to change their structure from a sole proprietorship to a corporation.

Being a sole proprietorship does not limit whether you have employees or not, although many sole proprietorships are one-person businesses. You can hire employees as a sole proprietorship, but you, as the owner, become the target for any claims made against the business as a result of any of the actions of your employees.

The flexibility associated with being the only owner is often attractive enough to keep people in business as a sole proprietorship, even after the company grows large in revenues.

Partnerships: Like a Business Marriage

Partnership is a wonderful term that evokes warm, comforting feelings. Who wouldn't want a partner to share the good and bad times in a business? Well, if you have ever been in a bad relationship, you know the damage it can do to your psychological and financial well-being. You should treat business partnerships with the same amount of respect.

When two or more people form a partnership, they are essentially married, from a business standpoint. Either party can obligate the other via the business, and everything the business and the partners own individually is on the line. In essence, a partnership is like a sole proprietorship owned by several people. All liability is passed to the partners.

A special partnership type, called a *limited partnership*, provides certain partners with a maximum financial liability equal to their investment. To maintain this limited financial liability status, these partners, called *limited partners*, cannot participate in the daily operation of the business. The *general partner* is responsible for the day-to-day management of the business. Limited partners invest in the company and rely on the general partner to run the business.

There are special laws that govern the operation of a limited partnership, and if they are not precisely followed, the courts may hold that the partnership was general, not limited. The formerly limited partner may find himself liable as a general partner for business-related debts. Be aware that you must complete and file special paperwork with the state to form a limited partnership.

WHAT?

Limited partnership A special form of partnership where a partner invests money and does not participate in the daily operation of the business. This partner is only liable for the amount of money that he has invested and no more.

Corporations: Share the Wealth

Creating a corporation is like creating a new business life. A corporation is a separate and distinct business entity that is responsible for itself. Upon formation, the corporation issues shares of stock to *shareholders*, the owners. The shareholders exchange money, goods, or expertise to receive their shares of stock.

A *board of directors*, elected by the shareholders, manages the corporation. This board then appoints *officers* of the corporation to handle the day-to-day affairs of the company. In essence, the board members represent the interests of the shareholders in the company operations. In many small corporations, the business owner is the primary, or only, shareholder and only board member.

The corporation pays taxes on its annual profits and passes the profits to the shareholders in the form of a *dividend*. The board of directors determines the amount of the dividends.

The major benefits associated with a corporate business form is that the corporation is liable for its own financial and civil liabilities. The shareholders only risk the amount of money they have invested in their respective shares of stock.

Using the earlier Dolls and Such example, assume that the business is a corporation with $500,000 in its bank account. If someone were to win a judgment against Dolls and Such for $1 million, the company would probably go out of business and only $500,000 would change hands. The person who won the legal judgment against the corporation would have no immediate legal basis for getting money from the shareholders personally.

However, this would not be the case with a partnership or sole proprietorship. As a partner or sole proprietor, your personal finances would be put squarely at risk in this scenario, and you could lose a lifetime of work. You might end up owing an additional $500,000 to the judgment holder if that situation ever came to pass.

Another major corporate benefit involves raising money for the business by selling shares in the corporation. Once the buyer and seller agree to a price per share of stock, the buyer simply purchases the number of shares needed to equal the amount of money needed. For instance, assume you need to raise $100,000. If you find a buyer who is willing to pay you $4 per share, then you sell them 25,000 shares of stock to receive the $100,000. Life is rarely this simple, but this example outlines the basic benefit associated with corporation finances.

To further illustrate the point, assume you still need $100,000 but don't know anyone with that kind of money on hand. Instead of selling 25,000 shares at $4 each to one person, you could sell 2,500 shares to ten different investors for $4 each and still get the money you need. You now have 10 shareholders instead of one, but you got the money you needed.

Publicly Versus Privately Held Corporations

There is a difference between a publicly held and privately held corporation. Publicly held corporations are traded on the various public stock exchanges, such as the New York

Stock Exchange, American Stock Exchange, and NASDAQ. The shareholders are typically large numbers of people who never come in direct contact with each other. They trust the board of directors to manage their investment for them.

Privately held, or *close*, corporations are more common. The shares are held by a few people, often family members, who also sit on the board and participate as officers of the corporation. The shares are also not offered to the general public.

Unless you are planning to create a very large business, you will probably create a privately held corporation with you and a few others as the only shareholders. If the number of shareholders exceeds 35, you must comply with the Securities and Exchange Commission (SEC) regulations for publicly offered companies, or choose to form a Limited Liability Company (LLC)—more on this topic later—that permits more than 35 shareholders. You will definitely need legal and accounting services.

> WHAT?
>
> **Close corporation**
> A corporation owned by a small number of shareholders, often only one. In this case, the corporation may be viewed as an extension of the individual. You must still act like a corporation with separate checking accounts, loans, and finances.

When a company "goes public," it offers to sell shares in the company to the general public. This is a common way for the founding members of a company to make oodles of money from the large numbers of stock shares they received during the startup stages. The founders often buy or receive this stock at the outset for a nominal price, sometimes pennies per share. When the company goes public, the shares may sell for dollars per share. You don't need to be a CPA to figure out that several hundred thousand shares sold at a public offering can add up to a lot of profit. This opportunity alone keeps many people actively working for startup companies, along with their associated risks, instead of working for larger, more stable companies.

> WHAT?
>
> The **Securities and Exchange Commission (SEC)** regulates public offerings of company securities. The SEC mandates strict guidelines for dissemination and content of company financial information to help assure investors that the information they receive on public companies is reliable and reasonably comprehensive.

Sub-S Corporations: A Little Bit of Protection

Let's say you want the legal protection provided by a corporation, but want the income to pass directly to you so you can declare it on your personal income tax statement. You can thank the IRS and Congress because they created the *Subchapter S corporation* for just this purpose.

In a Subchapter S, or S Corporation, instead of the corporation paying taxes on its income, the business income is passed onto the shareholders who then declare the income on their personal income tax statements. Subchapter S corporations retain all of the legal protection provided by a standard C corporation (any corporation that is not an S corporation).

So why opt for the S instead of C corporation? If you are personally in a lower tax bracket than the corporation, then passing the business income to you will decrease the overall tax paid. In addition, if the corporation loses money, you can use that loss to offset personal income earned from other investments you may have. However, if you don't plan properly or if the company does better than you expected, you could find yourself with a huge tax bill at the end of the year.

If you think the S corporation is right for you, check with an accountant and an attorney before taking the plunge. A little prevention goes a long way to avoid unforeseen problems down the road. Notice the decision is heavily based on how much revenue you anticipate the company will generate. This is why the strategic planning aspects of business are so critically important.

Limited Liability Company (LLC)

How would you like the advantages of a corporation or partnership without some of the restrictions regarding shareholders? That's what a new form of business organization, called a *limited liability company* (LLC), can provide.

Limited liability companies are now authorized in 43 states, with the remaining seven and the District of Columbia expected to approve a similar structure soon. The reason for their new popularity (only eight states authorized LLCs just two years ago) is that LLCs provide business owners with personal liability protection, just as corporations and partnerships do, and still tax profits at the individual level only, as with Subchapter S corporations.

What sets them apart from the popular S corporation is that LLCs do not have the same restrictions regarding shareholders. S corporations limit the number of shareholders to 35 and require that they be U.S. citizens; foreigners, domestic corporations, and co-owners of partnerships may not participate. LLCs, on the other hand, have no limits on the number of shareholders and do not place restrictions on the makeup or citizenship of its shareholders. In addition, LLCs can have more than one class of stock and can own stock in another corporation.

Because of these advantages LLCs are anticipated to exceed Subchapter S corporations, regular C corporations, partnerships, and limited partnerships as the preferred organizational structure. Since conversion to an LLC from another type of business structure can be costly, LLCs are generally recommended more for start-ups.

One concern about LLCs, however, is that there is no unified set of tax laws, since individual states created their own laws regarding LLCs, which were then copied by other states. The IRS has yet to provide a general set of national tax laws for LLCs. Check with the Secretary of State to find out more about the laws governing LLCs in your state.

> **Class of stock** Corporations can sell different kinds of stock (class) such as preferred or common at different prices. The various classes differ in when dividends are paid and under what circumstances.

This section relied heavily on "A Liability Shield for Entrepreneurs," Ripley Hotch, Nation's Business, *August, 1994.*

Professional Corporations: For Doctors, Lawyers, CPAs, and Such

There is a special corporation form that addresses the needs of professionals who share a practice, such as lawyers. The *professional corporation,* as it was initially called, provided special tax-related benefits to the participants. Many of the benefits have been reduced since 1981, however, and the growth in the number of professional corporations has declined. If you are a licensed professional who falls into this special category, check with your accountant to determine whether a professional corporation provides you any special benefits. Professional corporations use the letters P.C. after the company name to indicate what kind of corporation it is.

> Don't make your business organization decision based solely on the tax implications. The tax laws change on a regular basis, and the impact of the laws varies depending upon your personal income and your company's income levels.

Franchises: Paying for Their Experience

Although a *franchise* is not technically a business form, it is a way to start a business using the experience and training provided by an existing company.

The franchise process works something like this:

1. You decide you want to be in business.
2. You look around for business areas that interest you.
3. You find a franchisor who has developed a good business concept with a successful track record in helping people start similar operations.
4. You purchase the franchise rights to their procedures and name recognition in exchange for an up-front fee and a recurring annual percentage of your income.
5. After a few years, you start to resent paying the fee to the franchisor and begin looking for ways to sever the link.

(Number 5 may not always happen, but I have heard it from enough successful franchisees that you may as well go in expecting that reaction to occur eventually).

You benefit from the franchise relationship because it removes a lot of the risky trial and error associated with starting a new business. A successful franchisor, such as McDonald's, will know precisely how to run your business so you will have the best chance for success. That expertise is not free, but it may save you from going under while you work your way up the learning curve.

There are three basic franchise flavors: *distributor*, *chain-style*, and *manufacturing*.

WHAT? **Franchisor**
A company that has created a successful business operation and concept that offers to sell the rights to the operation and idea on a limited geographic or market basis. The buyer of the franchise rights is called the **franchisee.**

The *distributor franchise* is typically used with automobile dealerships where the franchisee (the dealer) is licensed to sell the franchisor's (such as Ford's) products. The franchisee is given some type of exclusive marketing arrangement for a specific geographic or market segment. The franchisee's main role is to sell the company's products, rather than become involved in manufacturing or other functions.

The *chain-style franchise* is used with fast-food establishments where the franchisee (the local owner) is licensed and required to prepare the food in accordance with the franchisor's (such as McDonald's) standards. The local store is often required to purchase all supplies from the franchisor and maintain quality standards, and (often) hit specific sales volume targets.

The *manufacturing franchise* is licensed to create a product (such as Coca-Cola) in accordance with the franchisor's (the Coca-Cola Company's) specifications. The franchise then resells the product at a wholesale price to the distribution channel.

> REALLY!?
>
> *Entrepreneur* magazine does an annual issue (January) on top franchises. Check it out!

A franchise arrangement allows you to start your own business with strong expertise behind you. This improves your likelihood of success and may decrease the amount of up-front cash required because many franchisors assist with the initial funding. However, it may increase the up-front total investment required (cash and loans), because you are buying a share of a proven business franchise concept. Unless you are dead set on "doing it your own way," you should consider franchising as a business option.

When you purchase a franchise, you'll need to set up a company just the same as if you started it from scratch. So you'll still need to evaluate which form of doing business is best for your situation: sole proprietorship, partnership, or corporation.

Oh No! You Want Offices in More Than One State

Like life wasn't complicated enough, you now want to operate your business with offices in several states. The good news is that this is possible. If your home base is in one state and the majority of your business is from that location, you can avoid the multistate headache. The bad news is, if this is not the case, you will need to perform some filings and registrations to qualify in each state where you do business.

There are firms that specialize in setting up companies that need to operate in several states at once. Contact a law firm and get a referral to one of their suppliers or simply contract the law firm to perform the needed paperwork for you.

> REALLY!?
>
> The Company Corporation in Wilmington, Delaware, offers online corporate registration via CompuServe and other online services. The $49 base fee they quote may not cover all the costs you'll have to pay, but entrepreneurs all over the country have found this to be one reasonable way to incorporate. Call 302-575-0440.

You could do all the legwork yourself; however, this approach could become a black hole for time and effort. You are probably better off farming it out to those who do it for a living. This is particularly important when considering a name for your organization because the name must be available in all states of interest. Read the next section about names. If you insist on doing it yourself, contact the secretary of state's office in each state of interest for filing guidelines and fees.

When to Use a Lawyer

When should you use a lawyer? I think the best answer to this question is "before you need one." By this I mean that prevention is the best cure for legal problems. If your business agreements are created and documented in a responsible way with both parties equally involved in the discussions, you can minimize the likelihood of future legal action.

You will also find numerous computer software packages on the market that will automatically generate a wide variety of legal documents for you, from a Bill of Sale to Articles of Incorporation. Most packages will even take into account the state in which you transact business and modify the language accordingly. Go to the library and check out past copies of *PC World*, *MacWorld*, or *PC Magazine* for their assessment of the various legal packages. They usually cost under $100 and pay for themselves with one use.

Lawyers will tell you that much of their income is generated in repairing the damage done by people who attempt to economize on legal fees up front and develop contracts and agreements on their own—only to find out that the document they developed doesn't accomplish its objective.

If you have the money (or even if you think you don't), have an attorney draw up the necessary filing documents for you. If money is a real concern, try taking your best shot at completing an important legal document on your own and then run it past an attorney for review.

You can purchase prewritten articles of incorporation, stock certificates, and corporation bylaws from the same companies that supply your attorney. Ask an attorney where he gets his "stash" of corporation documents, and you may be able to save yourself hundreds of dollars. Of course, you do inherit the hassle of putting the things together properly.

As always, if any agreement is for a large amount of money and binds you in critical ways, you should consult an attorney before getting too far down the road. A few hundred dollars up front can save thousands of dollars and hundreds of hours at a later date.

Special Opportunities for Women and Minorities

Governmental organizations, along with most large businesses, have implemented programs that provide special opportunities for minority-owned businesses. The definition of a minority and how that applies to the various business forms is inconsistent between agencies, so investigate your eligibility as a minority business enterprise. Getting the name of your business on a procurement list opens doors that you would otherwise have to discover on your own. These types of organizations are also known as Disadvantaged Business Enterprises (DBE) or Woman Business Enterprises (WBE).

These procurement programs are designed to ensure that a certain percentage of government-issued contracts go to these special business types. You are more likely to get a government request for a proposal if you are listed as a DBE or WBE than if not. This doesn't guarantee that you will get the business, but at least you get a shot at it. Contact the government procurement office, General Services Commission, or Corporate Purchasing to get the needed packet of information.

REALLY!?

The Small Business Administration has set up a program to help increase the number of government contracts awarded to smaller businesses owned particularly by minorities and women. Called Procurement Automated Search System (PASS), any business owner can complete an application to be listed in the government's database of potential suppliers. When an agency needs a type of product or service, they can search PASS for the names of potential vendors. Call your local SBA for information on PASS.

Dealing with the Tax Man

Taxes never go away. All you can do is try to minimize their negative impact on your profits. The impact of taxes on your choice of organizational structure is worth a brief discussion. I'll only present general concepts here about income taxes, so talk to your accountant about your specific situation. Remember, there are many other taxes a business will have to pay. You need to learn about all of them in your area—city, county, state, sales, franchise, and the list goes on.

All business entities, except for the C corporation, pass the income directly to you as the owner or major stockholder. You then declare it on your personal tax return. In corporations, all salary expenses (including the owner's salary) are deducted from the company's revenues prior to determining how much in taxes must be paid. You then pay personal income tax only on your salary, just as you would for any company.

Self-employed individuals really feel the bite of FICA and Medicare taxes, since they pay both the employee's share *and* the employer's share of these taxes.

In addition to income taxes, salaries have FICA (social security), unemployment, and Medicare taxes levied that the company must pay over and above the standard salary. This currently amounts to around 7.62%. The employee also pays these taxes. See Chapter 16.

> **WHAT?** **Dividends** Money paid to shareholders out of the corporation's profits (after taxes are taken out). This is a form of compensation to the shareholders for having made the investment in the corporation by purchasing shares.
>
> **Double taxation** Where the business pays tax on its annual profits and then passes the remaining profits on to you, the majority shareholder, who again gets taxed at the personal level; thus, the same dollar has been taxed twice.

In a corporation, however, *dividends* paid to shareholders are taxed twice; they are paid out of company income after the corporate taxes have been paid. The dividends are then paid to the shareholders who pay tax on the dividends because it is part of their personal income. This is called *double taxation* and it can get expensive.

Sometimes, corporations will try and come up with creative ways to avoid or minimize the financial bite taken out of their shareholder's dividends as a result of *double taxation*. Some people get so focused on avoiding paying taxes that they lose track of their primary concern: running a successful and profitable business that fulfills their personal and financial goals. We all hate giving Uncle Sam a nickel, but avoid the temptation to fiddle with your tax planning to the point that you lose focus on your business.

Individuals and corporations do not pay tax at the same rate. You will find that the break points between tax levels differ. Depending on your situation and the company's income levels, you may be better off leaving the money in the company and paying corporate taxes instead of paying yourself a large salary and paying personal income tax instead. Check out the following table to see the relative rates for personal and corporate taxes.

Single		Married Filing Jointly		Corporation	
Range	Rate	Range	Rate	Range	Rate
$0–21,450	15%	$0–35,800	15%	$0–50,000	15%
$21,451–51,900	28%	$35,800–86,500	28%	$50,001–75,000	28%
$51,901 and over	31%	$86,501 and over	31%	$75,001 and over	34%

Personal and corporate tax rates.

Single people should look at this table and smile. Check out the corporate tax benefit offered to single people between $21,000 – $50,000. The personal tax rate is 28%, but the corporation's is 15%. That 13% (28% – $15%) can be left in the corporation for business use at a lower tax rate than what a Sole Proprietor would have to pay.

The Least You Need to Know

It is a good idea to select the legal form for your business based upon your expected strategic goals. Each form has its own benefits; you want to choose the one best suited to your needs.

- ➤ Taxes are part of life for any business. Recognize that you'll have to learn about them or find competent help.
- ➤ Sole proprietorships, partnerships, and corporations are not the same. Choose your business form based on operational considerations, not tax considerations.
- ➤ Corporations provide the highest level of legal protection but can subject income to double taxation.
- ➤ Don't be afraid to investigate franchising; you may profit from other people's experiences.

Chapter 6

Additional Corporation Implications

In This Chapter

- How to set up a corporation
- Selecting a company name that works now and in the future
- Setting up a board of directors
- An overview of articles of incorporation and bylaws

There was a sense of destiny in the air as Susan made her way to her office. She said good morning to her assistant and anxiously looked for the folder that contained the artist's renderings of their company logo. She liked the name. Her husband had picked it from the final list of contenders. He had beamed when she told him that they would use it. It was fun to see him enjoy participating with her in the dream she had wanted for years. It surely made life at home easier.

The artist's renderings were beautiful. The colors were just what she wanted and anyone with half a brain would understand their offering. It had cost around $4,000 for the public relations firm to create the name and renderings. They were now ready to go.

At that moment Walter, the company attorney, walked into the room. He was holding a piece of paper in his hand and had a somber look on his face: even for Walter. He simply handed her the piece of paper and waited. The letter was from the secretary of state's office indicating that the name they had chosen was already in use by another company within the state and that their request for the name reservation was denied.

Susan's mind did a few somersaults and then landed. They were back to square one and $4,000 poorer than they were before they started. Why did they rush to have that logo created? Couldn't they have waited to hear back from the secretary of state? Susan's mind was racing. "I guess it's back to the drawing board again," she sighed. "But this time, let's send several potential names to the state for approval, rather than just one. I certainly don't want to waste any more time or money on choosing a name."

Setting Up the Corporation: An Overview

If you incorporate as a Subchapter S corporation rather than a C corporation, keep in mind that you can't have more than 35 shareholders.

Check the laws of your home state carefully. If you incorporate in another state, your state may charge stiff taxes to out-of-state corporations, negating a lot of the tax advantages of incorporating elsewhere. If you do business in more than one state, you may have to file tax returns and pay taxes in all of them.

Creating a corporation is like creating a new business life. The corporation has the ability to make commitments, incur debt, hire employees, flourish, if successful, and go out of business if not. You are the principle avenue through which this entity is created, and the responsibility for performing the proper legal steps involved with the corporation's birth is in your hands.

Corporations are created under guidelines established by the state in which the corporation will reside. Each state has its own regulations which govern the creation and operation of a corporation. The secretary of state office defines these guidelines and is your contact point for initial information.

First, determine who is going to be a shareholder in the corporation. How many of them will there be? Almost always, you need a minimum of one shareholder/officer of the corporation before the state will allow you to incorporate. Some states require a minimum of two officers. You will be asked for the names of the president, treasurer, and secretary. These can all be you. Just like the general store owner in a small town, you may have to wear several hats in your corporation.

Next, determine the states within which you intend to do business. Many states allow you to incorporate in that particular state but have your main offices and operations in another state. Delaware is one state that allows for this situation. The major benefits for "long-distance incorporation" are usually tax-related. If that state does not have a corporate income tax, or a small one, it is financially advantageous to incorporate in that state.

Nothing is free. Texas has no state income tax but levies a "franchise fee" that is the equivalent. It may not be called a tax, but it sure feels like a tax when you write the check. Check with corporations in your state of interest and verify the flies in the corporate ointment.

Corporation filing fees paid to the state for setting up your corporation vary widely, from as low as $40 to as high as $900+. (California, where else? Ouch!) Unless becoming a national company immediately is important to you, you are probably better off keeping the process simple and just incorporating in your home state. Startup life is complicated enough without adding more complexity than is necessary.

Your corporation must have a name that serves both a legal and marketing use. The name must comply with the state's legal requirements and should also convey something about your offerings to your customers. Naming details are covered in the next section.

Finally, you must file the *Articles of Incorporation* with the state. The articles outline the basic characteristics of the business and become the legal framework within which the corporation must operate. The business' purpose, planned duration of existence, and capital structure, such as how many share of stock have been issued and who owns what, are defined in the articles. (Read about articles of incorporation later in this chapter.) Once you file the articles and the fees are paid, you are incorporated!

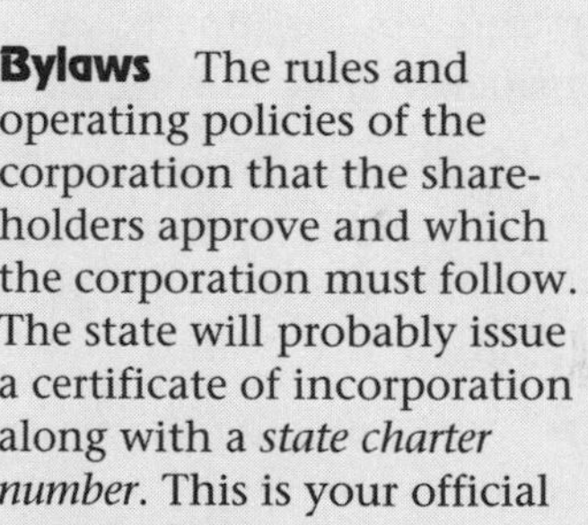

Articles of incorporation Establish the structure and stock ownership of the corporation. The articles are filed with the secretary of state.

Bylaws The rules and operating policies of the corporation that the shareholders approve and which the corporation must follow. The state will probably issue a certificate of incorporation along with a *state charter number*. This is your official record of incorporation.

State charter number The official number assigned to your corporation, like a unique Social Security number.

Congratulations! You have just given birth to a business with a life and identity all its own.

Establishing a trusty board of directors is a natural next step. If you plan to keep your company small, then you can act as your own board. This certainly keeps arguments between the board and upper management to a minimum. If you plan to grow past the "mom-and-pop" stage, then you should consider a board of directors consisting of advisors from the business community. The board of directors defines a set of *bylaws* that guide the internal operation of the company. Bylaws become the overall operating philosophy of the corporation.

What's in a Name? A Lot!

Just as a child must have a name, so must a corporation. However, unlike children, who can share names like Lisa, Tom, and Mary, corporations must have a unique name easily distinguished from other businesses in the state in which you incorporate.

The reason for such strict rules about similar names is to avoid confusion. For example, if a company is already doing business as Art Treasures, Inc. in Miami, Florida, it would have all the legal rights to that name. If you wanted to incorporate as Art Treasures, Inc. in another part of Florida, you probably would not be permitted to use this name because it would cause too much confusion. This protects both you and the other corporation. Once your company is successful, you don't want another company benefiting from your company's success and reputation. Here are some additional things to consider when choosing a name for your business:

- To be most effective, the company's name should also tell prospects something about the types of products or services you offer either by including the product name as part of the company name, as in Toys R Us, or by suggesting the benefits of buying from the company, as in Wall to Wall Sound.
- Avoid making the company name too complicated or obscure. Cute can work to your advantage, but if your company's name is too cute and nobody understands the joke, nobody will use your services. Make it straightforward but distinctive.
- The official corporation's name must indicate that it is a corporation, by including the word "corporation," "company," "incorporated," or "limited." The secretary of state's office can help you with this.

Public relations firms and advertising agencies often assist companies in finding a name that works for their situation. You may want to get a bid from a company that specializes in naming. After all, you usually keep your name for life.

Your company will carry the name for many years and you will spend a tremendous amount of time and money promoting it. Your customer "mind share" will revolve around the name. Treat it like gold, because it is! Jealously guard your company name, just like you would guard your own.

> REALLY!?
> You can use brainstorming software, such as IdeaFisher, to help come up with potential names.

Once you find the name you want to use, you must reserve it for a period of time (usually two to six months) by filing a *fictitious name form* with the secretary of state office in your state. There is a nominal fee for reserving the name. The office will perform a name search for you and tell you whether the name you want to use is still available, or whether some other company is already using it. I suggest giving the secretary of state several names to check at once, so that you don't have to keep going back to the drawing board if your top choice is already in use. You must incorporate within the two-to-six-month window or the name is forfeited.

You can see how complicated the naming procedure may be if you want to incorporate in several states, because the same name must be available in each state. Finding that one free name in all of the target states can be a frustrating and expensive procedure. Don't commission a designer for your corporate name and logo until you have the name reserved, or you may be throwing money away. Nothing is more complicated than trying to explain to a client the reason behind having two names.

> REALLY!?
> Unlike sole proprietorships, which typically involve just one piece of paper filed with the county clerk's office, a corporation is formed at the state level, by the secretary of state.

> My company started out as a sole proprietorship, which I decided to incorporate a few years ago. When I tried to incorporate under the sole proprietorship name, I found the name was already taken by a business in another city. We now have two operational names: one for the local community, Applied Concepts, and the other, Technology and Communications, Inc., for outside of the local area. We retained the local name due to its local recognition, but the headaches associated with having two business names should not be ignored. When you pick a name, make sure it is available from the start to prevent customer confusion.

Setting Up the Articles of Incorporation and Bylaws

How do you establish the articles of incorporation and the bylaws for your company? These two documents are where you put into words the overall intent of your corporation. You file the articles of incorporation with the state as part of the corporation formation procedure. The board of directors creates the bylaws and determines the company operating procedures.

Articles of Incorporation: The Basic Ingredients

The articles of incorporation need not be lengthy. They just need to be accurate and provide the state with the needed information to allow for incorporation. Most of the articles are easily created. Try this basic structure as a starting place. In the following articles, type the bold sentences and fill in the italic requests.

Article One: The Company Name

The name of the corporation is *(enter your company name).*

Article Two: The Period of Duration

The period of the company duration is *(enter the number of years, which is usually assumed to be PERPETUAL).*

Article Three: The Company Purpose

The purpose of the company is to *(enter the basic reasons why the company exists; most people simply use FOR ANY LEGAL PURPOSE).*

You can also be a little more specific and mention the types of products or services the corporation will be selling. However, if you ever decide to change the purpose of the corporation, you may have to go back and alter or amend your articles of incorporation. For this reason, it may be best to be somewhat general.

Article Four: The Capital Structure

The total number of shares that the company is authorized to issue is *(enter the number of shares)* **at a *par value* of** *(enter the par value of each share)* **dollars each.**

For example, you could assume that the company is authorized to issue 100,000 shares at a par value of $.01 each. Don't confuse *authorized shares* with *issued shares*. Issued shares are actually in the hands of a shareholder. Authorized shares are those that can be sold by the company, but need not be.

Try to keep this section simple unless you have specific reasons for creating a more complicated capital structure, and be sure to verify your capital structure with your accountant before finalizing your articles. You will need to file amended articles of incorporation should you ever decide to change your capital structure. In addition, if you have sold shares and then change your capital structure, you will need to convert the old shares to new ones.

WHAT?

Authorized shares The total number of shares of stock the corporation is permitted to issue. For instance, if 1,000 shares of stock are authorized at the start of the corporation, only a total of 1,000 shares can ever be sold to shareholders, no more than that.

Article Five: Initial Capitalization

Most business transactions are not considered binding, or final, until money has changed hands. For this reason, your corporation may require some form of consideration in order to officially start.

The corporation will not commence business until it has received for the issuance of its shares consideration of the value of *(enter the desired amount of money or valued services amount; usually not less than $1,000)*.

WHAT?

Consideration
A legal term for "something of value." That something could be money or the right to do something. Many contracts are not valid until some form of consideration has changed hands, and in some cases, that consideration may be as little as $1, to make the transaction official.

Article Six: Address and Registered Agent

The address of the corporation's *registered office* is (*enter the address*) **and the name of its *registered agent* at such address is** (*enter your name or the name of the person who is the primary contact for all company-related business including legal matters*).

The address must be a street address, not a P.O. box.

Article Seven: Board of Directors Information

The number of directors is (*enter the number of directors, typically 1 to 3*), **and their names and addresses are** (*enter the names and addresses of each board member*).

Registered Agent The official person to contact for all legal matters. The registered agent is located at the official corporate address, also called the registered office. In some states, the registered agent must be an attorney, and in others, you can serve as the registered agent.

Some corporations have a board of directors consisting of only one or two people, such as the owner and the owner's spouse, but then also establish an *advisory board* to give business advice and guidance. An advisory board works much like a board of directors in counseling the president, helping identify new opportunities, and giving feedback on the direction of the company.

The difference is that the members of the advisory board have no financial interest in the company, are not shareholders, and also assume no liability for the corporation's actions. In some cases, you may find that successful business people will be more likely to agree to serve on an advisory board than on a board of directors, because they don't want to be held liable for the consequences of the corporation's actions.

Article Eight: Name of the Incorporator

The name and address of the incorporator is (*enter your name, assuming that you are the person forming the corporation*).

This could be a third party with no interest in the company at all who is simply completing the paperwork for you, such as an attorney.

The incorporator must sign the articles in front of a notary public. Then, you file the articles, or a copy of them, with the state.

Bylaws: The Basic Ingredients

Your corporation now exists. What is it going to do and how will it conduct itself on a daily basis? This is the overall intent of the *bylaws*. They are the internal rules that govern employees' and officers' actions when the directors are not there to supervise. Violation of the corporation bylaws is usually treated as a grievous offense and can be grounds for dismissal in most companies.

Of course, when you're both the president and the board of directors, you can fire yourself whenever you want. If you have outside shareholders, meaning investors other than you and a spouse or close family member, be aware that they can use violation of the bylaws as a reason to bring in someone else to run the company if they hold a majority of the shares. If you own the majority of your corporation's shares, they probably can't fire you, but they can still cause problems for you. The moral of the story is: Set up bylaws that you should have no problem living by.

The first board of directors meeting is used to adopt the corporate bylaws. The bylaws can cover any areas of conduct deemed necessary, and generally includes company policy in areas such as:

- When and where shareholder meetings will be held.
- When and how the board will be formed.
- How frequently meetings are held.
- Voting rights of shareholders and directors.
- Procedures for hiring and dismissing company officers and a description of their respective duties.
- The overall handling of stock shares and dividends.
- Usage of the corporate seal.
- Internal approval procedures for legally committing the company.
- Definition of the company fiscal year, which is frequently the calendar year for simplicity's sake.
- References to the articles of incorporation as needed and procedures for amending the bylaws.

There is a lot of information contained within the bylaws that help to maintain consistency of company policy in the midst of the daily pressures. Make sure that the bylaws reflect the business and spiritual integrity of the organization; then stick with what you have or change the bylaws to better reflect your mission.

> **REALLY!?**
>
> Pull out your bylaws every six to twelve months to remind you of the direction in which you initially intended to steer the company. Daily pressures can take you off track, and this review will help you to keep company operations consistent over the long term.

Bylaws and Articles "In a Can"

Most bylaws and articles of incorporation include standard language, with only minor changes needed for specific company-related information. For this reason, many people decide to try to write

Be sure to verify your capital structure with a financial adviser before finalizing your articles. The software will simply work with the information you provide and does not verify its accuracy. If the information you type is incorrect, your articles of incorporation will be flawed.

their own using a computer program with the standard format for incorporating, which they then edit for their own situation. There are software packages out there, such as It's Legal by Parson Technologies, which will give you the standard language for under $50. Many software catalogs and computer retailers carry these programs, if you're interested.

While you may be tempted to save a few hundred dollars by using "canned" software to form your corporation, be aware that you could be creating serious problems for yourself down the line. You should always consider having significant documents (such as contracts and official paperwork) reviewed by your attorney to make sure you have established your legal structure the way you intend.

Establishing a Board of Directors: A Good Idea If You Choose Wisely

It has been said that human beings are reasonable in that we can always justify and rationalize our desires and actions. This is a dangerous trait when you run your own business. It is often helpful to have someone to report to, or you'll find reasons to take the company into business areas where no company has gone before, or should go.

This is a wonderful reason for creating a board of directors. A board of directors is a group of people who are not involved with the daily operation of the business but who have a vested interest in keeping the company on track. Board members commonly serve for one year, with three-year terms not uncommon.

Directors are required to act with the best interests of the corporation and its shareholders in mind. As long as they act with integrity and make decisions that any "reasonable" person would make given the same information, they are generally protected from potential lawsuits as a result of their decisions. This is the *business judgment rule* designed to protect directors from frivolous lawsuits filed by irate shareholders who may have lost money on their investments.

For example, if a board of directors decides to stop selling a particular product because it is losing money for the company and a customer becomes upset at that decision, the customer can still sue the corporation, but the members of the board of directors cannot be sued unless the customer can prove the decision was a poor one for the company.

Business judgment rule Protects members of corporate boards of directors from lawsuits filed by shareholders, customers, or others if the decision that caused the lawsuit was made in the best interests of the corporation.

With an advisory board, the members are still expected to act in the company's best interests and to recommend actions that further the corporation's goals, but the issue of liability doesn't come up. That's because an advisory board is much less formal than a board of directors and because the advisory board members generally receive no compensation for giving you advice. In most cases, no formal, written relationship exists between the advisory board members and the corporation. As a sign of your appreciation for their time and guidance, you should probably buy them dinner once in a while, but you don't have to give them shares of stock or big payments.

Directors generally serve on a board for indirect benefits, such as business contacts, prestige, and other related rewards. Typically, board members receive payment of travel expenses for attending meetings, as well as payment for serving on the board. Board members are frequently majority stockholders in the corporation, which ensures that board decisions are made on behalf of the shareholders and not simply to serve the company officers.

A diverse board is better than one comprised of people from the same industry or background; people with varied backgrounds bring different perspectives and contacts to the company. Board members who own shares will act in a more responsible manner because they have a direct interest in the company's success. Adding board members with financial, legal, managerial, and political experience can assist the company greatly when fast decisions must be made. This higher level of expertise shortens the information-gathering phase since the experts are often right there in the room.

It is a good idea to have the director stock ownership phased in over a period of time based upon participation and overall company performance. This means that board members receive a small number of shares on joining the board, which are added to over time, based on how well the company does and how much time the board members spend on company business. Setting up a stock ownership plan that takes effect over several years takes more time upfront but ensures that the directors are motivated to make your company, and you, succeed.

Finally, make sure that all board members agree to disclose any potential conflict of interest situations that may arise. Most organizations require that all board members sign a disclosure form upfront, either stating that there are no known conflicts of interest or explaining potential conflicts. Nothing breeds contempt and distrust faster than finding out that one of your confidants is cavorting with a competitor without your knowledge.

The Least You Need to Know

This chapter laid the groundwork to get you well on your way to incorporating. The process should now be clearer to you than before, so that whether you hire an attorney to prepare the documents or you do them yourself, you'll be more familiar with what's involved.

- Each state has its own regulations regarding incorporating. Contact the secretary of state's office in your state's capitol.
- The incorporation process is fairly simple and inexpensive in most states. Only one shareholder is usually required to incorporate.
- Picking the right name can hold up the procedure. Start with the name, verify its availability in the states where you'll be doing business, and reserve it until you finish the articles of incorporation.
- A board of directors will greatly assist your progress in developing the mega-company you envision. Look for board members from the start and choose wisely.

Part 3
Making Marketing and Sales Work for You

If you thought that marketing and selling were the same thing, you're in the majority, but actually, they're not. In this section, you'll learn what the difference is, why you should care, and how marketing and sales are the key to your success.

Now that your business is set up and you've filed all the necessary government paperwork, you need to get some customers. Customers will make or break you, because customers bring in money. In this section, you'll learn about getting customers and keeping them. You'll also discover the basics of selling, which everyone can learn to do effectively. Finally, you'll see how your competitors can help you succeed.

Chapter 7

Effective Marketing Makes Selling Easier

In This Chapter

- ➤ The difference between sales and marketing
- ➤ Target marketing and demographics
- ➤ Pricing strategies
- ➤ Promotional methods
- ➤ Distribution considerations

Jamie, the marketing consultant, brought them all into the room to report her findings. The company had seen a drop in its sales, yet it was spending more money on marketing and sales activities. The president felt that they were doing something fundamentally wrong. She had always believed that the harder you pushed on something, the more it moved. For the first time in her company history, the harder she pushed by spending more money and energy, the less she got back.

"Okay. Let's start at the beginning. It appears that you have a loyal customer base and that they all come from about four general industry groups. Would you agree with that?" asked Jamie. The president nodded.

"Then why are you spending all of this time and money selling into new market areas when you still have room for growth in your target areas?"

"We cannot depend on the same old customers for our livelihood. What if something happens to one of them? Then where are we?" the president inquired defiantly.

"Good point," said Jamie, "That would be true if your current customers and their respective market segment had minimal sales growth opportunity, but it appears that you are in the enviable position of having a firm market presence in a growing industry. You should first concentrate on taking care of business in your strong areas before moving into areas where you are unknown. Let me show you how a target marketing campaign to companies in your strong market segments can improve sales, decrease personnel requirements, and decrease cost. Interested?"

"What do you think?" said the smiling, yet doubtful, president.

Aren't Sales and Marketing the Same Thing?

Despite the fact that most people use the words sales and marketing interchangeably, the two activities really are different.

Marketing involves selecting the right product, pricing strategy, promotional programs, and distribution outlets for your particular audience, or market.

Sales is part of marketing and involves all the steps you take to get the customer to buy your product or service. It can be done in person by salespeople meeting the customer or by telephone, direct mail, or advertising that prompts the customer to place an order for your product.

Marketing consists of strategies to identify your customers, figure out what they need, determine what to charge them, tell them that you have what they need, and then sell it to them efficiently. In MBA programs, those are also called the "4 Ps" of marketing: Product, Pricing, Promotion, and Place of sale, which is also called distribution. If you want to get technical, they should really be called the "3 Ps and 1 D" of marketing, but let's not get nitpicky.

It is marketing's responsibility to identify the most likely customers, design the best product or service offering, set the product or service's price range, and choose the overall advertising message and presentation content most likely to get customers to buy. Specific marketing activities include market research, product or service development, analysis of pricing levels, creation of marketing materials and sales aids, advertising, public relations, and sales support.

Sales efforts work best when the salesperson addresses the customers most likely to buy, with a product they are most likely to use, for a price that is within their budget, with a presentation that delivers the right message in an easily understood format. Sales activities include contacting customers, making presentations, and getting the orders, among other things.

This chapter introduces you to the basic concepts of marketing and provides a background for the next chapter on the selling process.

Who Is Your Market?

We human beings like to believe that we are all different and that we are each unique, and on some basic levels, we are. However, in other areas, we fall into certain groups that think, act, buy, and react alike. We're not all lemmings who'd jump off a cliff at once, but we have certain characteristics that bind us as a group. These characteristics are often called *demographics* and include such things as age, income level, educational level, and marital status. Breaking down your target customers by demographic characteristics is called *market segmentation*. When marketing people often talk about the *demographic profile* of their ideal customer, they are looking for the common characteristics associated with their most likely customer.

A bank, for example, might segment its customers by age because people's banking needs change during different phases of their life. People over the age of 50 are more likely to be interested in retirement-related products than 18-year-olds, and 18-year-olds are more likely to be interested in college loan details than 30-something couples who are out of college and want to buy a home with a bank mortgage. Market segmentation helps the bank to group similar customers together and develop products that they will be interested in.

WHAT?

Demographics A set of objective characteristics that describe a group of people, including such things as age, home ownership, number of children, marital status, residence location, job function, and other descriptors.

Demographic profile Usually refers to a specific set of demographic characteristics that sales and marketing people use to target likely sales prospects.

Ideal customer profile A demographic description of the type of customer most likely to benefit from your product or service.

Market Segmentation Dividing the total available market (everyone who may ever buy) into smaller groups, or segments, by specific attributes such as age, sex, location, interests, industry, or other pertinent criteria.

Compiling information on potential customers is the challenge for market research companies. They gather information through mail and phone surveys and personal interviews to determine people's buying habits. As a business owner, you can then buy and use this information to develop effective marketing programs to sell to these potential buyers.

Anyone can buy these reports (unless the survey was paid for by a specific company for their use only). Check with your local public or university library first to see if they subscribe to any of these reports. Typically, the library purchases a wide variety of these reports and makes them available to the public. (Free is always the preferred route, and photocopy machines also exist in libraries.)

This type of information may be available for free from other sources, too, especially if it's related to general age, living conditions, income, and other generic topics. The federal government compiles this information in the form of a census every 10 years (the last census was completed in 1990) and makes it available at most libraries. The census contains substantial information about the American public and breaks the country into areas called Standard Metropolitan Statistical Areas (SMSAs). There are over 30 major SMSAs in the United States. Many companies decide to divide the country by SMSAs simply because the information on each SMSA is readily available and universally understood.

Target Marketing: Picking Your Customer

If you sell beef products, it wouldn't make sense to invest time and money displaying your products at a vegetarian convention. At the end of the convention, you'd think that your product had no place in the market and that it was causing a decline in American health. Obviously, people who don't eat meat aren't the best sales prospects for a meat product.

Identifying your customer is an important part of the marketing process. If you don't know who will buy your product and why, you have no idea who to contact and how to present your wares. When you don't know who your likely customers are, the result is a *scattergun marketing* approach, in which you blanket the market with a general message and hope that someone sees it and calls. This is not a very effective approach because it is costly, time-consuming, and results in few sales.

Target marketing focuses your financial and personnel resources on the people most likely to purchase what you offer. Let's say that for a particular geographic area there are 100,000 potential customers for your products or services. A direct mail piece sent to this group at $1.00 each would cost $100,000. From this mailer, you may get a 2 percent response (which is a typical response rate). This means that 2,000 people want more information from you. Of those people, assume 10 percent of those people, or 200, actually buy your product or service. So, for a $100,000 investment, your company sold your company's goods to 200 people. A little statistics and customer characteristics analysis will probably show that these 200 people have similarities that form them into a specific *market segment* (which we discussed earlier).

WHAT?

Scattergun Marketing A scattergun sends buckshot in a wide pattern hopefully hitting something. Scattergun marketing sends marketing information everywhere hoping that someone will hear it and buy (the opposite of target marketing).

While promotional methods such as direct mail are discussed later, I should point out that you just spent $500 per customer to get each sale. Now, if you're selling a $10,000 item, you've done well, but if you're selling a $20 item, you've lost big bucks.

In order to develop a target marketing approach, you first need to be able to define which markets contain your best potential customers. This means that you need to know something about what you're selling and who needs it most.

For example, you may find that your market segment is mostly women between 25 and 45 years of age, or that they are mostly college educated or work in specific industries. You can also use certain circumstances as market segmentation criteria; for example, people moving to a new location usually need new telephone equipment. So, to contact people most likely to purchase a telephone system, your first step may be to identify people who are moving or plan to move shortly.

Target marketing does not waste time, money, and effort approaching people who are not good prospects. As a result, you get much better results from your marketing efforts. The types of results you get will vary widely from situation to situation, but you will always find target marketing a more efficient marketing effort than the scattergun approach.

Target Marketing A marketing approach that involves focusing your marketing efforts on those groups of potential customers most likely to buy your products or services.

Pricing Strategies Can Make or Break You

Price is an interesting phenomenon in our capitalist society. It often means more than just the amount of money that is paid for a product. It is often viewed as a status symbol or a measure of worth over and above the number of dollars that change hands—the most expensive suit wins. Pricing a product too low can make it appear inferior and can make people avoid it, even though it's of comparable quality.

Do not ever let your ego dictate price for your products. I have seen several companies with a substantial jump on the market fall flat due to the faulty belief that people would pay more for their product simply because it was new, different, or because their name was on it! Price your products based on more than just what you would *like* people to pay.

Ultimately, the customer pays a price that is consistent with his *perceived value* of the offering. If the name on the product is perceived by the customer as having high value (such as designer clothing) then the customer may be willing to pay a high price to wear those designer duds. Other pricing strategies are cost-based and market-based. You can calculate *cost-based* prices by determining the costs of producing a product or delivering a service and then adding a profit margin. You determine *market-based* prices by studying what similar products or services cost and asking a similar price.

Perceived value The overall value that the customer places on a particular product or service. This includes much more than price and considers other features such as delivery lead time, quality of salesmanship, service, style, and other less tangible items. With a perceived value pricing strategy, you set a price for your product or service by determining what people are willing to pay yet making sure that you can still cover all your costs.

It takes a lot of information about your product costs, your competitors' pricing, and how customers decide what and when to buy in order to accurately and comfortably fix pricing for your offerings. Here are some basic rules that may help you to determine the best price for your service or products:

- Don't ever price the product below your cost. You need to make a profit on virtually every sale in order to stay in business. Some people think that if they sell huge amounts, they'll come out okay in the end. Wrong! You can't lose a nickel on each unit and expect to make up the profit in volume.
- If you have a new company or a new product, you generally cannot match price with an established company with a similar offering. This is because they are already known, trusted, and are a less risky choice for the customer. For the same price, their offering is considered a better purchase.

- You generally have to price lower than the established competition until you get a foothold in the market.
- You can generally sell intangibles such as service, deliverability, and location for up to 20 percent over a competitor's price. Over that point, the customer will probably treat your offering as too expensive for their perceived value.
- Don't always price your offering on a *cost plus profit margin* basis. Although this approach is easy to compute, it usually leaves money on the customer's table that you could have otherwise had in your company bank account. *Market-based pricing* is generally more complicated but best ensures the most profit on each sale. In other words, if you do a better job producing the product and lower your costs, market-based pricing would give higher profits, while cost-based pricing would cut sales price and profit.
- Quantity discounts are an effective way to encourage your customers to purchase more of your product at a given time. However, watch the discount amounts, or you may find yourself selling a lot for a minimal profit.

> WHAT?
>
> **Cost plus profit pricing** When your price is calculated using the cost to the company plus whatever profit margin is reasonable for your industry. So a widget that costs $1 to produce with a desired 50 percent profit margin would sell for $1/.5 = $2.
>
> **Market-based pricing** When you price offerings at a level set by what everyone else is charging, rather than by costs. With this strategy, you can generally make more money assuming your competition is charging reasonable rates and you can keep your costs down.

Obviously, you can set your prices wherever you want, but your best price will mean more sales for you, because you will have figured out what your customers believe is a fair price for your goods. In return, they will buy more.

> REALLY!?
>
> Profit margins for a company are available, sorted by Standard Industrial Code (SIC), from the Dun & Bradstreet report, from Robert Morris Associates' *Annual Statement Studies*, or the annual report of publicly traded, established companies. Most publicly traded companies will send you a copy of their annual report if you call their Investor Relations Department.

You must answer several key questions when determining a pricing strategy:

1. What are your competitors offering your potential customers in terms of their basic product/service price and the price of any add-on services?
2. How much does it cost you to supply the product or service desired by the customer (including those additional intangibles just discussed)?

3. What additional features do you offer your customers that your competitors do not, and are these features worth more money?

The costs associated with a product vary depending upon where it is in the *product life cycle*. The next section provides a brief overview of a new product's typical life cycle. You can use this model as a guide in determining your pricing, distribution, and marketing message strategies.

I have a friend who prides himself on his hourly consulting rate of $300. When I asked him how many hours he billed a month, he said three, on average. This means that he makes $900 per month from his consulting work. Another colleague, on the other hand, bills at $110 per hour and works 30–50 hours per month, on average, which equates to $3,300 to $5,500 per month of income. Who is better off? It depends on each person's needs, but if the intent is to make money, then the lower billing rate is the way to go.

The Product or Service Life Cycle

Every product or service goes through a *life cycle* from its introduction until the time it is discontinued or taken off the market. The life cycle usually refers to products, but services go through a similar evolution. The life cycle is divided into four basic stages:

Stage 1: Market development (aka embryonic) The product or service is new to the market, having recently been introduced. Sales are slow at this stage and usually difficult to close due to potential customers' lack of familiarity. Only potential customers who have shown a willingness to experiment with new products or services are good prospects for this stage. That group of experimenters is often referred to as *early adopters* because they are the first to try something new.

WHAT? **Price erosion** When so many competitors have entered the market that everyone has to keep dropping their price to win sales, eroding the market price and profit margins.

Stage 2: Market growth Where sales are increasing steadily and there is a general awareness of the product or service. Competition usually starts to show up at this point.

Stage 3: Maturity Overall demand starts to level off as customers purchase the offering as a routine part of doing business. Customers have a high degree of familiarity with the offering. *Price erosion* can happen at this point due to intense competition from what is now a hot market for the product or service.

Stage 4: Market decline Customer demand for the product or service starts to decline due to improved variations of the product by other companies, new technology, or other market forces that make the product inferior or obsolete.

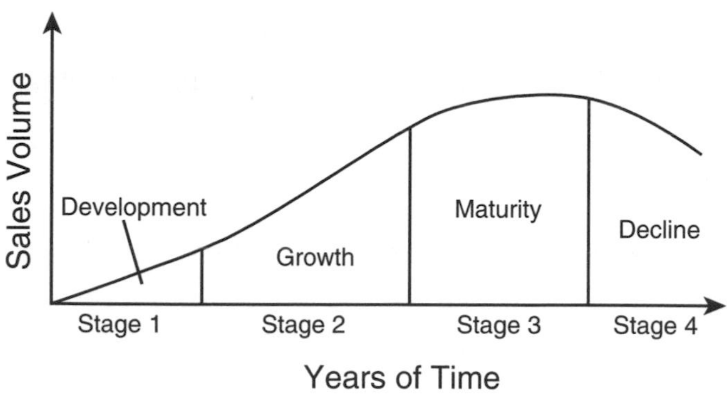

Product/service life cycle.

While most products or services go through a life cycle in a matter of years or a decade, fad products such as novelty gifts (the mood ring or pet rock) may go through an entire life cycle in a very short period of time (such as a single Christmas buying season). Durable goods such as microwaves may have an extended life cycle caused by the level of technological sophistication and a high level of consumer acceptance.

Notice that the perceived value of your offering will change over the life cycle. In the early days, when customers are just learning about what you are selling, only a small segment will take a chance by making a purchase.

In the growth stage, with demand for your offering increasing, you may be in the driver's seat. This means you can charge a premium price since you have something everyone wants.

By the time you enter the maturity stage, you will probably have encountered competitors who have developed similar products, forcing you to compete on price and service. For example, the personal computer industry is in the maturity stage of its development. Notice the rapid price erosion combined with improved performance that this industry has experienced. This is typical of an industry in the maturity stage of the life cycle.

The product life-cycle concept affects your pricing strategy. Once you determine where your product or service offerings fall on the product life cycle, you can make a better choice about your long-term strategy. The price you set for your rates as a new consultant will be different than for an experienced, nationally known consultant.

Use the three different strategies—cost, market, and perceived value pricing—to choose the price level that will generate the most sales. Then make sure that your price is consistent with your life-cycle position.

Determining Your Marketing Message and Positioning

There are these two guys in their sixties who play racquetball with me regularly, and they whip me every time. As if getting beaten weren't bad enough, at the end of the game, I'm totally exhausted and they're only slightly winded! One time, I finally put aside my pride and asked about the secret to their racquetball success. They replied, "It isn't the speed with which you act as much as the position from which you act."

Positioning is everything in sports and in business. I don't mean the geographic location of your company, necessarily, but the way your company is perceived by your customers.

> WHAT? **Market positioning**
> Creating a positive image in the minds of potential and existing customers. The purpose of market positioning is to have potential customers perceive your product or service in a particular way that makes them more likely to want to buy from you.

Take a moment and think about the hundreds of marketing-related messages that bombard you on a daily basis. How do you sift through the irrelevant ones and focus on the ones of importance to you? It depends on the way the product is presented to you and whether it communicates a beneficial message of interest to you. The *marketing message*, the essence of your positioning goal, is the key to customer perception.

The message should be simple, easy to remember, and easy to understand. The only way you can effectively position your company or your product in your customer's mind is to understand their thinking and lifestyle. You must know your competition's marketing approach and make sure that your company is seen as different from the others, or make customers more comfortable with your totally new company or product; by making it look a lot like your competition.

Typical positioning statements look something like:

- Lower price with superior quality
- More convenient and better-stocked store shelves
- More fun at a lower price
- Earn your college tuition in exchange for several years of training

The range of positioning statements is infinite and limited only by your creativity. Your marketing message clearly and simply conveys the *positioning benefit perception* you want your customers to understand. Spend a lot of time thinking about this and try several variations out on colleagues. The marketing message will appear in almost everything you produce and create the perception your salespeople will work with during the sales process. If your message is off, you are in trouble because your customers won't even think of you when they need exactly the products or services you provide!

Stay True to Your Message: Consistency Is Appreciated

Change may be a natural part of life, but it generally causes confusion when dealing with marketing messages and positioning. It takes months (or years) to create a solid market positioning in a customer's mind, and you should not tamper with it in a careless way. Confusion is a dangerous thing when dealing with customers.

Decide on a positioning and stay with it unless you are absolutely sure it doesn't work. You can tamper somewhat with the message as long as all the adjustments convey the same positioning benefits to your customers.

If you know someone who changes careers on a regular basis, you know how hard it is to discuss this person's professional capabilities. She may be brilliant, but if she cannot explain her qualifications in a simple way that means something to the listener, this person will remain an enigma. Enigmas are interesting at cocktail parties but rarely get hired for important projects.

The same is true of your offerings. Keep the positioning consistent, and make sure your marketing message accurately conveys the customer benefits

> BANKRUPT
>
> Because potential customers must see your message numerous times before taking action to buy from you, don't change your message too quickly or too frequently. If you do, customers will get confused about who your company is and why they should do business with you. On average, people have to see your message seven times before they recognize they need to buy what you're offering.

associated with the positioning. You will get tired of using the same message well before your customers will. In fact, just as you get bored with it and want to change it, this is when the customers start taking notice.

Promoting Your Company and Products

Getting the public's attention is crucial to marketing success. Here are some ways you can bring attention to your company's offerings (some are even *free*).

Publicity Is Free

Newspapers are always hungry for stories. It takes many words to fill a newspaper on a daily basis, and you wouldn't believe what a large percentage of those news stories are provided by companies looking for a write-up. The key is looking for something that your company is doing that will interest the paper's readership. If you can find that, you may have the basis for a story about your company. That is *free* advertising with credibility attached because it comes from a third-party, objective source. This free advertising is called *publicity*.

This is a wonderful opportunity, but it takes work. You have to train yourself to continually watch for chances to turn daily occurrences into something people want to read or hear about. Once you find a situation where your company would be a potential source of information for a reporter or editor, the first step is making contact with the media to let them know. It will probably not happen on the first try, but just as with any type of advertising, repetition works. It may take several contacts before the editors and reporters recognize your company and/or personal name and think of how to use it as a story.

There are public relations (PR) firms that specialize in making the desired media contacts for you. Many of the PR firms in your area will already know the editors, which often makes it easier for them to persuade an editor to profile your business or to quote you. Although it will cost you money to hire a PR firm, their services will probably help to improve sales for your company. Look at their fee as a marketing investment that will yield results in the form of sales. If money is tight (and it usually is, isn't it?), then get to know the editors yourself. You can work on them to run your story.

There needs to be a "hook" or interesting angle to any story you propose to the *media*. Stories such as "Local entrepreneur sells mom's cake recipe for lots of dough," or "Austin-based business closes a large baking deal" are both newsworthy pieces that could result in free publicity. Okay, okay, these aren't the best headlines in the world, but you get the picture.

To get started, create a written announcement (officially called a *press release*) and contact the business editor at the publication where you'd like to be featured, or the business editor at the radio or TV station of interest. The press release must contain your company contact person's name, address, phone, and fax. The title must convey the essence of the release and should be one-page long (two pages maximum, unless you are better established). Your company should be prominently mentioned, and the first paragraph should be short and to the point.

WHAT?

Publicity Mention of your company or offering in newspaper or magazine articles, television, or radio shows. There is no cost for this coverage, other than the fees you may want to pay a professional public relations firm to assist you.

Media Includes reporters, journalists, editors at publications, and assignment editors or news directors at television and radio stations.

Establish a Public Relations Program

Publicity is just one aspect of a complete program for dealing with the media and your customers. Here are a few tips to help you start creating a public relations program.

- Start studying the local media to learn about the types of stories they regularly cover. This gives you an idea of what may be of interest.
- Ask around for sample press releases written and sent out by other companies and compare them to yours. Watch to see what stories actually appear in the press.
- Keep a running list of items that may have significance to the local public.
- Outline possible story ideas when you think of them, even if it is just a few sentences long. These moments of inspiration are often fleeting and lost if not promptly recorded.

Working with the media is fun, but it can also be a mixed blessing. The advantage of media exposure is that everyone hears about you for free, but the disadvantage is that you have no control over what information the media decides to use. If you want to ensure control over where and when a particular message appears in the press, try advertising.

Use Community Events to Promote Your Company

You and your company are unique, and there are tons of opportunities for getting your name and offerings into the public eye. We have already discussed publicity, and here are some other ways that contribute to the community and get your name out there in plain view:

- Sponsor a local sports team such as little league, softball, or soccer. Every uniform will have your company name on it.
- Speak at Rotary, Chamber of Commerce, and other community-oriented organizations. Make sure your company name is on all literature handed out at the function.
- Keep your eyes open for cooperative events such as donating food for people participating at a civic function or donating cups and water for a 5K race. Why not sponsor the race? Give away some of your products or services in conjunction with a local radio or television station.
- Finally, trade shows are a way to display your offerings but at a cost that can be substantial. See if you can share space with another company to offset the substantial investment involved with many trade shows.

In the early '80s, I developed a novelty gift product that I sold nationwide. I put together a press release that included the product's box, a press release, and a black and white photo of the product. We got exposure in dozens of newspapers, magazines, and national television coverage. I was ecstatic until the following month. I was sued by over 14 people whom I had never met or had contact with in my life. They had seen the various media coverage and decided that I had stolen their product and were intent on getting their proper justice.

In no way, shape, or form had I known of any of their products prior to this point, and I certainly had not stolen anyone's idea. The legal hassles associated with this fiasco eventually put the company under since we simply weren't capitalized to handle the unexpected legal expenses that amounted to tens of thousands of dollars.

What About Advertising?

Advertising is good for increasing awareness of your company and its offerings. Unless you're in retail, don't expect to close many sales directly from your advertising. The point of advertising is to firmly plant your marketing message into the consumer's mind so that they think about you when they are looking for what you offer. Advertising also gets the company in front of a wide variety of people in a timely manner.

Marketers (or marketeers) call this *mind share*. This is the part of a person's thought process occupied by perceptions associated with your specific company. The greater the mind share, the more likely people are to contact you when they are looking for what you offer. If you have no mind share, then they won't even know to call, and the entire marketing/sales effort falls onto your shoulders. You develop mind share by using advertising, publicity, promotion, and personal experience with your company.

> WHAT?
>
> **Mind share**
> The portion of a person's thought processes that includes perceptions of your company's offerings. 100 percent mind share means that any time a person needs your type of offering, she thinks of your company.

Push and Pull Marketing Strategies

Advertising is useful for creating a *pull marketing strategy*, which means that the customers "pull" your product through the distribution channel by asking for it. A pull strategy is expensive since it requires massive marketing to your potential customers to alert them to your product's availability.

At the other extreme is the *push marketing strategy* that requires you to convince distributors to carry and promote your product, hoping that customers will purchase it. A push strategy may show faster results but is very dependent on the activities of the specific distributor.

> WHAT?
>
> **Pull and push marketing strategies** A pull strategy convinces your potential customers to request your offering through their suppliers. In essence, the end user pulls your offering through the distribution channel by putting pressure on suppliers to carry it in their inventory. A push strategy sells your product to distributors, who then promote it to their customers. A pull strategy is driven by customers. A push strategy is driven by distributors.

Keep the following points in mind when you consider advertising:

- Many companies provide money to distributors for cooperative advertising. If you mention their products in specific ways in your ads, they will pay for a portion of the ad. Include enough suppliers and the entire ad can be paid for by the suppliers. Contact each of your suppliers for their specific restrictions.
- Yellow Page advertising is a must for any business, such as a restaurant, trying to reach the general public. The book only comes out once a year, so you should plan in advance to be included. Check with colleagues about their success with the various ad types; take the plunge and hope for the best.

- Placing an ad just one time in a paper or on TV or radio is generally useless. You need to repeat your ad on a regular basis to get the best results, so plan for 6–10 insertions, or don't waste your money.
- Advertising firms specialize in making companies like yours succeed with advertising. They also have an art department that can design an ad for you.
- Contact each publication, radio, and TV station you may be interested in advertising with and ask them to send you a media kit. The kit includes demographic information about the people who read each publication, listen to specific radio programs, and watch individual TV shows. Typical information includes age, sex, education, and marital status. This information lets you determine whether the people who will see or hear the ad are the ones most likely to buy from you. Notice how the pieces are beginning to fit together.
- Ask each media supplier if they have ever run ads like yours before and what type of responses they received. This may help you to determine if it makes sense to invest in advertising there.

Infomercials are currently popular as a means of marketing products (such as the Victoria Jackson line of cosmetics) and services (such as the Psychic Friends Network) and must be effective, based on the rapid increase in the number of infomercials currently on television. There's a lot of money riding on the success of some of these infomercials; some cost hundreds of thousands of dollars to produce, and they are generally beyond the financial reach of the conventional entrepreneur. This doesn't mean that this avenue should not be pursued, but only that the startup costs should not be ignored. Producing a half-hour or hour-long commercial is extremely expensive, and on top of that, you add the cost of buying the TV time.

Advertising can be a useful tool when used properly, but it can also drain massive amounts of cash from your company with minimal financial return. Make sure that wherever your ads appear, they are being seen or heard by serious potential customers for your company's product or service offerings.

Your Selling Approach: Retail, Distributors, Mail Order, or Direct

How does your customer buy your product? That is the question. Is it better to pay commissions to independent sales representatives, sell products at wholesale rates, or to simply sell it to your customers with a direct sales force?

Using Distribution Channels

The *distribution channel* has a profound impact on your contact with the customer, the profit margin available, and the lead time for delivery.

The distribution channel(s) you use to get your product or service into the hands of customers will affect the markup and profit margin you can expect. Markup and profit margin are related, but definitely different; be sure you understand each before pricing your products.

Markup is added to the cost of a product, while profit margin is a calculation of what percent of a product's price is profit; the difference is the product's cost. Because there are many businesses involved in the process of getting a product from the manufacturer to you, there are also many different markups being added at every step of the way.

A product typically starts at the manufacturer who actually produces the product. The manufacturer adds a markup to the cost of producing the product and sells it to a distributor. The distributor is responsible for getting the product to a wholesaler, who may sell within a particular city or region. Each adds another markup in order for their own businesses to make money. Retailers, who are the only members of the distribution channel to have direct contact with customers, also add a markup. So from the manufacturer to the retailer, there could be several markups along the way, resulting in a retail price that is passed along to the customer.

There are industry standards for what kind of profit margin and markup are reasonable, as a guideline in setting your own pricing guidelines. Many clothing department stores have at least a 100 percent markup, meaning they sell their clothing for double what they buy it for. Advertising and marketing agencies, on the other hand, may mark up their

WHAT?

Distribution channel However your product or service gets from your facilities into the hands of customers. Different ways of distributing your product include direct sales, using employees to sell your offerings, retail stores, mail order, and independent sales or manufacturers representatives.

WHAT?

Markup The percentage increase you add to the cost of a product or service in order to come up with the price you charge customers. A 100 percent markup means that a shirt costing you $10.00 would cost customers $20.00. You calculate markup by adding ($10.00 × 100%) + $10.00. 100% is also expressed as 1. So ($10 × 1) +$10 =$20.

Profit margin The amount of profit you make on a sale, expressed as a percent of the product's price. Using the previous shirt example, the profit margin on each shirt can be calculated by subtracting the cost of the shirt from the purchase price and then dividing by the purchase price. ($20–10)/20=10/20=.50=50% profit margin.

Why start from scratch? Why not look at how your competitors sell their offerings to get some ideas about what has been tried before and what has worked well for existing companies? Do they have retail storefronts, or do they sell through a distribution channel to many retail outlets? What distributors already carry your competitors' products? Ask the retailers; they will tell you who they buy from and their alternate sources.

By law you have to ship a prepaid order in 30 days or be forced to offer a refund to a customer who doesn't want to wait any longer. So while it may improve your cash situation to produce according to how many orders you receive, make sure you can deliver in 30 days or less.

services from 10–20 percent, and commercial suppliers may have markups of only 5–10 percent. It all depends on the industry you're in.

The best part of using third parties, such as independent distributors or sales representatives, is that they are out selling your products while your employees can stay focused on internal company activities such as marketing and creation of new products. A few minutes spent evaluating the positive and negative aspects of the various distribution channels should help you in deciding your course of action. Read about sales and the use of sales representatives in Chapter 8.

Using Mail-Order and Direct-Mail Methods

Do you want to take on the opportunities and headaches associated with mail order? You get the order along with its payment and then are responsible for getting the order in the hands of the customer. You have 30 days from the time you receive the order until you have to ship it, which gives you plenty of time in many cases to produce or acquire needed products, instead of stockpiling a huge inventory.

A big downside is the customers can cancel the orders after you have shipped them. Credit-card fraud is also a real problem with mail-order sales, which means that you may never get paid for the order. Accepting credit cards is crucial for mail-order sales, or you'll risk having even worse collection problems if you rely solely on checks for payment. Many companies wait until a check clears before shipping the product to the customer as one way to combat bad checks.

Since there are huge upfront costs required to create and mail a catalog, companies have to be confident they will receive enough orders to at least pay for production and mailing of the catalog. With response rates in the 0.5–3% range, you must have a high profit margin on the products sold to cover the initial investment.

The Least You Need to Know

The marketing and sales aspects of any new business require the most scrutiny. A few-months delay on sales can put a company out of business. Anyone investing in your company will want strong assurances that the marketing and sales side of the business is well thought out and reasonable. Spend your time here, and everything else will come easier.

- ➤ Marketing lays the groundwork by communicating why customers should buy your service or your product. Sales closes the deal and brings in the money.
- ➤ Price is not the only buying criteria used by customers; they look at the total value and benefits of your offering.
- ➤ Create a simple, yet clear, marketing message that describes your company's market positioning and stick with it.
- ➤ Advertising and promotion are important to positioning your company in the marketplace. A company or product's position affects how people perceive it.
- ➤ The distribution channel that you decide is the best way to get your products in the hands of customers will have a significant impact on how quickly sales will occur.

Chapter 8

Without Sales, Nothing Happens

In This Chapter

- ➤ What are sales
- ➤ Standard sales procedures and qualification steps
- ➤ Evaluate direct and distribution sales
- ➤ Selling services

"So what happened?" asked the board member who provided the initial funding for the company.

"The sales just didn't come in as expected," said the president, a professional engineer and former operations manager. "We've been through three sets of salespeople and can't seem to find a good group. They all seem to just want more money and don't bring in the bacon."

"Have you ever been with them on a sales call?" asked the board member.

"Not really," replied the president. "I have been working with our technical people to make sure the product can do what we promised. Selling is what I have sales managers for. Why pay them if I have to do everything myself?" He knew he was on shaky ground.

"So, let's make sure I understand. We have a product and a production facility that works perfectly due to your involvement, but we have nobody who wants to buy what we build. Is that correct?" Heads nodded around the room. "What is wrong with this picture and what are your plans to correct it?"

A New Definition of Sales

Picture a salesperson. What do you see? A fast-talking nonlistener who is always looking at your pocketbook? A slick dresser who continually promises to do things in "your own best interest" but who is obviously only interested in selling you something—anything—whether you need it or not?

When you go into a retail store to find a particular item, do you ask the salesperson for help or tell her that you are "just browsing" when she offers to assist? If you are like most people who do not use her help, it may be because you have had bad experiences with salespeople before and prefer not to have something you don't need forced on you.

Of course, these are the horror stories, the examples of poor salespeople who do their employers and their customers no good whatsoever, but understanding the sales process and what it takes to succeed at selling is important in running a business. So whether you will be selling for your company directly, or whether you will just be overseeing the sales department, this chapter can help.

Selling is an integral part of doing business. To succeed, you must give it the attention and respect you give to other areas of the business such as operations, marketing, and finance. This doesn't mean that you must do the selling yourself, however. If you lack the interest or the ability to sell successfully, find someone who can. I call sales the money funnel since no cash comes into the company unless someone has sold your product or service to a customer and you have the customer's money.

Manipulation and Selling Are Not the Same Thing

Most of us have had someone convince us to do something we later realized was not in our best interest. We felt manipulated by the whole process and by the salesperson involved.

> WHAT? **Manipulation**
> Customers often feel as if they are not in control of the sales process, that they will be encouraged and persuaded to purchase something they don't really need.

Manipulation has nothing to do with sales! If you manipulate someone to buy your offering and they don't want it, they will resent you, your company, and its offerings for a long time. That single sale could cost you a fortune in future revenues, not only from that one customer who will never buy from you again but also from everyone he tells about his buying experience with you.

Sales is the process of matching your products or services with a customer who truly needs them. You are helping the customer solve a problem by providing a service or a product that will make her life easier. It could be as simple as selling a pair of shoes for a special party or as complicated as setting up an international experiment on the space shuttle. If the customer has a need for your offering, and you provide a credible product or service that meets his needs, within his budget, then he *will* buy! It is just that simple. If he doesn't, there is either something wrong with your offering, how it is being presented to customers, or who it was being presented to.

Manipulative selling may earn you a fast buck, but it also eliminates the chance for a future sale to that customer. Professional selling is the action of solving a customer's problems through your company's offerings. It is service-based instead of manipulation-based.

Many new salespeople have shifted from average performers who just did their jobs to outstanding performers who liked what they did by simply making this conceptual shift. The difference between these two approaches is trying to sell something to a customer without caring whether she needs it or not versus determining first whether the customer has a need that your product or service can meet. If it turns out that the customer has a need for what you're offering, the sales process begins. Obviously, there are more satisfied customers that result from professional selling than from manipulative types of selling.

The Difference Between Closing and Selling

The sales process takes place in a number of stages. Look at the way you buy anything. You will go through your own set of questions and stages before actually forking over your money. You may evaluate the available information, read about the product in magazine or newspaper articles, ask knowledgeable friends for their opinions, call your mom for her advice, and eventually decide on a purchase.

Professional selling involves numerous small events and exchanges of information that must occur before the sale can happen. At each step along the way, the salesperson makes small requests for customer action or *closes*, which eventually leads to a sale. For example, asking to meet with someone face-to-face is a small close in that you are asking the customer to take an action that leads in the direction of the sale. If the customer agrees, you are one step closer to getting them to make a purchase. Asking the customer to provide you with detailed information about their needs is another small close, because you are asking the customer to take steps toward buying your product or your service. Once the customer is satisfied that buying your product or service is the right decision, they will commit to a purchase.

Close A request by the salesperson for a specific action on the customer's part. Asking for the order is the ultimate close, but there are smaller closes that occur at each stage of the selling process to gradually move the customer closer to the sale.

People expect to be asked reasonable questions that help them solve their problem, and they also expect you to ask for the purchase. If you don't ask for the order, you can't blame them if they don't give it to you.

Everyone Has to Sell, but Not Everyone Closes

It is important to ask for the order at the right time in the sales process, or the salesperson can alienate the customer. Nothing is more irritating to a customer than to be continually asked to buy something before she is ready. Eventually the salesperson's lack of sensitivity gets in the customer's way of making a rational decision. At this point, the customer may leave simply because it is too much of a hassle to buy from this salesperson.

Everyone in your organization should support the sales process by providing information, support, service, and guidance when requested by the customer. When it is time for the final order to be placed, the salesperson takes care of writing up the sale. Everyone in a company needs to be part of the selling process, but only a few really need to close—beware of the difference.

Aggressive selling is closing when it is inappropriate to close and is rarely effective because it turns off the customer. *Professional selling* is closing when it is necessary to move the customer forward to a new sales stage, and the customer is comfortable moving ahead to the next stage. The moral of the story is: Don't rush customers into making a decision, or you may lose them forever.

Is Your Offering a Special or Commodity Item?

Your company's approach to selling is largely determined by your market positioning and message. (This was covered in Chapter 7.) Offerings with plenty of competition, where the products and services are pretty much the same, require that features such as price, delivery, warranty, and stability be emphasized to set your company apart. Specialty products and services, such as high-technology electronics or tailored clothing, require a higher level of personalized service and credibility as part of the sales process because each product is so different from the others on the market.

Where does your product fit? *Commodities* rely more on the distribution channel to effectively get products in the hands of customers, as well as established customers who use your product on a regular basis. There is little or no difference between commodity products which include milk, lined paper, and lead pencils.

Specialty products require a higher level of technical and sales sophistication because the product's competitive advantage must be explained well. The salesperson has to know about the benefits of the competitors' products and services and how they compare to his own company's offerings in order to sell the customer on why his is better.

Four Critical Criteria for Closing the Deal

All the sweet talking, wining, dining, and fancy brochures in the world will not close a sale from an *unqualified prospect* (they have to be able to buy). I have seen more new, and even experienced, salespeople invest valuable time on prospective customers that were really never qualified to purchase in the first place. Here is a list of four criteria you can use to determine whether you are dealing with a qualified customer. A qualified customer is someone who is interested in buying from you and has the means to do so. If you don't know the answers to these four key questions, you haven't qualified the potential customer. Get the answers, or you may waste a tremendous amount of time and energy on a prospect who cannot buy from you.

WHAT?

Unqualified prospect An individual who says that they need your product or service but who has not yet confirmed that they are able to make the purchase decision. To be sure you are dealing with someone who can buy from you, work through the four qualification criteria.

1. Does Your Customer Need What You Have to Offer?

If your customers don't need what you offer, then you can't blame them for not buying it. Would you buy something you didn't need just to make the salesperson happy? No way, and they won't either!

Make sure you really understand their needs and that they understand what you have to offer. Your challenge is to accurately identify your potential customers' needs and make sure your marketing message addresses them. If you determine you cannot meet their needs, get out of their way.

You may even want to help the customers find an alternate source if your offerings are not what they need. Doing this makes the potential customers feel good about your company, because you are truly doing something that has no immediate reward for you (since you know they aren't going to buy from you right now). In the long run, your willingness to help find a better source may pay off with the customers coming back to buy from you later, because you've demonstrated that you really have their needs at heart.

2. Are You Working with the Decision Maker?

Ultimately, a single person will authorize the purchase of your offering. If you are not dealing with the person in charge of the budget, who can say "yes" and sign on the dotted line, then you are only dealing with someone who has the authority to say "no" to the sale.

Instead of wasting time and energy convincing someone who is not authorized to make a decision to buy from you, first determine who the decision maker is. Then work to meet with that person. Meeting with anyone else but the decision maker doesn't get you any closer to making the sale.

3. Is There Money Budgeted for This Purchase?

If there is no money available to pay for a purchase, there is no potential for a sale. It is perfectly okay to ask whether money is already in the budget for this purchase. You may find the money is coming out of next year's budget, and that the sale is on hold until the next fiscal year starts. Or you may find that there is no money currently budgeted for this project, which should set off warning bells in your head. Or you may find your customer needs to spend the budgeted money by the end of this fiscal year, which provides an added incentive on his part to move the sale forward. This is called a *pending event.*

A pending event is something expected to happen in the future that is affecting when a decision needs to be made. Typical pending events include ending fiscal years (when budgeted money needs to be spent or lost), moving offices, and mergers. If there is no pending event, the customer can, and may, take forever to make a decision. If there is no critical deadline, you may spend a lot of time trying to convince a customer to buy.

4. Is Your Customer Politically Open to Using Your Offering?

There are times when you can have everything in place, the deal looks like it can't help but close, and then it falls apart. It is almost like an unknown power stepped in and killed the deal. That is probably just what happened. Many companies have divisions and subsidiaries they are supposed to buy from, and if it is discovered they are planning to buy from another company, someone may try to kill the deal. Why would a company buy from you if they have a subsidiary that offers the same product at a comparable price? They won't! Not because the product isn't right. Not because you did a poor job of selling. Simply because they have a company policy that says all purchases must first be made from an internal business partner. Period.

Try to find out about these barriers to your sales early on and save yourself a lot of frustration and anguish later. You can do this by researching all the divisions of a large company to determine whether there are groups providing the same service or the same product as you are. It may also be useful to know who the company is currently buying from, to know whether you'll be able to win business away from them.

Selling Is a Nine-Stage Process

Baking bread can be a frustrating and exhilarating experience at the same time. It is an art form, and anyone who has failed in the bread-baking process can verify this. There are specific steps you must follow in precisely the right order and at precisely the right time. Reordering the sequence or trying to rush the process invariably leads to a poor-tasting loaf.

The sales process is similar; there are specific stages a sale will go through before the deal is either lost or won. Trying to perform these steps out of sequence usually leads to poor results, and skipping a step usually leads to disappointment. Plan your sales strategy to include moving the customer from one stage to another, with small closes along the way rather than trying to rush them forward to the final close. Let me walk you through these stages and explain what occurs and what you should accomplish.

1. The Suspect Stage

At this stage, you have heard from a friend of a friend that perhaps Company A may need your products or services. Let's say that you provide business consulting services, for example. This is the first stage in the process, and it usually occurs as a result of your marketing efforts, such as a direct mail letter, advertisement, or phone call.

When you don't know much about Company A, but you think they may have a need for your services, they are considered a *suspect* or a *lead*. There really is no close at this stage other than to make contact with a person on the staff at Company A to verify he has a need for your services.

2. The Prospect Stage

If you make contact with a representative of Company A and learn they do indeed have a need for the services you provide, you have just received confirmation and can move Company A to the next stage as a *prospect*. In the first stage, you just *suspected* that Company A had a need and now, after receiving confirmation, you know for a fact that they have a need. They are now a prospective customer.

Confirmation from a prospect can come in the form of a response to your direct-mail campaign, a request for additional information, or a phone call made by your salesperson. The close for this stage is to have Company A agree to an in-depth discussion about their business needs. Not *your* needs, but their needs!

3. The Entree Stage

In the entree stage, you have your first major interaction with the prospect. This contact is often made in person. For technical sales in particular, personal contact is usually required in order to explain very complex products and features.

This stage enables you to learn more about the prospect's need for your services and lay the ground work for the next stage. Here you qualify Company A regarding money, time frame, and the decision-making process. Your close for this stage is to have the prospect detail for you exactly what they intend to buy: how many, for what purpose, when, at what price, and so on. The more you know about their plans and needs, the better the job you can do in convincing them that you are the best choice for this project.

4. The Discovery Stage

In some cases, there is no need for a discovery stage because the prospect has already indicated their needs to you and has requested a specific proposal or quote from you. When this happens, you can proceed to stage 5, where you put together a written quote or proposal explaining what approach you would take to addressing the prospect's situation.

When you are dealing with larger companies, you may find you have to speak and meet with several people before being ready to send a proposal. Often, this is because there are many layers of management who need to give their "okay" to whatever project you may be trying to win. This may mean many presentations, meetings, or visits just to be sure you've spoken with everyone involved in deciding which company the prospect should hire. And when you're meeting with numerous people, you have to repeatedly go through the process of learning what each person's needs and concerns are.

If you haven't already collected this kind of information in stage 3, be sure and determine what the prospect's situation is, what they think may be the best way to improve the situation, what kind of budget they have, how quickly they want the work done, and what the most important factors are that they'll use in picking a supplier. Armed with this information, you can write a proposal that shows you truly understand what their situation is and that you can provide a solution that's also in their budget.

5. The Proposal Stage

Once the propect's needs have been defined and the overall sales criteria have been established, it is time for you to present your best solution: your proposal. This can be in the form of a formal written document or bid, or you can simply tell the prospect that the shoes cost $75. In either case, you now explain to the prospect that you recommend a specific solution to improving his situation, and the cost is such-and-such.

6. Initial Trial Close Stage

In the initial trial close stage, you ask the prospect for his reaction to your proposal, and whether he plans to buy from you. Don't take "no" as final at this stage. "No" may only suggest that you missed something or that the prospect needs time to consider your proposal. Ask for some feedback on your proposal and just listen to what the prospect tells you. You may be surprised at what you hear.

7. The Budget Stage

Many large purchases must go through an approval process at the prospect's company, which can take anywhere from a few hours to a few months, depending on the company and the offerings involved. This stage is often nerve wracking and requires patience. Unfortunately, all you can do is maintain regular contact with the prospect to ensure that nothing stops the positive momentum toward the sale.

For a small purchase, this stage can be as simple as running a credit card through the machine and getting an approval code.

8. The Close Stage

This is when you ask for the order and either get it, find out what is missing, or simply lose the deal to another company. All prior closing stages lead to this point. If you read the situation properly and had valid information, you stand an excellent chance of winning the sale. This is an exciting and scary time, particularly when the sale involves a large amount of money.

Many salespeople are very skilled at getting prospects to this stage but then lose out on a sale because they simply don't ask for it. Few prospects will ask to sign a contract on the spot or issue a purchase order unless specifically asked by the salesperson. So don't leave the prospect hanging at this stage: just ask for the sale.

And if you get a "no" or a "maybe," go back to the discovery stage to find out if you missed some crucial bit of information or if the prospect's needs have changed. Then go through the rest of the stages again.

9. The Post-Sale Stage

You've made the sale and the deal is closed. Everyone should be happy, right? Check back with the decision maker to make sure things are going okay. Make sure the customer is still happy with his choice and isn't having doubts or misgivings. This is an often overlooked and critically important stage to building long-term customer satisfaction.

It is much less expensive to keep an existing customer than to find a new one. Your most valuable assets are your repeat customers. Guard them jealously. To ensure that they continue to be repeat customers, check back with them after each sale to confirm they are pleased with their purchase, if for no other reason than to show your customers that you have their best interests at heart and weren't just after the sale.

A Sales Channels Overview

Salespeople are important people in your organization. Just as important, in many cases, are the people who support the sales team. You may want to have a few salespeople responsible for finding new ways to distribute your product but also have a number of support people who are solely responsible for serving existing customers and distributors.

These two tasks, finding new customers and supporting existing customers, require different skills. The support person has a relatively routine job that revolves around meeting delivery deadlines and keeping account information up-to-date, but the salesperson has to go out and create opportunities on a daily basis.

There are a couple of different options, however, for how your sales staff gets new customers. You can use independent distributors to expand distribution of your product quickly through its own sales channels, or you can build a direct sales force that deals directly with customers. Both approaches have pluses and minuses.

Distributors as Sales Agents

Using distributors or independent representatives removes you and your sales force from direct customer contact. The advantage is you now have a sales force of hundreds or thousands selling your product or service. A disadvantage is that it is more difficult to get customer feedback, because you have a barrier between your company and the customer.

You do lose control when you use distributors or reps to perform the sales function for your company. Major problems can erupt when distributors make commitments or promises on your behalf. Be sure that you define upfront each party's responsibilities in order to avoid situations like these.

It is critical to have this customer feedback so you can accurately determine whether there are new products or services you should be developing. Can you trust the distributor or rep to make that assessment for you? In most cases, the answer is no, so you have to decide whether the additional sales from using this independent organization is worth giving up direct contact with customers.

Using distributors usually means you need to hire fewer salespeople to cover a comparable geographic area or market, allowing you to keep your costs down. However, you need to interview and qualify distributors as carefully as you would a full-time salesperson, because that distributor is going to be representing your company. Make sure you are comfortable with that.

Tips for Using Your Own Sales Force

When is it time to set up your own direct sales force instead of selling through distributors? That is a good question and one each company must make based on its own set of circumstances.

Here are a few things to consider when making the choice:

1. The overhead associated with an internal sales force is substantially higher than with distributors. Those overhead costs eat into your profits every month, whether the sales are there to support that overhead or not.
2. You gain more control over your customer relations when you sell direct. This provides you with better management information for decision-making.
3. Selling direct does not take advantage of established customer relationships your distributors may have in place. Your direct sales force will have to generate its own contacts and relationships, and that can take a longer time to develop, delaying sales in the process.
4. Sales for highly technical products and services are often handled better by an internal sales force you can train fully and who will be less likely to make promises your company can't live up to.
5. Some companies start out selling direct on a smaller scale until they determine the proper sales strategy for their offering. They then approach larger distributors about introducing their products or services through the distributor's sales channels.

You have more control and flexibility with an internal sales force, but you also have higher expenses. You need to examine your marketing strategy to decide which approach makes more sense for you right now.

Selling Services Instead of Products

Services provide an interesting sales situation. The customer is buying something of value, but when the project is completed, she may not have anything tangible to show for it. For example, the result of your service contract with a customer may appear in the form of a new organization structure, better-trained staff, a new logo design, or a piece of software. These items clearly contribute to the company's success, but they are less obvious to the customer.

You have to keep in mind that services solve people's problems through your expertise and experience. Since the customer doesn't walk away with a tangible product, he must walk away with the belief that he benefited from using your service. Benefit-oriented selling is an important part of any sale, but critical when selling services such as consulting or training.

Clearly defining the *scope of work* from the beginning is critical to success when selling services instead of products. Since the customer may not have something tangible at the end of a project, it is important to clearly define at what point the project is complete. More than one company has been left holding the bag when they submit an invoice the customer feels is too high or should not be paid at all, because the customer doesn't feel he got his money's worth. The company providing the service may have done everything they were asked to do, but if the customer thought he was getting something else, it becomes difficult to get paid.

WHAT? **Scope of work** The agreement on exactly what services will be provided to a customer. For instance, the scope of a project may be to write a press release or to paint a building. Mailing out all the press releases or painting the business owner's house would be beyond the scope of work, meaning that those activities were not included as part of the agreement and would have to be paid for separately.

To avoid situations like these, the best policy is to get it in writing. In your proposal to your potential customer, state clearly what you are offering to do for them and at what price. Make the desired outcome as specific as possible, such as through the delivery of a final report. If there is nothing tangible you can provide to signify the completion of a contract, such as is the case with service contracts and warranties, set a specific time period during which your services will be offered. Once that period is up, your services stop.

Always avoid vague, ambiguous statements like: We will edit the new corporate brochure until the customer is happy with it. This one is a time bomb just waiting to explode. What happens after you've done 25 versions of the customer's brochure and he just can't make up his mind? Is your work done or do you have to continue to edit and re-edit until the customer is satisfied? If you had stated exactly how many rewrites you would provide as part of the agreement, the answer would probably be no, you don't have to keep working forever, but with vague statements like the one I mentioned, you would probably never get paid.

Instead, use carefully chosen and specific wording, such as: We will provide an initial design followed by a professionally created first draft, and then a second final version of the brochure that includes any requested customer changes. Establish milestones, that is, measurable targets or events that demonstrate you have provided the service and reached your objective.

Advance payments (retainers) or down payments are always good, but particularly valuable with contracts for service. People have convenient memories, and a little cash on the line always seems to keep the memory of both parties active and on track. It's also an excellent sales qualifier. Any prospect who is unwilling to pay a percentage of the total project cost is not someone you want to do business with. A charge of 25 percent is the suggested minimum, with 35–50 percent not out of the question. Submit invoices on a regular basis (determined in agreement with your customer) if you are billing on an hourly basis, so you receive regular payments for your work.

The Least You Need to Know

Sales are necessary for a company to survive, and selling can be fun and informative. As a company president, you are the top salesperson. If you are not highly sales-motivated, then you should hire someone who is.

- Selling is a process, not an end in itself.
- Closing and selling are not the same thing.
- The four customer qualification criteria must be in place, or you may waste time on a prospect who doesn't have decision-making authority.
- Every sale must go through nine specific stages before the customer is willing to make a commitment.
- Selling direct or through external sales representatives requires different approaches.

Chapter 9

Dealing with the Competition

In This Chapter

- Evaluate your competitors
- Determine when competition poses a real threat
- Find competitive information
- Determine the best defense against competitive pressure

My boss sat back in his chair and reflected for a moment. His eyes brightened, and he smiled as he moved forward in his chair.

"I was on a plane going to Minneapolis," he said, "and two guys behind me were talking about a large sale they were working on. Then one guy says the name of the company and the contact's name, and I realized that this was one of my customers. He then outlined the entire sale situation from the dollars involved, the basic technical requirements, the time frame within which a decision would be made, and who would make the decision. In short, he told me everything I needed to know to steal away the sale."

"What did you do?" I asked inquisitively, knowing that my boss liked inquisitive people, and it really was a good sales story.

"I called the customer immediately on arriving at the airport, told him that I had heard he was looking for some equipment and that I had what he needed at a price that just happened to be 5 percent cheaper than the bid provided by the guy on the plane," he replied. "I closed the deal that afternoon before the other guy even had a chance to claim his luggage."

This is a paraphrasing of a true story (except the luggage part). There is always some competitor out there who will take your lunch away, and you may not even know how it happened!

Is the Competition Real or Just a Nuisance?

It is easy to overreact when dealing with the competition. You may treat them as insignificant (watch your ego on this one) or as a major threat (watch your paranoia on this one). Both of these approaches are inappropriate unless you know something about the competitor. You need to have an honest understanding of your competition's strengths and weaknesses before deciding how you should respond.

In general, *direct competitors* pose either *strategic* or *tactical* threats to your business. A strategic threat can affect you negatively down the road but may only make itself a minor nuisance at the present time. A tactical threat takes money out of your pocket today when your customers go to your competitor instead of to you to spend their money.

> WHAT?
>
> **Direct competitor** A company who sells the same product or service that your company does, going after the same customers.
>
> **Nuisance** A weak competitor who will take up a lot of your time but really poses no threat to you.

A strategic threat can easily become a tactical pain in the butt if you don't pay attention to it and take the proper actions to protect yourself. A tactical threat, if large enough, can cause major problems for you. This is especially true when you have a small customer base that provides most of your sales. If your competition takes one customer, which they will definitely try to do, they can hurt you both today and down the road when others wonder what is so special about them that they took a major account away from you.

When you start up your business, you are in the enviable position of having no major competitor take you seriously. This provides you with a tremendous amount of freedom since nobody will be aiming to eliminate you in sales situations. You know that you are doing okay when competitors start to know your name and change their marketing strategy to go after you.

Because you are just starting out, you should be collecting as much information about the companies in your particular market segment as possible. Sit down with the information and try to imagine the picture that your prospective customers have in their minds about each of your competitors. This is generally created by your competitors' marketing message and positioning. (See Chapter 7 for more on this topic.)

How does your offering compare to the competitors'? If you were a customer looking at two companies, would you see them as direct competitors or as two companies in separate market segments? From this approach, you can get a first cut on who to treat as a competitor.

Accumulating Competitive Information

The Central Intelligence Agency calls it information; I call it the essence of competitive action. No matter what you call it, information is the key to making informed and appropriate competitive decisions.

Information is everywhere, and all you need to do is keep looking for it, collate it, and, finally, put it into some semblance of organization and order. It is amazing how fragments of information can give you an excellent overall picture of a competitor.

I had the dubious honor of serving our country as a nuclear weapons electronics technician (a 35F-20 for those who care). As part of this military honor, I received a top Secret/Crypto security clearance. As part of the indoctrination, I was told to keep my mouth shut and my ears open at all times and to report any shred of information to a specific party. When I asked a central intelligence person the value of this procedure, he told me that each little piece of information by itself is meaningless, but when it is combined with dozens of others from different sources, a pattern and picture begins to emerge that clearly identifies specific tendencies.

Where do you start looking for competitive information? How about the Yellow Pages? Who is listed in the category you would choose for yourself? Are they also listed in another category? If so, why? How many are there? How do they position themselves in the ad? Is it a display ad or simply a small-column ad? Grab last year's Yellow Pages and compare it to this year's. Has the number of competitors increased or decreased? Did some of the advertisers advance to a display ad? Did their positioning change from last year to this year? Look at how much insight you can obtain about your market by simply looking at the Yellow Pages.

Scour the newspapers and trade publications for advertising, articles, and quotes from any of your potential competitors. Ask your friends to do the same. They may find something that you missed. Start a folder for each of the competitors (they really deserve at least a manila folder, don't they)? Your local library may also keep files on local companies that you can scan for free. Every time you find a piece of information, write it down if you heard it, or photocopy it if you found it in print. Date and place the information in that folder. I promise that you won't exactly remember it later, and the mind has a convenient way of changing its perception of reality over time.

REALLY!?

Useful sources for competitive information include the following:

- Yellow Pages
- Newspapers and magazines
- Your customers and your competitors
- Annual reports
- Social gatherings and networking functions

Ask your customers what they know about your competition; how do they like dealing with them? What do they like? Dislike? What is their satisfaction level? Why don't they use you for the same products and services in which they are using your competition? Notice this discussion opens up another level of communication with your customers, which is always a good idea.

Ask customers for pricing information when you have either lost or won a bid; they just may give it to you. Notice that if they give you this information, they will probably share it with your competition in the same way. I have actually had clients give me a complete competitor's bid with all references to the company deleted. In this way, the information appears generic in nature and does not reveal the source, yet provides valuable insight into the competitor's overall offering. Guard this customer confidence like a diamond! It is a tribute to your client-vendor relationship when a customer opens up in this way, and you should treat it with the high degree of respect it deserves.

There are companies that specialize in accumulating information about companies, for a fee. They are called *clipping services,* and their job is to review a set number of publications for information regarding certain companies. You tell them which companies you want them to watch for and which newspapers or magazines you want them to read. They will generally photocopy an article that appears and send it to you on a regular (usually weekly) basis. This service is not free, but it may pay for itself in aggravation avoidance.

Finally, you can call your competitors and ask for information. A lot of times, they will send it to you. Don't use a fake personal or company name. If you misrepresent yourself, you are toying with *industrial espionage,* which is really scary. Penalties for fraud and misrepresentation can be severe and can seriously damage your business and your credibility. Just give them your name, number, and address and hope that you're talking to someone who doesn't know who you are. This is probably a safe bet when you first start out and will become more difficult as your success builds along with your reputation. With public companies, just call the investor relations department and ask for a copy of the company's annual report.

> REALLY!?
>
> One of the biggest clipping services is Luce Press Clippings. They can be reached at 1-800-528-8226. Bigger is better in this case because they scan a wider selection of publications on a regular basis.

Open ears, focused attention, closed mouths, and organized details are the secrets to accumulating competitor information. It's a job that requires constant diligence and doesn't take up much time once you begin.

Comparing Yourself to Them

Okay, so you've played super-sleuth and acquired a wealth of information about your competition. Put down your pipe, Sherlock, it's time to get into the trenches and start analyzing the information you've collected. How do you compare to the competition from your customer's perspective? When you find the answer to this question, you are on your way to determining your own position in the marketplace.

Here's an exercise that will help you find some answers. Take out a pad of paper or create a spreadsheet to automate the easy calculations that will follow.

- Divide your spreadsheet into four columns: A, B, C, and D.
- In column A, write down the top 10 criteria your customers probably use in deciding who to buy from. Characteristics may include technical competency, service, phone support, convenience, credit terms, years in business, depth of offering, price, and so on.
- In column B, place a number that corresponds to the amount of importance you believe a customer places on this particular item, based on your experience. Make 1 stand for most unimportant and 10 stand for a must-have. Although these are your opinions, they are still worthwhile to note. Your chart should look something like this:

		Your Company		Competitor #1	
Ⓐ Characteristics	Ⓑ Importance (1-10)	Ⓒ Effect (1-10)	Ⓓ Result (B x C)	Ⓔ Effect (1-10)	Ⓕ Result (B x E)
Years in Business	4	3	12	6	24
Credit Terms	7	8	56	8	56
Hours of Operation	7	8	56	8	56
Depth of Offering	6	6	36	8	48
Prior Experience with Company	8	5	40	6	48
Certification	5	8	40	6	30
		Totals	**240**		**262**
		Sale Price	**$75**		**$95**

In this example, Competitor #1 has a superior market position compared to your company, as indicated by the higher total (262). This higher total helps to justify the higher product price.

- Create individual columns for each of your competitors and your company. These columns will contain a number between 1 and 10 that gives your *subjective assessment* of how well each company meets customers' needs. (See columns C and E in the example.)
- Create another column for your company and each of your competitors. For each company and each of your competitors, multiply the subjective assessment column's number (column C and E) by the importance number (column B) and insert the result in each column you've just created.
- At the bottom of each column, total all of the numbers in the column for your company and each competitor. This final number provides a *relative weighting* assessment of how each competitor compares against the others and your company.

How does the number in your last column compare with those of your competitors? Is your number higher or lower? The same? How does your price compare with the others when compared against the summary numbers, such as in columns D and F in the example?

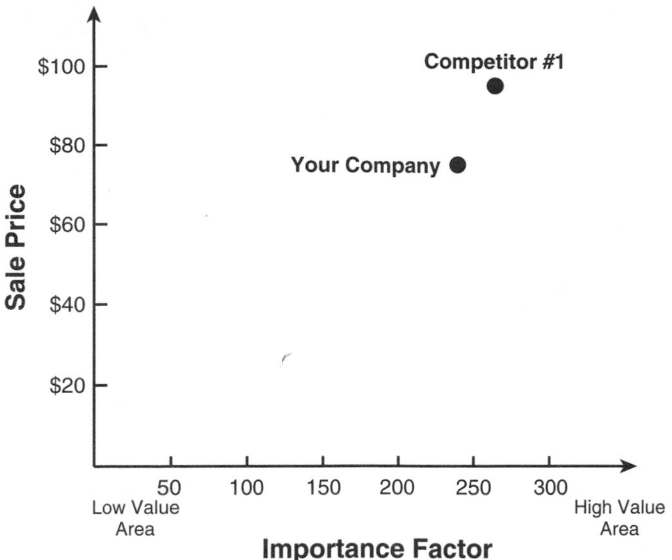

The results of your relative weighting assessment.

You should now have a pretty good idea of how you stack up against your competition. You may be less expensive than they are, but you don't offer the extra services that they do. You can deal with this lack of services by either adding services (and potentially having to raise your prices) or emphasizing in your marketing program that customers will get a bargain when dealing with your company.

On the other hand, if your price is too low and you have a higher total value, you may want to consider raising the price on your offering. Why leave money on the table if you don't have to?

> **REALLY!?**
>
> The pricing section of Chapter 7 outlines the difference between price and customer-perceived value. If you haven't read that section, you should take a few minutes and read it in the context of comparing yourself to the competition. Customers buy value, not price. Check it out.

Let Them Undercut Themselves While You Charge a Premium

Here is the best of all worlds: Your competition has decided to gain customers by dropping their price. This often starts a *price war* where all companies try to keep their customers by matching or lowering their prices even more. This is a dangerous cycle that usually winds up with suppliers hurt, the customer confused and dissatisfied, and substantially lower profit margins all around. The airline and computer industries go through this cycle on a regular basis. It tears the entire industry apart and takes years (if ever) to recover lost finances, and there's really no reason for it.

> WHAT? **Price war** When all competitors compete based on price and keep undercutting their competitors to get sales. As each company lowers its own price, others drop their prices to compete, resulting in profit margins in the industry as a whole falling to critically low levels.

There is a way to beat this cycle if it happens to your industry, but it takes amazing courage and fast reflexes. Instead of lowering your price, keep the price where it is. Beef up your extra services and sell the increased quality that you can provide for the higher price. Any experienced corporate business person knows you have to make a reasonable profit margin to stay in business. So instead of automatically dropping price as a reflex reaction, try this approach first, but continue to monitor your sales carefully. If you can't keep sales up, then you may just have to join the fray and hope that you survive.

Are You a Specialty Store or a Superstore?

Are the other folks in your industry large companies with deep pockets and a wide selection of offerings (*superstore*)? Or are they smaller companies that provide a specialized, niche offering that a few people use (*specialty store*)? It's important that you understand where you want to fit in the continuum between the two types of businesses. Note that these terms apply equally well to service or product businesses. You could be a full-service health club (superstore) or a specialty massage practitioner.

If you're trying to be a superstore but don't have the money to provide the required variety and volume of products needed, you will probably go out of business. The financial demands of making a business of this size work will affect your ability to maintain appropriate inventory or personnel expertise levels. Once your "shelves" appear naked or you don't provide a proper service level, customers will take their business elsewhere.

If you are a smaller business that tries to cater to everyone's needs, you will probably fail. Not because you lack skills or ability, but because your customers will expect more than you can offer. In addition, your smaller quantity of purchases will keep your costs, and prices, higher. The superstore firms will clobber you on price alone.

It is interesting that the superstores are wary of the specialty stores eroding their business in key areas. A specialty store can provide a much higher level of personalized service to customers than a superstore can ever hope to. The specialty store can also charge a little more for the service because the customer perceives it as having more value. In this way, the specialty store keeps margins high and expenses low, which is always a good way to run a business.

> REALLY!?
>
> Suppliers often lower prices to purchasers who buy in big volume. They'd rather deal with selling huge quantities to the big store and will charge you more because it's inconvenient to deal with a little store. The cost of providing a product is smaller when sold in larger quantities. This volume buying allows major corporations to get great prices on products and services that you can't match.

In technical areas, a specialty store may be one that customizes computer equipment or software for the customer, while also selling the software. The company makes money on both the software product and the service. The customer wins because she knows that her purchase will be handled in a low-risk, professional manner. Customers will pay for the service, especially if they have tried the cheap route before and been burned.

In retail, a specialty store may be one that deals only in candles and related items. The customer may be able to find a cheaper candle in a superstore, but could he find "just the right one?" Probably not, and that is the benefit of a specialty store. People expect to pay more for the added selection and service. Value is what sells; don't shortchange yourself on that count.

A typical service-oriented superstore would be one of the "Big 6" accounting firms that provide a wide array of accounting and consulting services. The local tax preparation service would be the industry's specialty store, since they do taxes, and only taxes, and may or may not charge a premium for the specialization.

Trying to be a superstore when you should be a specialty store is sure-fire trouble, as is the reverse. If you don't have the broad range of products or services to qualify as a superstore in your industry, stick with serving a small niche as a specialty store. You'll probably make more money by establishing a reputation as a specialist in a particular area, rather than a generalist who tries to do everything.

Market Makers and Followers: It's Cheaper to Be a Follower

Market makers are those companies with the financial backing and marketing know-how to create whole new business opportunities. Some examples of current market makers include larger companies such as Microsoft, MCI, and General Foods. They have the deep pockets required to pay for the process of educating consumers about a new product or service. The gradual increase in customer awareness required to create new market opportunities is both expensive and time-consuming. Larger corporations can afford to be the leader in creating whole new markets, but you don't have to be a leader to succeed in a new market.

Even if you have a product that is unique and innovative, you still may have a difficult time convincing the public to buy it. Be prepared. Generating enough interest in your product (or service) to result in sales may not be worth your effort unless you have an established distribution channel. That is, unless you have a way to get it quickly out to the people who want to buy it.

Getting your product into a distributor's hands may be one of the most difficult challenges you'll face, especially if you have a kind of food to sell. Competition for retail "shelf space" at grocery and convenience stores is brutal, with most grocery stores charging the manufacturer for the privilege of being able to sell their products there. Sounds unbelievable, doesn't it. The grocery stores know that they are the key to reaching your potential customers, and they have thousands of products to choose from, so why not ask for a fee to showcase your product? I'm sure that this information helps to justify the high cost of Twinkies and Devil Dogs. If you offer a service, distribution is less of an issue because there are fewer ways that you can provide your service to your customers; you either perform the service yourself, such as hairstyling or copywriting, or you have sales representatives making contacts for you, lining up new customers.

It is always cheaper, and less risky, to piggyback your offering on something that is already accepted and trusted in the market. Instead of trying to create a new market or introduce a totally new kind of product that no one has ever seen before, let the big folks spend their money doing that. Let them increase understanding and awareness of this new market opportunity. Then you can jump in later with your own product and benefit from all the money they've spent marketing to the public.

When you are starting out, try first to be a market follower. You can become a leader later when you have the big bank account and market acceptance.

Using Market Segmentation to Your Advantage

Within every market and industry are smaller pockets of opportunity called *market niches*. Larger companies don't waste their time trying to meet the needs of a small portion of the market, but you may want to. Niches can be very profitable if you have the right offering.

These market niches are often like a vacuum in that once you make your product available, everything you produce will get sucked into the niche, too. You can also easily establish a strong reputation that will make it difficult for larger competitors to compete with. Too cool! Even though niches may have fewer potential customers, they are often easier to sell to.

> WHAT?
>
> **Market niche** A segment of the market that has an existing need for a product or service that nobody is currently offering.

Alliances Are Often Better Than Competition

The Chinese have a saying that goes something like this: Who knows you better than your enemies. This also applies to business competitors.

It is not uncommon to find that you and your competitors, or even your noncompetitors, have more in common than it initially appears. They may address a particular market niche much more effectively than you, and vice versa. Combined, you may offer something that is truly more powerful than each of your individual strengths. You can cooperatively market your offerings. You can share mailing and administrative costs and aid each other in new product development activities.

Let's say, for instance, that you are a corporate bookkeeping service that doesn't prepare taxes. It would make sense for you to align yourself or partner in some way with a tax preparation service. The benefit is that your customers will perceive you as providing a higher level of service: bookkeeping *and* tax preparations.

There is a potential downside to all of this cooperation. You have to share sensitive company information with them to a much larger degree than you would otherwise do with a competitor. You need to weigh the pros and cons of doing this, but if the benefits of the alliance outweigh the risks you should go for it. One way to look at partnering opportunities is as a defense against the strong-arm tactics of the superstores that may try and muscle in on your territory. Working with other related companies, you make it more difficult for the superstore to win customers.

The Least You Need to Know

Competition is what makes the American economy thrive. It continually keeps us on our toes and drives us to higher levels of performance. You can view competition as a nuisance or as an opportunity to improve your products or services on a regular basis.

- Competition will always exist, but that's not necessarily bad. Comparing your products and services to those of your competitors will help ensure you stay on top of what customers want.
- Watching your competitors provides insight into what's going on in your market and what they believe customers want. This information can help you plan for the future better.
- Customers purchase value not price. Just because your competitors drop their prices doesn't mean that you have to. A price war can often present an opportunity, depending upon your particular market segment and product offering.
- You may find that working with your competitors against other common foes is a better strategy than trying to "go it alone" against everyone.

Part 4
Dealing with the Financial Aspects

I know that you're tempted to skip right over this chapter because it has that ugly word on it—financial. Yes, I know that financial stuff can be boring and confusing if not explained well. But have no fear, this chapter won't be that bad. More importantly, if you skip it, you could lose a lot of money.

There are many different ways to figure out if you're succeeding in business, and one of them is to look at your financial situation. Unless you read this chapter, you won't know how to do that, will you? So stick with me and I'll help you through it. If you have to put it down every once in a while to take a breather, I'll understand, but make sure you come back to it!!

Chapter 10

Making Sure That You Are Making It

In This Chapter:

- The critical need for accounting procedures
- Basic accounting principles
- An overview of balance sheets and income statements
- An introduction to ratio analysis
- Cash flow analyses
- When to use a CPA

Jake, who lived in Tulsa, was in Chicago for a business seminar and was excited about seeing his friend Dan. They worked on cars together in high school and now owned their own auto repair businesses. It was great to talk about business—they shared the same problems and could still be honest with each other since they were not competitors. Dan's business was in its fifth year of operation. Jake started his about two years ago and was clearly not making it. Things were tough, and this seminar was his last shot at turning things around before he had to "bag it" and get a "real job."

"I don't understand," said Dan. "You're a great mechanic and you love working with people. What's wrong with your business that you aren't making ends meet?"

Jake looked out the window and back at Dan. "Good question. I'm busy as all get-out and often have to turn business away, but at the end of the year, my accountant tells me I don't have enough money to pay myself what I need. Something's wrong, and if it doesn't get fixed soon, I go back to work for the dealership."

"What is your percentage profit margin?" was Dan's initial question. "And how does your pricing compare with the competition in town?"

"I have the lowest prices around," said Jake proudly. "I dropped our prices 20 percent last year, and that was when things really cut loose. We're doing more work than ever, and my sales are twice what they were last year. I even had to add space to my garage to handle the new business."

Dan smiled, then looked Jake squarely in the eye. "High sales and profits do not always go hand-in-hand. If you can't keep your profit margins where they need to be, you're in trouble. What's your percentage profit margin? What percentage of your sales is wrapped up in fixed expenses and what percentage markup do you apply to your parts inventory?"

"I don't know," replied Jake. "I let my accountant take care of all that financial stuff for me. I do cars; he does numbers. I just tell him what I want our prices to be and he takes it from there. That's what I pay him for."

"So he makes your financial decisions? What does he know about the car business? Does he care if you don't make money? Do you really not review your financial statements more than once a year? I have a bad feeling that you're a great mechanic who never made the transition to being a business manager. Let's get a copy of your financial statements and compare them to mine. I'll bet we can get an idea of where things are going wrong," said Dan warmly. "Your business means too much to you to let it go under due to bad pricing and financial decisions."

Jake nodded with a somber look on his face, silently hoping that Dan would buy lunch. He started to realize that managing the business like a hobby instead of a business may have hurt his dream of independence. This time, he would stay awake during the seminar's financial analysis segment.

An Overview of Accounting Principles

Most business owners treat accounting as a necessary evil. I understand completely, because I did the same thing. Because I did not treat seriously the accounting aspects of managing my company, I made a few financial decisions based on bad information, much to my regret. I now believe in the value of accurate accounting, and I encourage you to learn from my mistakes.

This chapter won't make an accountant or bookkeeper out of you, but it will introduce you to accounting terms and methods. You'll also learn enough to manage an accountant in a way that is valuable to your own business situation.

You Mean Accounting Really Is Important?

Communication is a wonderful thing—when it works. When communication is hazy, there are grounds for confusion and hard feelings. Communication takes on a new importance when it's about money. People treat money as a basic necessity of life, and threats to their money generally are treated as a threat to their person. So how do you communicate about money when working with a business?

This is the purpose of the highly structured world of accounting—to provide business managers and others with the information they need in order to manage the business or evaluate the results of their investments. Accounting is how business keeps score, and, just like keeping score in baseball, there are numerous rules and procedures to accurately reflect the results of the actions on the field. If you are publishing financial information to outsiders, you need to consider an additional set of special rules (called *GAAP*, or *Generally Accepted Accounting Principles*), but for managing a business you need to make sure your accounting system makes sense.

You need to accumulate information that is timely, reliable, and useful, and you don't want to take valuable time away from making money to keep score. Fortunately, principles and policies have been developed that can make accounting for your business easier. If you don't know those principles and policies in your industry or business, consider consulting a professional who has the necessary experience to help you set up good, efficient systems. Once good accounting systems are established, keeping the records becomes a clerical task that can be delegated or performed by an outside bookkeeper if you aren't interested in keeping the books yourself.

The following sections provide some basic accounting concepts so you can understand the considerations involved in setting up and maintaining your accounting systems. Time spent planning and developing good procedures can save you countless hours of frustration down the road.

Accounting Periods and Their Use

Accounting periods are periods of time, like months, quarters, or years, that allow a company's financial reports to be compared from one time frame to another. It's a good idea to review your company's performance on a regular basis so you can become aware of potential problems, such as running out of cash or lower sales figures, before it's too late.

Accounting periods also provide a basis for comparing company performance from one period to the next, from quarter to quarter or from year to year. In order to file your tax returns, you have to determine in what month you want your year to end, so you can report your profit or loss for that year.

For starters, you need to determine when your company will evaluate its financial performance. Most companies, small and large, look at their basic financial statements on at least a quarterly basis (every three months) to measure their progress towards long-term goals, and most managers review their financial statements on a daily or weekly basis. It's always good to know where your sales are coming from and how your money is being spent.

Calendar fiscal year

When the company's financial reporting period is the same as the calendar year, which extends from January 1st to December 31st.

The next question is, "When does your company's financial year begin and end?" A year in a company's history is a *fiscal* year. Unless there is some reason to do otherwise, as recommended by your accountant, keep your fiscal year the same as the calendar year, from January 1st to December 31st. This means your quarters will end on March 31, June 30, September 30, and December 31. And of course, you'll need to consider whether the Internal Revenue Service has any relevant rules before you can comfortably select a fiscal year end.

When Is It Really Sold, and What Did It Cost?

Assume that your client pays you today for work you intend to perform in 60 days. First off, kiss this client and keep him happy—this type of client is rare, indeed. Second, take a look at whether you should declare that money as *earned income*. (In other words, can you spend the money today, or should you wait?)

In the accrual accounting world (don't worry, we'll define accrual soon), when you receive payment from a customer for work that hasn't been completed yet, for accounting purposes, you need to show that payment as "unearned income" until the work is done. When the earning process is complete, the accrual basis of accounting will report that transaction as income.

WHAT?

Income
Generally seen as money received from a customer. However, you should also consider whether the work is done, or the product has been delivered. Even though you have the money in your bank account, if the customer can cancel his or her contract and get the money back, you have not truly earned the income.

Earned income Money you have received from a customer for work performed or for products provided. You've done everything the customer requested, according to some formal or informal agreement, and you can consider the money yours.

If the customer can cancel his order, then the money really hasn't been earned yet, has it? You are essentially holding the money for him until you complete the work. In short, if you haven't finished earning the money by meeting all the terms of your contract with the customer, you shouldn't consider the revenue from those sales as truly yours.

If you have a noncancelable contract along with a nonrefundable advance, then the money you received is yours. At that point, you can include it as revenue.

If you use the cash basis of accounting (described in the next section), you don't need to know the difference between collections and "earned income." In the cash-based accounting world, everything you receive from sales is considered income when it is collected, and you don't make any special accounting entries to show when it is "earned."

Which Accounting Method Is Right for Your Business?

Here's a fundamental accounting question: When do you actually incur an expense? Is it when you use the product or service, or when you pay for the product or service? The answer is different, depending on whether you use the *cash basis* or *accrual basis* of accounting. These are two approaches to accounting, and you need to know which one is more appropriate for your business.

Revenue
Money you receive from customers as payment for your services or the sale of your product.

The cash basis of accounting recognizes sales and expenses when money is actually received or spent. The accrual basis of accounting focuses on the earning process, and matches sales revenue to the period when the earning process is completed. The accrual basis also matches expenses incurred to generate those sales to the period in which the income is reported.

If your business has inventory, the IRS says you must use the accrual basis of accounting, so that decision is made for you. However, if you run a service business, especially if you are a small business, you may find that keeping your books on the cash basis is much simpler.

Here's an example to illustrate the differences between the two methods.

Assume you run a small consulting firm, and you have only one project going on right now. Last month, you spent $400 on supplies and office expenses, paid your staff $1,000, and billed your client $2,500 for the project. This month, your client pays the bill (and the check clears the bank!). Under the cash basis of accounting, you show a loss of $1,400 last month since you paid for the supplies and salaries then, and you show a profit of $2,500 this month since you collected the payment now. Under the accrual basis, you match the expenses incurred last month with the revenue earned last month, and show a profit of $1,100 ($2,500 in revenue less $1,400 in expenses).

If you have a fairly simple business, with expenses incurred close to the time sales revenues are collected, the cash basis of accounting may give you information that is accurate and timely enough to let you run your business. But most larger businesses use the accrual basis of accounting, for some or all of the following reasons:

- They have inventories, and the IRS makes them use accrual accounting.
- There are long lags between the time expenses are incurred and the time sales revenues are collected, and the business managers feel that cash basis accounting gives them a distorted picture of operations.
- The business sells a small number of large items, and showing earnings based on collections results in dramatic swings in reported performance from month to month, even though the underlying operations may not be fluctuating nearly as much.

- The business has more than one owner, and the owners want a clear picture of the earnings of the business, not just the cash collections. (Cash basis accounting gets particularly messy when partners split up.)
- Their accountant talked them into it. (Accountants believe the accrual basis of accounting provides better information on the results of business operations, even though an accrual basis system may be more complicated or costly to maintain.)

So how do you track money owed to you when you're using the cash basis of accounting? Very simply, you complete work for a customer and you bill them. In some businesses, you'll receive payment right away, such as if you are running a restaurant; customers pay after they eat. You keep track of who owes what by having waiters and waitresses use those little order slips. At the end of the night, you total the amount on all the order slips collected and match them with the amount of money in your cash register. You then deposit most of that money in your bank account and keep some in the register to use as change the next day.

Most businesses, however, have to wait to receive payment. You may bill a customer on the first of the month and have to wait 30 days until your check arrives. To keep track of who owes what, just create a file of all the invoices sent out to customers. As customers pay, you deposit their checks in the bank and take their invoice copies out of the file. You can always check to see whose invoice is outstanding by looking in that file. Once more than 30 days has past, you'll want to give the customer a call and find out if there is a problem.

Accrual accounting imposes an additional accounting step; now you have to use the accounting system to track when a customer is billed as well as when the collection comes in, and you may be making accounting entries at times when no cash has changed hands.

Furthermore, accrual accounting may report handsome profits while you have no cash in the bank to pay suppliers—because your customers haven't paid you yet. When managing any business, large or small, remember that "cash is king," and track your bank balances and expectations about cash flows using the techniques discussed later in this chapter. Many businesses have shared the sad experience of running out of cash before all the bills have been paid—try not to join them!

Accrual accounting may also impose tax complications. No one likes paying taxes on reported income before the cash from those sales has been collected, but that can be the way accrual accounting works. Your accountant or tax advisor can give you suggestions on techniques to minimize this source of pain.

The following table summarizes the advantages and disadvantages of cash basis and accrual basis accounting.

Cash Basis	Accrual Basis
Advantages	
Relatively simple to use.	Provides a conceptually more correct picture of the results of your business operations.
Understandable to anyone who report has balanced a checkbook.	Consistent with the way bigger companies their financial results.
Reports income when you have the cash to pay the taxes.	Accepted by the IRS if your business has inventory. Simplifies accounting during change in ownership.
	Makes reporting to outsiders more compre hensible (bankers, potential investors, and so on) since they are used to accrual-basis statements.
Disadvantages	
Can distort the results of operations, possibly leading to bad business decisions.	Can be costly and time consuming.
Not acceptable by the IRS if your business has inventory.	May not match reported income and cash availability.
Not comparable to the way apply bigger companies report their financial results.	Requires some thought to understand and the accrual accounting concepts.
Complicates accounting during changes in ownership.	

Understanding the Various Financial Statements

Find a comfortable chair and make a pot of coffee; it's time to learn the language of accounting. It's not nearly as fun as the language of love, but stick with me. Even if you intend to use an accountant to manage your records, you still need to understand basic financial terms so you can make reasonable financial decisions on your own.

Understanding financial statements isn't difficult. Yes, even you can pick it up. Effectively using financial statements also gives you a preview of good and bad times before they hit, so you can take proactive measures if necessary.

This section introduces you to financial statements and explains their basic purpose. There are three basic financial statements: the *balance sheet, income statement,* and *cash flow analysis*. The balance sheet shows you how much you own and how much you owe at a particular point in time, which is usually calculated on the last day of the year. The income statement shows you the amount of money brought in and spent during a specific accounting period, which is usually a year. And the cash flow analysis shows exactly how much you actually received in revenue and how much you spent on a monthly basis.

While bankers are most concerned with your balance sheet, because they want to be sure you will have enough resources to pay off the loan they've just given you, you really need to watch your cash flow statement carefully. Your cash flow statement keeps you informed about how much money you have in your bank account to pay all your bills.

A Chart of Accounts

One of the procedures accountants use to make record-keeping easier and more understandable is to summarize transactions so that similar transactions are grouped together. This is done by using a *Chart of Accounts*, which lists all the possible categories of transactions and organizes them to make producing financial statements easier. Accounts that summarize the assets and liabilities of the company will be grouped together and form the balance sheet. Accounts that summarize the sales and expenses of the company will be grouped together to form the income statement. And those statements, taken together, describe the financial condition and results of operations for the company.

If you are using the accrual basis of accounting, you also need a financial statement that details cash flow activity, which is likely to be different from the activity shown on the income statement. Cash basis companies may not need as elaborate an analysis to generate a good understanding of their cash flows, but they should still be aware that lags between billing and collection can adversely affect their cash position. Depending on the size of your business and the complexity of your collections, a cash basis company may need to develop a full-fledged cash flow analysis report, too.

Remember, it doesn't matter what a great deal you got on the inventory, or how much you saved by buying in volume, *if you can't sell the blooming inventory*! Don't let quantity discounts blind you to the true needs of your business.

The Income Statement

Your *income statement* (or *profit and loss statement* or *P and L*) tells you whether your business is profitable or not. The income statement totals the amount of *revenue* and then subtracts the expenses associated with making that revenue. The result is the *pretax profit.*

Income statements show you how much money you made and how much you spent during a particular period of time. Most businesses prepare year-end income statements so they can see how they did during the year. But you can also prepare income statements for any period, such as quarterly or the year-to-date.

Expenses fall into two categories: *cost of sales expenses* and *operational expenses*. Cost of sales expenses (also called the cost of goods sold, or COGS) are those directly related to producing your product or providing your service. These generally include the cost of raw materials, the cost of labor to run the machine that produced the widget you sold, and other expenses required to sell the product or service.

Gross profit The amount of money left after you cover the cost of sales. Out of gross profit, you pay your operating expenses. Gross profit = Revenue – Cost of Sales.

For example, say you sold a coffee mug for $5 and it cost you $2.50 to purchase it. The cost of sales is $2.50, which is what you paid for the mug. The *gross profit* calculation associated with this single mug's sale is: **Revenue – Cost of Sales = Gross Profit**, or $5.00 – $2.50 = $2.50 Gross Profit. Because the costs of producing your product will change depending on how much you manufacture at a time, cost of sales are called *variable expenses*. Just as things usually cost less when you buy them in bulk, producing a product in large quantities works the same way. The more you produce, generally the lower the cost per product and the higher the gross profit.

Operating expenses are also called *fixed expenses*. Operating expenses are those expenses associated with just running your business. No matter how much you sell this month, you will still have these expenses. These include your salary, your rent payment, the cost of the electricity in your office, insurance, administrative salaries, and other similar costs of operating the company. Fixed expenses are paid out of the gross profit.

Now that I've given you an overview of what the income statement provides for you, let's take a look at one.

A Simplified Income Statement
Jackson Surveying—Income Statement
Period Ending December 31, 19XX

Income Statement

Item	**Dollar Amount**	**Description of Its Income Statement Function**
Sales	$250,000	All revenues
Cost of Sales (variable costs)	$95,000	Variable costs associated with the revenues
Gross Profit (Gross Margin)	$155,000	Sales - Cost of Sales
Operating (Fixed) Expenses:		All nonvariable expenses:
Salaries	$65,000	Usually administrative and executive salaries
Rent	$18,000	What you pay to keep your doors open
Marketing and Sales	$55,000	What it costs you to sell your offering
Total Other Expenses	$138,000	Total of All Other Expenses
Pre-Tax Profit	$17,000	Gross Profit - Total Other Expenses
Federal/State Taxes	$5,950	Taxes due on the Pre-Tax Profit
Net Income	$11,050	Pre-Tax Profit - Federal and State Taxes

A typical income statement.

Remember our earlier coverage of accrual and cash-based accounting? Look at the income statement and notice how the relationship between expenses and revenues is directly linked to profit calculations. Unless the two are synchronized, there is no way to accurately determine if you made money during the time period you're looking at.

The Balance Sheet

Whereas an income statement reflects the flow of money in and out of a company during a specific period of time, the *balance sheet* shows the amount of company assets and liabilities at a particular point in time. The balance sheet is based on a fundamental equation of accounting: **Assets = Liabilities + Owner's Equity**.

> WHAT?
>
> **Depreciation** Since nothing lasts forever, accountants assume that everything you own declines in value over time. So every year, a portion of an item's value is subtracted based on how long it is expected to last. Computers, for instance, are expected to last just three to five years. So every year for three years, one-third of the value of the computer is taken as an expense on the balance sheet. Buildings, which have a much longer useful life, have a much smaller percentage subtracted each year.
>
> **Liquid assets** Things of value such as available cash that you can use today to pay off debts or purchase items.

Assets are those items of value the company owns, such as cash in the checking account, accounts receivables, equipment, and property. The value of an asset is based on its initial purchase price minus any applicable *depreciation*. For example, cash is an asset. You obtain the cash either from selling stock, obtaining a loan, or selling your services or products. Cash is money you can spend on the spot. It is called a *liquid asset*; you can use it immediately to pay off a debt or to purchase items. Other common liquid assets include accounts receivable and inventory. Liquid assets are often called *current assets*.

Fixed assets have a longer life and are more difficult to convert into cash quickly. Typical fixed assets include buildings, machinery, and land. The value of an asset is based on its initial purchase price less any depreciation. Different fixed assets have different depreciation terms, or depreciable lives. Check with an accountant to determine the proper depreciable life of a given item.

Liabilities are amounts that you owe. Typical liabilities include loans, credit cards, taxes owed, and other people to whom you owe money. Short-term liabilities, which are paid back within 12 months, are also called *accounts payable*. Long-term liabilities include mortgages and equipment loans.

Owner's equity is what is left over when the liabilities are subtracted from the assets. Take what you have, subtract what you owe, and you are left with owner's equity. This is the number that you want to maximize since it reflects the value of your company. The initial investment of your company stock and retained earnings are added together to calculate owner's equity.

The amount of *net income* (see the income statement figure) determined at the end of the year is added to an equity account named *Retained Earnings*. You add the current year's net income to the prior year's retained earnings to calculate the current year's retained earnings. Ideally, retained earnings become cash used by the company to promote further growth.

The following table is an example of how to organize your accounts in preparation for making your balance sheet.

Typical Balance Sheet Accounts

Assets	Description
Cash	Bank accounts, petty cash, investments.
Accounts Receivable	What other companies owe you on a credit basis, to be paid within 30 days.
Inventory	Raw materials, finished goods, product being built, retail merchandise, training manuals, and so on.
Fixed Assets	Land, buildings, machinery, office equipment, depreciation expense.
Liabilities	**Description**
Short-term	Must be paid in less than 12 months. Includes unpaid wages, taxes, credit cards, short-term loans and long-term notes with less than 12 months left on their term.
Long-term	Due over a period that is longer than 12 months. Includes mortgages, equipment loans, bank loans, and other longer term financial obligations.
Equity	(Assets – Liabilities = Equity)
Capital Stock	Owned by shareholders. Includes common stock and preferred stock.
Retained Earnings	Current and cumulative year's net profits or losses as accumulated from prior and current year income statements.

So here you are with accounts and numbers. Now look at the following figure to see how to put them together to create a balance sheet.

A Simplified Balance Statement Jackson Surveying—Balance Sheet Period Ending December 31, 19XX	
Current Assets	
Cash in Bank	$15,000
Accounts Receivable	$25,000
Inventory	$18,000
Other Current Assets	$7,000
Total Current Assets	$65,000
Fixed Assets	
Land and Building	$250,000
Machinery	$75,000
Office Equipment	$35,000
Accumulated Depreciation	($25,000)
Total Fixed Assets	$335,000
Total Assets	**$400,000**
Current Liabilities	
Credit Cards	$3,000
Wages Payable	$9,500
Taxes Payable	$3,000
Line of Credit	$5,500
Total Current Liabilities	$20,000
Long-Term Liabilities	
Mortgage Loan	$185,000
Machinery Loan	$55,000
Equipment Loan	$30,000
Total Long-Term Liabilities	$270,000
Total Liabilities	**$290,000**
Owner's Equity	
Common Stock	$45,000
Retained Earnings	$65,000
Total Owner's Equity	$110,000
Total Liabilities and Equity	**$400,000**

This typical balance sheet shows the format for organizing all your balance sheet accounts.

As your company grows, the numbers on your assets and liabilities and equity line will grow larger and larger. This will be due to purchasing new equipment, increasing your accounts receivable because of higher sales, or improving your cash situation. Companies just starting out will have a very small number on their assets and liabilities and equity line.

Owner's equity, what your company is worth, is calculated by subtracting the liabilities from the assets. This means that as your assets (what you own) increase and your liabilities (what you owe) decrease, your equity will increase. This makes logical sense, and the balance sheet puts it into a form where it can be precisely calculated.

Although your balance sheet may not change drastically from week to week, it's a good idea to review whether you are taking on more debt or increasing the value of the company on a regular basis. Most software packages can easily provide you with a balance sheet and income statement whenever you want to look at it.

Cash Flow Analysis

A *cash flow analysis* is your most important financial statement because it tells you whether you have enough cash to pay your bills. Although tracking your assets and liabilities is important over the long term, when you're just starting out, the key challenge is keeping the money coming in.

A cash flow analysis, or cash flow statement, looks a lot like an income statement. The major difference is that your income statement focuses on earnings from operations, while the cash flow analysis also reflects investments, borrowings, repayments of loans, and other balance sheet changes. Cash flow from operations may also be significantly different than reported earnings, especially if you are using the accrual basis of accounting.

The reason you need both an income statement and a cash flow analysis is that you may have a really good month of sales and then a really bad month of sales. So bad, in fact, that you had to get a loan to cover your expenses. If you were watching your cash flow analysis, you could see when you started to run out of money during that month. However, since an income statement looks at a longer period of time, the good months and bad months even out. So you wouldn't know by looking at your income statement that August almost put you out of business, but your monthly cash flow analysis would alert you to potential problems.

SAMPLE
PROJECTED CASH FLOW

	January	February	March	April	May	June	July	August	September	October	November	December	1995
Revenues													
Rooms	5,642	3,100	12,500	5,700	5,850	17,760	6,960	15,150	12,740	11,830	31,005	12,188	140,425
Food and Entertainment	186	186	186	186	186	190	190	190	190	190	190	190	2,260
Net Revenues	**$6,718**	**$3,853**	**$14,449**	**$6,784**	**$6,953**	**$20,386**	**$8,211**	**$17,443**	**$14,727**	**$13,701**	**$35,317**	**$14,104**	**$162,646**
Cost of Sales													
Rooms	100	1,891	7,625	3,477	3,569	2,664	1,044	2,273	1,764	1,638	4,293	1,688	32,025
Food and Entertainment	0	0	0	0	0	0	0	0	0	0	0	0	0
Gross Profit	**$6,618**	**$1,962**	**$6,824**	**$3,307**	**$3,384**	**$17,722**	**$7,167**	**$15,171**	**$12,963**	**$12,063**	**$31,024**	**$12,416**	**$130,621**
Expenses													
Director Salary	201	201	201	201	201	3,000	3,000	3,000	3,000	3,000	3,000	3,000	22,007
Payroll Taxes & Benefits	0	40	40	40	40	600	600	600	850	1,335	1,585	1,585	7,316
Staff Support	19	19	19	19	19	20	20	20	20	20	20	20	235
Advertising & Promotion	146	0	0	146	0	0	0	3,000	0	2,709	0	0	6,000
Depreciation	0	0	0	0	0	666	666	666	666	666	666	666	4,660
Supplies & Postage	330	0	0	330	0	0	0	793	0	132	0	0	1,585
Professional Fees	0	0	0	386	0	539	0	0	0	0	0	0	925
Printing	200	0	0	200	0	0	0	480	0	80	0	0	960
Telephone	263	263	263	263	263	892	892	892	892	892	892	892	7,560
Equipment Rental & Repairs	133	133	133	133	133	134	134	134	134	134	134	134	1,600
Travel	353	353	353	353	353	1,034	1,034	1,034	1,034	1,034	1,034	1,034	9,000
Vehicle Operation	482	265	1,068	487	500	1,518	595	1,295	1,089	1,011	2,650	1,041	12,000
Miscellaneous Items	237	237	237	237	237	237	237	237	237	237	237	237	2,840
Total Operating Expenses	**$3,471**	**$2,618**	**$4,776**	**$3,902**	**$2,853**	**$10,590**	**$10,228**	**$14,101**	**$11,522**	**$16,876**	**$17,093**	**$15,885**	**$113,917**
Net Income (Loss) Before Taxes	**$3,148**	**($657)**	**$2,049**	**($595)**	**$531**	**$7,131**	**($3,062)**	**$1,070**	**$1,440**	**($4,813)**	**$13,930**	**($3,469)**	**$16,704**
Provision for Income Taxes													
Federal Income Tax	0	0	0	0	0	0	0	0	0	0	0	0	0
State Income Tax	0	0	0	0	0	0	0	0	0	0	0	0	0
Net Income (Loss)	**$3,148**	**($657)**	**$2,049**	**($595)**	**$531**	**$7,131**	**($3,062)**	**$1,070**	**$1,440**	**($4,813)**	**$13,930**	**($3,469)**	**$2,849**

A typical cash flow analysis.

Using the Financial Statements

You now have tons of information neatly arranged in little columns. So what? How do you use it to your financial and management benefit? Try these suggestions on for size:

Use last year's cash flow analysis as a guide to estimating what your sales and expenses will be this year, by month. Use it as a goal-setting tool to help improve your company's financial situation month by month.

Use your income statement to estimate year-end totals for sales and expenses so you can compare where you are today to where you expect to be by the end of the year. Are you ahead of where you thought you would be sales-wise? Are your expenses growing faster than you had originally planned? Watching and comparing these numbers will help manage your business' financial situation better.

The same goes for your balance sheet. Do you intend to pay off some of those start-up loans this year? Will you be buying a new building for your business? Create a projected balance sheet for the coming year: estimate what your balance sheet will look like once you pay off those debts during the year or after you buy your building.

To CPA or Not to CPA, That Is the Question

Face it: you probably don't want to be an accountant or bookkeeper. You could go out and buy one of those green eyeshades and a pocket protector, but you still have to spend your evenings and weekends putting the numbers into the computer and paying bills. It is more fun to be out there working with customers, isn't it? It should be, if you're trying to start a business. Is it in your best interest to spend time doing accounting and tax returns when you could be helping to make sales for the company? Probably not.

Let's divide the accounting world into three basic regions: *bookkeeping, tax accounting,* and *managerial accounting.*

Bookkeeping involves accurately tracking where your money is coming from and where it is going, getting the numbers into the right accounts and with the proper values. You can hire a bookkeeper to manage your record-keeping or invest in a computer program to do much the same thing. Bookkeepers are not necessarily accountants, though they do help organize all your information for use by your accountant.

Tax accounting is a type of accounting concerned solely with how much money you will have to pay in taxes, so you can keep as much of your profits from Uncle Sam as possible. Tax accountants can help you take steps to minimize your tax bill.

> Whether you select a CPA or a bookkeeper to help you track and manage your finances, be sure you trust that person. And no matter what you do, don't hand over signature authority to someone else. You should be the only one able to write checks for the company so that you steer clear of embezzlers and stay on top of where your money is going.

Managerial accountants help you use your financial information to make business decisions. Generally, these accountants are on staff at a company and are responsible for record-keeping and reporting.

While you will want to stay closely involved with monitoring your financial statements, you can certainly hire a tax accountant or bookkeeper to help in those areas. Tax returns are becoming more and more complex, requiring a dedicated effort to take the best advantage of legal deductions. An accountant, even a CPA, will generally pay for herself in this area.

Bookkeeping is time-consuming, tedious, and relatively inexpensive to turn over to a third party. You should ask your accountant if she wants do both your bookkeeping and your tax planning. Accountants sometimes throw in free tax-return preparation when they do your bookkeeping, since their software can generate a tax return based on the numbers they've been tracking for you.

You may want to act as your own accountant in the early days to save money, but if you're not good with numbers, find someone to handle this for you right away. Otherwise, you can do the company financial records a lot of damage that you'll have to pay to correct later. The wide array of accounting software packages on the market, such as Quick Books, DacEasy or M.Y.O.B, make the basic bookkeeping process easier. They all sell for under $200 and come with a payroll module that helps you calculate how much to deduct from your employees' paychecks.

A Certified Public Accountant (CPA) is an accountant who has passed certain experience and testing requirements as set by your state *board of accountancy*. Investors use an independent accountant, who is usually a CPA, to verify the accuracy of your business financial statements. The CPA audits your financials, giving an extra level of assurance to potential investors and shareholders that the numbers represented are accurate.

Consider these suggestions for your starting point in dealing with accounting professionals:

1. Automate from the beginning. Get a computer and a software package that will help track your sales and expenses.
2. Use an accountant, not necessarily a CPA, for your tax return. This will certainly pay for itself if you will be depreciating equipment.
3. Farm out the bookkeeping aspects if at all possible. Talk to your accountant, and you may get the bookkeeping and tax return as part of an inexpensive package deal.
4. Graduate to a CPA when you need to work with external financial companies that will require the independent audit verification. You probably won't need a CPA early on, but you will once you look for outside funding.

The Least You Need to Know

Accounting is the tool used to determine the financial health of your business. It is a necessary and integral part of your business and you should pay close attention to it from the start. You are in business to make money. No matter what other altruistic motivations you may think you have, if you cannot make the financial aspects of your business work, you are out of business.

- ➤ Financial statements include an income statement, cash flow analysis, and balance sheet.
- ➤ Accrual and cash basis accounting will provide different profit and loss information for the same accounting period.
- ➤ Bookkeeping is basically clerical in nature; financial accounting involves analyzing financial performance and comparing current results with prior accounting periods.
- ➤ Bankers don't expect you to be an accounting wizard, but you need to be comfortable with financial terminology.
- ➤ When in doubt, get an accountant. You may not need a CPA right away, though.

Chapter 11

Working with Banks

In This Chapter

- Your banker is an ally, not an enemy
- A banker's perspective on lending money
- The importance of a business plan
- Working with the SBA

"These guys have absolutely no vision," said Bill. "This is a great idea, and all I need is $25,000. That's nothing to a bank their size, but NO-O-O! They want all of this supporting documentation before they will consider the loan. Why do I bother with banks in the first place?"

"They have money, and you need money. Isn't that right?" asked Bill's father.

"Sure, but why make it so complicated? It makes me want to pull my account and take my business to another bank that appreciates a good deal," said Bill. "I know this business. They have no idea what they're throwing away."

"That may be the key to your problem," his father said quietly. "If they don't understand the opportunity, can you blame them for not seeing its value? After all, whose job is it to convince them to give you money? Theirs or yours?"

What Does a Bank Bring to the Table?

In a word: money! As your company grows, its need for cash will also grow. Banks are storage houses for money, which is the one element most lacking in a new company. To get an idea of what it is like to be a banker, think about the last time you lent someone money and they were slow in paying you back. How does it feel to be a banker? Are you going to be more cautious the next time you lend someone money? Keep that feeling in mind when you talk to your banker, and you will have a much better understanding of her side of the desk.

So where does a bank fit into a new business' life? In the beginning, you will most likely have to turn to sources other than a bank for business financing. When you are just starting, the bank has no experience with you, and your company has little to no financial track record on which they determine risk. On what basis is the bank going to lend you money? Your good intentions? Your smile? Initially, expect the bank to provide checking services and accept wire transfers, federal tax deposits, and credit card deposits, along with other standard banking services. Over time, the bank will see your record of frequent deposits and a growing bank account, thus documenting solid growth and financial performance. Then, the bank will be more willing to risk loaning your company money. When you want a line of credit or a loan secured by a business asset of some type, you will need to work with a bank.

Banks exist to serve customers, but as the old joke says, "The only way you can get a loan is to prove you don't need it." Consequently, many startup companies have difficulty getting a loan from a bank—even if they have the best idea in the world.

You'll have to deal with banks anyway, loan or not, for your business checking account, payroll tax deposits, credit card processing, and other administrative details. It's a good idea to start *now* to develop a good relationship with your bank—and with the loan officers at your branch. Why? Well, one of these days your business will be well-established and a banker who understands your company can be a great resource in supporting your profitable growth. Start now, long before you are asking for money, to lay the groundwork that will help convince your banker that you are a solid customer and a good business risk. Besides, bankers see a lot of different businesses, and you may be able to get some good business advice from your banker at the best price: *free*!

Why don't banks lend to companies just starting? They have to be convinced that they will get their money back, with interest, when it is supposed to be repaid. Startup companies are notoriously bad about paying loans back on time, if at all, and after the turmoil in the banking industry with the savings and loan crisis of the mid-80s, loan officers tend to shy away from risky situations. Yes, they may be missing a golden opportunity to support your business in the early stages, but they also miss the opportunity to lose the money they'd loan you if your company doesn't work out the way you hoped.

Don't take it personally, but recognize it as part of the business environment you're not likely to change, and build your strategies accordingly. If you need financing to start your business, you will probably need to get it from investors or nonbank sources (which are discussed more in Chapter 12).

After you establish a track record in business, how do you deal with a bank? The next few sections boil down the lessons it took me several years and a lot of rejection to learn. I hope these lessons make it easier for you.

Make the Loan Officer an Ally Instead of an Enemy

Who would you rather give money to—someone who treats you with contempt and antagonism every time you meet, or someone who appears to appreciate you for what you have to offer? Would you give money for a risky venture to someone you barely know, or someone you have known for awhile and trust? The answer to these questions is simple, and my point is probably already made. Meet the loan officer responsible for your account when you first open the account—before you need money. Keep him updated on your progress and help him become more familiar with your company. You'll find that bringing him into the loop early will make him an ally when you need to ask for a loan. Don't wait until you're desperate for money to bring him up to speed on your activities.

It's also a good idea to get to know other loan officers at your branch, so if your main contact leaves, you don't have to start from scratch getting to know someone else. These days, people don't stay at one job very long, so it's likely that by the time you're ready to apply for a loan, your original loan officer will be working somewhere else.

Make sure that this first meeting goes well—no matter what! Appear to know what you're doing, even if you're feeling doubtful. The doubts will pass, but the initial impression on the loan officer will stay. Look and act like the president of your own company, someone who deserves as much money as you want! This meeting doesn't have to be lengthy, but you must leave a positive impression so the loan officer will remember you when you need to borrow money.

Banks Will Give You Money Only When You Don't Need It

Banks make money by lending it to individuals and businesses. The loan officer's obligation to the bank is to make loans to the businesses that are most likely to pay them back. The state's Office of the Comptroller of Currency, or OCC, controls banks' lending policies. The loan officer has to walk the line between pursuing the best business opportunity for the bank and complying with regulatory agencies such as the OCC.

From a bank's perspective, lending money to a small business provides risks and advantages that are different from those associated with a large company. Let's take a look at some of these.

When you request a loan for an amount greater than the loan officer's lending authority (which can be as little as $15,000 or as much as $100,000, depending on the bank), the loan officer has to get approval from her supervisor or from a loan committee that makes decisions regarding larger loans.

The smaller business loans have a higher risk associated with them because the business is usually newer and may have fewer assets to be used as collateral. This increases the interest rate the small business must pay, which increases the revenue banks receive. Small businesses are also of interest because funds from a loan can usually be covered by money from company checking and savings accounts at the bank. Since small businesses are likely to keep their money in one bank, banks are becoming more willing to lend them money.

Larger companies have large lending needs that require extra attention from the bank (401K, lock box, and so on). These lending services generate fee income for the bank, but the loans are priced at a lower interest rate because the larger customers are in a better negotiating position. However, larger businesses rarely have all their money in one or two accounts—it's invested in several other places.

In addition, it is generally safer for a bank to invest money in several ways, rather than all in one basket. Several small business loans spread the risk over several businesses, so that even if one business owner starts to have trouble repaying his loan, the whole bank is not threatened.

The primary reason banks have conservative lending policies is that loan defaults are expensive. They can only provide loans that are an acceptable risk in the eyes of their depositors and the regulatory agencies to whom they report. They are not in the business of providing high-risk, high-profit, potential venture capital loans.

As a small business owner, you must create a track record in advance that will qualify your company for a loan when you need it.

- Keep your personal and business financial situation healthy by using standard accounting practices and watching your cash flow.
- Try to get a small line of credit early on to get your credit established with the bank. A business line of credit will usually get increased when you pay it off on a regular basis.

Calling your loan officer and saying, "I need the money tomorrow" is a red flag that something is out of control with the company and its management. A panic situation raises questions about your managerial ability. Plan ahead to make sure that you can get a bank to lend you money when you really do need it.

REALLY!?

To give you an idea of how much a default costs a bank, consider a company with a $10,000 loan that defaults. The bank has lost the $10,000 plus the interest on the loan, which is generally 2–3% in profit to the bank. To make up that loss, the bank has to lend an additional $333,333 just to get its money back. A $333,333 loan would generate close to $10,000 in interest income in a year.

Bank Loans That You Can Get

Now you understand the world of finance from the bankers' perspective. How does this translate into your ability to get money when you need it? Here are some loan options for you to consider.

An *unsecured line of credit* can be given on a personal basis to the company officers. This is essentially a personal loan to officers (based on the personal credit history of the individuals) who then loan it to the company. This loan will not be given directly to the company since the company has not proven it could pay the loan back. The officer then arranges reasonable repayment terms with the company. If you are the officer of a corporation, make sure the loan conditions, such as the interest rate and the term of the loan, are similar to those you would see in normal business transactions.

A *secured line of credit* is the next best option. In this scenario, the bank loans the company money to purchase an asset such as new equipment or a new building. The asset is then used to secure the loan until the company pays it back, just like a house secures a mortgage, which is simply another kind of loan. In this case, the company typically must provide at least 20 percent of the purchase amount. (A $50,000 purchase requires $10,000 invested by the company and $40,000 by the bank.) If the loan can't be

> The value of assets is usually discounted when used as security for a loan. As my banker says, "We are in the business of lending money, not selling items to recover debt."
>
> Notes, or loans, secured by larger assets such as major equipment and property are considered long-term and can have a 36–60 month repayment period.

repaid, the assets are sold to recover the bank's investment. Liquid assets, such as a certificate of deposit, a receivable note, or inventory are the most desirable and easiest to loan against because they are the easiest to sell if the company defaults on the loan. Next best are fixed assets such as equipment and computers.

You may also be able to get *short-term loans* (under a year) by using receivables or inventory as your collateral. This type of loan is really a line of credit with special provisions. You provide a monthly summary to the bank showing that your company has a certain level of liquid assets—accounts receivables from customers, inventory, or CDs—that can be used as security on the loan. The bank will only loan 70–80 percent of the value of the assets, which is recalculated each month. The danger is that if your assets are declining from one month to the next, you could have to shell out some additional money.

For example, assume that you secured your line of credit last month with $50,000 in receivables, giving you $35,000 in credit (70 percent of $50,000). If your receivables drop to $40,000 the next month, your collateral would be worth only $28,000 (70 percent of $40,000). The $7,000 difference between the $35,000 and the $28,000 value of your assets would have to be paid to the bank *immediately* to meet the terms of the original loan agreement. This can be a tough check to write if you haven't planned for it.

> When calculating the value of your inventory, bankers use 50 percent of the retail price as the value. They don't consider the inventory worth full price because the bank would have to sell it for less if you went out of business.

As Usual, You Need to Sell Them on You and the Company

People naturally avoid risk, and bankers make risk avoidance an art form. There is only one issue ever discussed with a loan officer: How will the bank get the money back if the loan defaults? Where will the money come from? A new company has no established source of cash. The entire business is assumed very risky. The only thing the loan officer has to refer to is the business plan.

Your bank wants to be sure you've thought through all aspects of your business and believe it can work. If you don't believe in it, why should they? Can you imagine giving $50,000 to someone who is wishy-washy about where they plan to go, how they'll get there, when they'll arrive, and how they'll pay you back? I can't! I've done that and been burned. Your business plan is your opportunity to explain what you want to do and how you intend to succeed.

The bank is going to expect something from you before they give credit. First, you must do your homework and prepare a comprehensive business plan with realistic sales and expense projections. Next, you must provide personal financial statements to give the bank an idea of your own financial situation, separate from the company. Any person with 20 percent or more ownership in the venture will be required to personally guarantee the debt, meaning that they agree to repay it if the company defaults. Period. Later on you will have more negotiating room, but early on, this is the norm.

Your challenge is to convince your bank that you are credit worthy. As a new business owner, your personal credit history along with a well thought out business plan are the best cards that you can play. My banker told me that the loans I received in my second year of business were based on my personal credibility, personal asset value, and the strength of my business plan. So far, so good!

Banks will evaluate you based on the five C's of lending:

Character What are you like? Confident? Ethical? Self-assured? This is treated as a very important consideration when first starting out. Make the initial meetings count!

Capacity or cash flow Can you repay the debt? Do you have the cash flow to support the monthly, or periodic, payments required?

Collateral What can the bank take if the loan defaults? Make it clear that you don't intend to default, but that the bank is covered should the worst happen.

Condition What is the general economic condition of the area and what is the intended use for the money? Real estate ventures in Texas were tough to fund in the late 1980s.

Capital What is the company's net worth or equity?

Commercial Checking Accounts: A Different Animal

Balance your commercial checking account just like your personal checkbook— but try to do it more often! Your company writes checks and makes deposits like you do in your personal checking account, but the rules are slightly different. You can shop around and find a better deal on fees and transaction costs on business checking accounts, but make sure the rules and requirements fit your needs. Don't overlook the important factors of convenience and security—after all, you hope to be taking lots of money to the bank, so make sure the bank you select is accessible and safe!

Keep the following in mind when you set up a commercial checking account for your company:

- You are charged for your commercial account based on the number of transactions and the average account balance.
- You can expect to pay around $.03 for each check that you deposit, along with a transaction fee for the deposit. (Can you believe it? Only a bank would bill you for giving them money!) The rate billed for each check will vary based on whether it is local, in-state, out of state, or from your cousin Vinnie!
- You will also be billed for each check you write.
- You will receive a statement from the bank that outlines the charges billed to your checking account for those transactions. This statement is in addition to the basic checking statement listing all the checks and deposits that have cleared.
- Banks charge transaction fees for each deposit you make and check you write, but they also give you interest on the money in your account that you can use to pay for those transaction fees. By keeping enough in your account to offset transaction fees, you save some money.

You should shop around to get the best checking account for your company, based on whether you expect to have lots of transactions or just a few, and whether you can maintain the minimum balance to avoid additional charges.

Where Does the Small Business Administration (SBA) Loan Fit In?

The SBA requires that you keep thorough records. All funds disbursed must be accounted for by the bank and the borrower. The record-keeping load is substantial, so be ready for it.

When nobody else will help, the Small Business Administration (SBA) will come to the rescue. Maybe. It used to be difficult to get an SBA loan, but the SBA has changed and may be able to help if the loan amount is under $100,000. What used to generate a one-inch folder of paperwork is now down to a two-page application as part of the LowDoc loan program. This is good news, but you should understand the process to see how the SBA can help you in the early days.

The SBA doesn't give you money. A bank actually issues the check. The SBA just guarantees the bank that the loan will be repaid and charges you a 2 percent fee for the insurance policy. A guarantee from the SBA that the loan will be repaid makes the loan very attractive to a bank.

Don't assume that you need an SBA guarantee to get a loan. Fill out a loan application at the bank of your choice, which will require your personal financial information and a business plan. Should your loan not meet the bank criteria for lending (the 5 C's), the bank can then turn to the SBA for a loan guarantee. If the SBA approves, the loan is funded from the bank with a guarantee provided by the SBA. The bank approves the loan if the SBA provides an 80–90 percent repayment guarantee.

> **REALLY!?**
>
> Think of the bank as the initial approval gate keeper. The SBA will only consider giving you a guarantee if three banks have already rejected you for traditional financing. So you have to go to banks first to get rejected and then to the SBA, which will rely a lot on the bank's assessment of your situation.

There are several different SBA loan types, and they change on a regular basis. Contact your local SBA office and sit through one of their introductory talks (around one hour long). It provides a solid basis for understanding the procedure and how to work with a bank to obtain a loan. There are preferred SBA vendors who do a lot of business with the SBA, so get a listing of them and work with one of the preferred banks from the beginning.

Big Banks and Small Banks: They Are Not the Same

Which is better—a small bank with easy access to the lending managers, or a big bank with deeper pockets and higher approval levels? The answer is: It depends.

All banks have lending guidelines, but the internal policies are more flexible with a small bank. The officers are more likely to bend the rules in a small bank than in a big one. With a small bank, you get to know the officers better and quicker, but the loan amount that can be approved may be smaller.

Start where you already have a relationship. If the big banks give you grief, go to a smaller one. You might look like a large fish in a small pond, so beware that the pond may not be deep enough as you grow.

Average small business loan amounts are in the $25–50K range, which is well within the reach of any bank. Be aware that since it takes just as much paperwork to process a $25,000 loan as a $250,000 loan, most banks would prefer to process the larger amount, where they will earn more interest on the loan.

The Least You Need to Know

Be prepared to sell the banker on the financial validity of your business idea. Remember, they don't know you from Adam when you first come in, so make your visits count. "Give me $50,000 because I'm a good guy" will never get the money!

- You will almost certainly need the assistance of a bank as your business succeeds and your cash requirements increase, so get to know the officers of your bank now.
- Your personal credit history and business plan are your best selling points when trying to get money in the early stages.
- The five C's determine your credit worthiness. Make sure that you have effectively addressed all of them to increase your chances of success.
- The SBA requires the same amount of preparation for a loan guarantee as a bank does. Apply for a loan at a bank first, and if you are turned down, the SBA may be able to help get it approved by guaranteeing repayment for you.

Chapter 12

Cash Is King

In This Chapter

- The value of cash to an organization
- Turning receivables into cash
- How success can hurt your business
- Using credit to your advantage
- Selling stock to raise cash

Laurie stared in disbelief at her conference room table. She had heard of this happening to other companies; she couldn't believe it had happened to hers.

"We're out of money," she said. "I can make payroll, but I don't have enough left over to pay our suppliers."

"That's impossible," said Philip, the VP of Sales and Marketing. "We just had three of our best months this quarter. In fact, our current revenues are triple that of last year at this time, and our income statement clearly shows a profit for this quarter. What gives?"

"The earnings are right, but we haven't collected on those large sales over the past few months. And remember, we've had to pay our workers and suppliers even though we haven't yet been paid by our customers. It'll be great when all those sales are collected, but if we keep growing like we have been, we're likely to need even more cash."

"So, are you trying to tell me that our marketing success has put the company in jeopardy?" cried Philip.

"Not at all," said Laurie. "We simply did not plan for the rapid increase and came up short with our lines of credit and other ways of getting cash into our bank account. It was mine and Jerry's responsibility to plan for this, and we got caught with our pants down. We need to tell our vendors our dilemma. I think honesty is the best policy. Let's just hope they will let us stall our payments. We can't let it happen again!"

Everyone nodded their heads at the seriousness of the situation. They had been so happy being successful that they had forgotten that cash is king.

When You're Out of Money, You're Out of Business (Usually)

Love may make the world go 'round, but it's cash that keeps a business going. Try to keep an employee around when you cannot pay him, and you will understand that cash is the business equivalent of air. Lose your employees, the good ones, and you have substantially hurt your business. Once they're gone, they're usually gone for good.

Let's look at your vendors. How long will they keep providing you with the materials you need if you cannot pay your bills? About as long as a snowball would last in a west Texas desert. Once again, you cannot blame them for putting a stop to your credit line. Guess who is paying her employees out of her own pocket because she gave you credit and you can't pay? Your vendor! She has to cover her own behind just like you do. See Chapter 14 for more insights regarding providing credit to risky customers.

Now, what about you? What happens if you cannot pay yourself? How long will you keep the business alive and pay your employees when you are not being paid yourself? A few months, maybe, but when it becomes a way of life, you will be seriously tempted to pull the plug and "get a real job," not because you don't love what you do, but simply because that's what an organism does when its air supply is taken away.

A cash problem hurts your employees, your vendors, and you personally. Lack of cash may cause your usually professional employees to become disgruntled, may cause the quality of your product to decline somewhat, and may lead to your own loss of enthusiasm. The result is that your customers will be affected, and they probably won't like it. Their opinion of your company may drop as employees become more snippy over the phone or in person. Unfortunately, customers don't really care why the quality has declined; they just recognize that it has, and they may decide to take their business elsewhere if it continues.

All this because you forgot that cash is king! Income is great. Equipment is wonderful. Receivables are heartwarming. Inventory gives you something to count on boring weekends and at the end of the year. But cash is what makes it all work on a daily basis.

How Success Can Kill a Business Without Funding Sources

How good can it get? Here you are with a 300 percent increase in sales over the last six months. Your people are flying high, and you just can't seem to do anything wrong. As a matter of fact, the projects coming your way are larger than you ever thought you would have, and it looks like you'll get them all! Your initial dreams have come true, and you're on the verge of becoming unbearable to everyone around you. Don't worry. Life is about to humble you, unless you have taken the proper steps to deal with the growth.

Have you ever met someone who told you that they were so successful they went out of business? If not, you should look for such a person and buy him dinner (or a drink, depending on how he dealt with the loss). Just as you don't need to go through a windshield to learn that seatbelts are a good thing, you don't need to go out of business to learn the dangers of rapid growth.

Picture this scenario: You used to provide $10,000 per month in services and all of your customers paid cash on delivery or by credit card. When you completed the sale, you got the cash. Everyone was happy. Then customers began asking for credit terms. After all, your competitor offered them credit, and they have consistently used your company instead. It wasn't such a big deal, and they were stable. Why not offer them credit? So you did.

Let's look at what just happened when you agreed to accept credit terms instead of cash. You took the cash you would have received this month and told the customer that they could pay you next month, at the earliest. However, you still need to pay your employees and vendors at the end of this month. Where is that money going to come from? Unless your company has lots of cash on hand (and wouldn't we all like that situation?), it will have to come from you. When the customer pays, you will simply pay yourself back and all is fine. Sort of....

Now let's be really successful and bump your monthly sales to $30,000. Wonderful! And who is going to provide the cash needed to cover the month-end bills? You? Do you have the $30,000 on hand to lend the company? Even if you do have the cash at $30,000, you may not when sales hit $50,000 or $100,000.

My point is this: Someday you will no longer be able to personally provide this kind of cash advance to the company. Uh-oh! There go your employees and all those wonderful vendor relationships. When they leave, they place everything that made you successful in jeopardy. In short, the whopping success that you enjoyed has just put you precariously close to being out of business. Isn't it amazing how a few short (or very long) weeks can turn your business on its ear? That is exactly what will happen if you don't take steps to avoid a cash crunch.

I'm not trying to talk you out of making your business as wildly successful as you can imagine. I'm just trying to convince you to open your eyes to the fact that success can destroy all that you have built if you don't also deal with its potential risks.

Factoring, Credit Terms, Loans, and "Float"

Here you are, all dressed up to go to the dance with a hot date and no cash to pay for the cab. Now what do you do? You go to someone and borrow money against your next paycheck or income tax refund. Well, the same thing can be done with a business, and it's called *factoring*. With factoring, a company gives you a percentage of what customers owe you, sort of like a short-term loan.

WHAT?

Factoring The process of receiving money now for payments your customers are expected to make to you in the next few weeks. There is a cost for having that money now though, which is paid in the form of a percentage fee to the factoring company or factor.

You can also improve your cash situation by providing your customers with an incentive for paying their bills early (or even on time) and extending payments to your own vendors with whom you have credit. This improves your cash position by improving the *float* between when you receive money and when you must pay your bills.

Finally, you can get a *short-term loan* that is secured by your receivables from a bank or other funding source. This technique is less expensive than factoring and provides greater stability, along with other benefits.

Factoring Receivables

If you need cash now to cover business expenses, there are companies out there who will provide you with cash for your receivables, in exchange for a fee. This procedure is called *factoring*, or discounting, of receivable notes.

The general procedure is as follows:

1. You close the deal and the customer agrees to pay you for it.

2. The company that plans to factor your receivables issues an invoice to the customer (usually on your letterhead), which the customer is to pay.
3. The factoring company immediately gives you cash worth between 80 and 95 percent of the receivable value.
4. The factoring company then gives back a portion of the fee (usually up to 10 percent of the initial 15 percent discount) if the customer repays within the specified time frame.

For example, assume that a client contracts from you $10,000 worth of whatever you offer. You can realistically expect to receive that money within 45–60 days, which can put you in a bind depending on your company's cash situation. You could factor the note using the previously outlined procedure and have the numbers work out as follows:

1. You close the deal for $10,000.
2. The factoring company issues an invoice to your customer for $10,000 and indicates the terms in which the payment should be made to the factoring company.
3. The factoring company writes you a check for between $8,000 and $9,500.
4. If the customer pays within the allowed 30 days, then the factoring company writes you another check for around 10 percent (or $1,000) when payment is received. (The longer it takes for your customer to pay the factor, the less of a rebate you will get back.)

Assuming that you receive an 85 percent factoring rate with a 10 percent rebate for payment received within 30 days, you would see $8,500 immediately and $1,000 within 30 days. You give up 5 percent, or $500, to get your money upfront instead of later and for pushing the collections issue over to the factoring company. Collection becomes their problem, not yours.

If you are in a cash crunch, factoring can save your hide. However, here are the down sides, and they are not trivial. If you factor on a regular basis at 5 percent per month, then you are paying 5% × 12 = 60% annual interest on your money. Wow! That's big bucks for the convenience of having your cash earlier instead of later. On the other hand, if you need it, you need it.

You can minimize the sour taste that factoring percentages can create by performing your own factoring services. If you have substantial personal resources, you can use them to replace the need for factoring. You can buy the receivables from your company with your personal funds and provide the same terms as a factoring company. At least, the interest is going into your favorite account (yours!) instead of into some other company's.

Unfortunately, you can only factor up to the limit allowed by your personal resources. You then need to look for other options.

Using Credit Terms to Enhance Your Cash Position

Timing is the secret to success, and that is particularly true when working with money. The time that money is in your hands, or in someone else's, either makes you money or costs you money. You must make every possible effort to turn your sales into cash as quickly as possible, paying as little as possible to get your money faster, such as by factoring or offering fast payment discounts.

You have an excellent opportunity to improve your cash flow by simply changing the way you pay your bills and collect receivables from your clients. If you must pay in 30 days and your clients pay in 60 days, you have a problem. On the other hand, if they pay in 10 days and you pay in 45 days, you are in excellent shape. You accomplish this by simply offering your customers a discount (such as 2 percent of what they owe you) for payment within 10 days. Many companies will jump at the chance to save the 2 percent, and it's certainly cheaper for you to offer this discount than to pay a factoring service 5–15 percent for the same result!

Think about it. Plot out on a piece of paper the timing of payments made and received. Assume a $10,000 sale is made today. Mark on a calendar when you expect to provide the products or services, when you plan to receive the payment made under your credit terms, and when you have to pay your vendors and employees. Notice that the arrows for money going out and money coming in have a delay between them that doesn't work in your favor. You must pay the suppliers before you have received payment. Now mark where payment would be received with a 2% per 10-day incentive. Isn't life easier when the cash is in your hands, instead of in your customer's account?

Don't tell the IRS that I told you this, but you can improve your cash position for a two-week period, if needed, by holding your monthly payroll taxes until the middle of the month. You have to pay them on time, or you pay dearly for your transgression, but you can keep the cash in your account up to the last minute to cover other debts. Sometimes, providence will shine on you when that big check you've been waiting for arrives just in time. This keeps you from having to factor at all, but it can keep you up nights worrying about the big check.

Loans Designed for This Situation

You can imagine that every business has exactly the same problems in turning its receivables into cash. It should not surprise you that people, even banks, provide loans designed to cover exactly this short-term timing situation. It is essentially a line of credit secured by the receivables, and you are expected to pay it down as quickly as possible. See

Chapter 11 for information on this type of loan. The interest rate will be around 9–13% annually, instead of 60%, and you will establish a credit history with your bank. That always pays off in the long run, since the bank can become an integral partner as your success requires higher and higher borrowing levels.

Equity Funding Sources for a Corporation

A good credit history always pays off in the long run, because a bank that is comfortable with you as a borrower can make life much easier as your business grows. In return, investors now own a portion of the company. This is called *equity financing*.

Equity funding is obtained through three basic means: selling shares of stock to private investors, selling shares of stock to professional investors such as venture capitalists, and "going public," which involves selling shares to the general public on one of the stock exchanges.

One reason to incorporate is to be able to sell stock for funding purposes. Notice that a stock sale makes the shareholders owners of the corporation and you do not need to repay their stock investment. They are taking a risk with their investment and get a say in the company operation in exchange. Taking out a loan still keeps the company 100 percent under your ownership and control, but you have to repay the debt.

> **Equity financing**
> WHAT?
> When someone gives you money in return for owning a portion of your company. You are giving up equity in the business in return for capital. You don't pay back equity financing. Investors get their money back by selling their shares to someone else. The other kind of financing is *debt financing*, which is when you get a loan that you must pay back later.

Pick Your Investors Well

Selling shares of stock looks pretty good on the surface: you sell a portion of the company in exchange for some cash. All you give up is a little ownership in the company to get the cash you need. What is the downside? As usual, it comes down to who you choose as your investors.

The more sophisticated the investor, the better an ally she will make down the road. A professional investor knows the pitfalls associated with running a business and can assist in guiding you through potential minefields. However, professional investors also tend to be demanding and relatively heartless when you do not perform as expected.

Other forms of funding that apply to non-corporations include loans and "buying in" investments where partners pay to become a member of the partnership.

From their perspective, not living up to your plan indicates a lack of business control. A professional investor will take you to task if needed because she has a vested interest in your success.

Your Uncle Billy, on the other hand, may not need monthly reports from you on your progress and may purchase your company's stock on his faith in your ability alone. This makes getting your initial funding easier, but may hurt you down the road. Let's say that the company has a rough quarter, for reasons that are outside of your control, such as flood or war. Billy may not understand why that dividend check you promised didn't arrive. He may not understand why you need more money due to the unforeseen circumstances. In fact, Billy may not have deep enough pockets to fund the next round of investing.

Be forewarned that many family conflicts have erupted over investments made in businesses that ultimately went under. Do you really want to be responsible for risking your Uncle Billy's retirement fund?

Professional investors also bring a wide array of business expertise and contacts to the table. This broadens the resources available to you as the founder, while also opening up potential new marketing opportunities. In short, if you can get a trustworthy professional on your side, that is a better route than Uncle Billy.

Never knowingly involve someone in your business that you do not trust. You will be busy enough worrying about expanding your business; you do not need someone questioning your every move and undermining what you do. Stall, work harder, cut expenses, and play with cash float before getting involved with an investor who may be a potential headache down the road.

Ultimately, it is your job to increase the value of the shareholders' investment. This is done by improving the company's sales while decreasing the cost of making those sales. In short, your job is to make the company more profitable from one year to the next. If the profit that the investors see is not substantially greater than what they could get from other investments such as the stock market or bonds, then why should they invest with you? Your job is to give them a better return on their investment than they could have with traditional methods.

The Various Stock Exchanges and How to Access Them

The likelihood of selling stock in a successful public offering is slim to none in the first few years of operation. The reason? You have no track record for an investor to evaluate. In general, you should not consider making a public offering until your company has seen at least 4–8 quarters of profitable operation, with profits growing in each quarter. The first time you sell shares to the public is an *initial public offering* (IPO) and an excellent means for new companies to raise large amounts of capital for expansion.

A company needs $5–10 million in sales to make an IPO worthwhile, because the $250,000 to $500,000 cost to handle the offering makes it almost impossible for smaller companies. Those expenses include legal and filing fees, public accounting fees, document printing (not a trivial item), and underwriter fees.

The *underwriter* is critical to the success of the offering, and receives a hefty fee for that assistance (around 9–12 percent of the offering). Start looking for an underwriter today if you plan to go public in the next few years. They will advise you when and how to go public so you get the most money for your stock sale. Ask other companies that had successful IPOs who they would recommend.

The basic procedure for a public offering is as follows:

- Have at least four profitable quarters with sales of at least $5 million a year.
- Find an underwriter who sees your company vision and believes in what you have to offer.
- The underwriter then prepares an investment *prospectus* and SEC registration statement, while coordinating accounting and legal activities.
- The underwriter then handles the marketing and sale of the stock. He gets 1–2 percent of the initial offering amount and another 7–10 percent of the total value of the actual stock offering.

>
> **Underwriter** A company that handles all the paperwork and filings associated with marketing your stock. Underwriters must be licensed to sell stock, so they are usually affiliated with an investment firm or brokerage.

As the business owner of a public company, you must do the following:

- File quarterly and annual reports with the SEC, along with annual certified financial audits.

- Create quarterly *proxy statements* for new shareholders and shareholder and annual financial reports.
- Announce and hold shareholder meetings.
- Send out dividend statements, checks, and tax reports.
- Complete special paperwork for the stock exchanges themselves.

In short, going public requires a lot of additional paperwork and staff. Consider these costs before deciding to go public.

There are four basic public exchanges used in North America: the New York Stock Exchange (NYSE), the American Stock Exchange (AMEX), the NASDAQ, and the Canadian Stock Exchange. The New York Stock Exchange is usually for more established companies; the American Stock Exchange is another alternative for medium to large companies. The NASDAQ is where most new companies find a stock-trading home. The Canadian Stock Exchange is becoming a viable alternate funding avenue for firms based in the United States. Stocks are often priced at low investment amounts (under $1.00), and the restrictions are less stringent than those of NYSE, AMEX, or NASDAQ. Your underwriter is your guide into this world.

The Least You Need to Know

Every successful business will eventually need sources of funding as the business' financing needs grow larger than the founder's bank account. Expect this situation to occur, and plan accordingly.

- Cash is the lifeblood, or air supply, of an organization. Without cash to pay employees or vendors, you are out of business.
- Cash will become scarce at some point in your business growth—of that you can be certain. Set up credit lines today that will help you when it happens.
- Factoring is a convenient, yet expensive, way of turning receivables into cash.
- Banks will give you short-term lines of credit secured by receivables, but the amount of credit will vary from month-to-month.
- A private stock placement is possible, but unlikely, in the early stages of your company. If you need lots of money, look toward an initial public offering (IPO), which requires one or two years of profitable operation and an experienced underwriter.

Chapter 13

Setting Up for Credit Card Sales

In This Chapter

- Comparing standard terms with credit card sales
- Typical installation and monthly charges for the privilege
- Protecting yourself from fraud
- Telephone sales versus in-person credit card sales
- Determining the right credit card setup for you

Jamie was pumped up! Sales were going through the roof and things appeared to be financially on track. So why did his accountant want to talk with him? What could possibly be wrong? His trusty accountant, Raymond, was smiling but also shaking his head.

"Jamie, how would you feel about having another $1,000 in your pocket this month without lifting a finger?" asked Raymond. He knew Jamie well enough to already know the answer.

"Sure, and what's your cut for bringing this opportunity to me?" asked Jamie.

"Not a nickel. This one is on the house. Do you remember those two large training contracts you signed last month? The one for $17,000 and the other for $15,000? Well, guess what? The clients decided to charge the sales to their American Express card, and American Express charged you 4.5 percent for processing those charges! These clients both have great credit records

and probably would have jumped on the 2 percent discount we offer for payment within 10 days. In short, you gave up at least 2.5 percent of the sale price because your salespeople wanted to get credit for the sale before the end of the quarter!"

"Hmmm," Jamie thought. "2.5 percent of $32,000 is around $800, and 4.5 percent of $32,000 is worth close to $1,500. The sales reps just cost me enough to pay for a trip to Hawaii! What do you suggest?" asked Jamie.

"Let your salespeople know that credit card sales cost the company extra money because the credit card company charges a processing fee. Cards should be used only for sales under a certain dollar level and limited to specific situations, such as for new customers without a solid credit history with our company. If you don't set some limitations on credit card sales, you are giving money away to credit card companies when you could have had the cash in your pocket. Credit cards are an excellent way to avoid collections problems with new customers, but they get expensive with customers whom you know will pay."

"Thanks for the feedback and information, Raymond," said Jamie as he walked out the door. "Let's make sure I don't give up another trip to Hawaii."

Are Credit Card Sales Important to Your Business?

Credit cards are becoming the new form of legal tender. I know people who carry credit cards, a checkbook, and an ATM card but little to no cash. It is important to consider whether offering your clients the opportunity to pay using a credit card, instead of cash or a check, is a good thing.

For those of you who plan to go into retail businesses, you have no choice. You must offer credit cards as a payment option or you'll risk losing sales. Period. However, if you'll be selling consulting services costing tens of thousands of dollars, then a credit card will probably not be the best way to get paid, and you should request a credit application and check.

People obtain credit cards from a bank that provides a line of credit to the person whose name is on the card. The line of credit is generally unsecured, meaning the bank has nothing that it can take and sell to repay the person's debt should they default on their payments. The only recourse is to cancel the card, trash the person's credit record, and bother him until he pays. The credit cards are issued as a VISA, MasterCard, Discover, or some other brand name. American Express produces its own card and provides its own credit processing operations.

When a person purchases something from you and pays using a credit card, he is using his line of credit from the bank. The bank is essentially agreeing to pay the person's obligation to your company and takes the responsibility for obtaining payment from the person whose name appears on the card. In short, the bank is giving the person a loan that he uses to buy a product or service from you. In return for taking responsibility for collecting payment from the cardholder, the bank charges a fee to you, the business owner.

> REALLY!?
>
> CNET (1-800-223-4608) and FirstNet Corporation (1-800-866-9113) are two credit card processing companies you may want to check into.

So, you can generally think of the buyer who uses a credit card as someone with a line of credit from a bank. The company whose name appears on the card, such as Citibank or Chase, handles the processing and marketing of the card. A business processes a customer's purchase using the credit card and signed receipt. In return, the bank deposits the amount of the purchase (minus the fees) into your bank account.

Sounds pretty simple, doesn't it? Run the card through the credit card machine, punch in the purchase amount, and press Enter. You've just gotten paid. Too cool! Too easy! What's the catch?

The catch is that there's a cost to this great service. Let's see who gets a piece of that simple little transaction. Assume you are processing the transaction electronically, which is truly the way to go unless you only do a few transactions per month.

> WHAT?
>
> **Merchant number**
> A number given to your company that is used to identify which account should be credited when a customer makes a purchase. It also verifies that you're allowed to accept credit cards in payment. When you call your credit card processor for authorization to charge a customer's credit card, she will ask for your merchant number, the customer's card number and expiration date, and the amount of the purchase before giving approval.

First there is the cost of the machine used for processing the cards. It comes from a credit card transaction processing company and is essentially a small computer terminal that connects you directly to your credit card processing company. This company is often a bank or one of their sales representatives who acts as a liaison between your company and the credit card processing network.

The credit card processing company will typically charge you an application fee ($65–$100) and a programming/installation fee ($35–$50). For these fees, you'll be able to accept payment by VISA, MasterCard, and probably Diner's Club and Carte Blanche, but not American Express or Discover.

American Express has been, and probably still is, the preferred credit card for business-related expenses. American Express claims that over 70 percent of Fortune 500 companies use their card and that many require all business expenses be placed on the American Express Corporate Card. They also claim the average American Express charge is between 34 percent and 72 percent higher than charges on other credit cards. Be aware that in the past, however, American Express charged higher fees than the other credit card companies.

Try to find a company that will provide access to VISA, MasterCard, Discover, and American Express as a single service. If they don't want to do this, at least get them to tell you how to set up your machine so that it will process all the different credit cards.

American Express has its own processing network that they call the Electronic Draft Capture (EDC) network. This is their way of processing customer purchases made using their card. Call 1-800-847-8848 for American Express EDC processing and setup procedures. Once American Express receives and completes your request for American Express credit card transactions, you must contact your terminal provider (the folks who are renting you the credit card processing machine, such as CNET or FirstNet) and make sure that they program your machine to process American Express transactions.

American Express will charge you a fee for the privilege of being set up on their network, usually $65–$100. They will also send you a box full of supplies that include an imprinting machine (the other folks didn't offer one for free) and the sales/credit receipts. Of the organizations I worked with in setting up my accounts, American Express was by far the easiest and classiest group to work with.

But wait, there's more! The Discover Card also has its own network and requires the same actions. Call Discover at 1-800-347-2000 to start the process and get the electronic terminal to also read and process Discover transactions.

Should you simply buy your own terminal instead of renting it? Good question, and one that depends on your volume, monthly rental fee, and current cash situation. Rent for a few months and see how it goes. If after six months you start to resent the monthly charges, you should either go back to a hand processing system in which you manually call in each charge for verification or buy your own electronic terminal.

So here you are with your credit card terminal and some receipts, ready to sell your product or service using credit card processing. You thought the analysis was over, but it is really just beginning. In addition to the setup charges and terminal costs, the credit card companies also want a percentage of the transaction amount as their compensation for guaranteeing the charge. Read on to find out how much you'll have to pay for this privilege.

What Does It Cost You on a Monthly Basis?

First, you pay a monthly fee for the electronic terminal ($25–$40) that is automatically deducted from your bank account by the service company. You are also going to pay a monthly service fee ($5–$10) for the reporting of your account activity during the month. This is also automatically taken from your company checking account.

The credit card company then charges your company a percentage of the transaction amount for each purchase. This fee varies between service providers, credit card companies, the type of transaction involved, the size and frequency of the transaction, and whether the transaction is processed electronically or manually using a paper system. *The bank will charge you a transaction fee for each deposit made to your account.* The table shows typical discount and transaction fees for the various credit card types.

Table 13.1 Typical Discount and Transaction Fees

Credit Card Type	Discount Rate (percent of purchase amount)	Transaction Fee (cost to deposit in bank account)
VISA	1.8–3.0%	20 cents
MasterCard	1.8–3.0%	20 cents
American Express	4.0–4.5%	Varies
Discover	1.8–3.0%	20 cents

Here is what you get for the fee and how the process works when you have an electronic system.

1. You run the card through the credit card machine (called *swiping* the card). The terminal reads the card number and card type off the black magnetic strip on the back of the card.
2. The credit card terminal requests the transaction amount and expiration date of the card. You type in both when requested and tell it to process the transaction.
3. The terminal dials the proper phone number to the card processing company and sends the information to the computer, which then confirms the card isn't stolen and the cardholder has enough money available on the card to process the charge.
4. If everything is okay, the computer responds with an approval code that you write on the sales receipt.

A $100 American Express charge will net your company $95.30 [$100 – 4.5 percent (discount) – $.20 (transaction fee)]. You get the money right away, but you essentially pay a 5 percent fee for the privilege, user convenience, and security. Some small businesses will not accept American Express or other credit cards because it costs so much and eats away at profits. Look at what it's costing you in slow or no payments each year to decide if you should accept credit cards.

5. The credit card processing company then deducts the proper percentage from the purchase amount and deposits the rest in your business checking account. You essentially get the money right away instead of waiting for 30 days and taking the risk the customer won't ever pay.
6. Most banks also charge businesses a transaction fee for each deposit you make, so you'll also be charged for credit card deposits.
7. The processing company sends you a summary statement every month that outlines all transaction dates, sale amounts, credits applied (product returns), discount rates applied, and net deposits. This statement is handy for reconciling your bank deposits, invoices, and receivables when you have customers paying by different methods.

Covering Your Legal Butt

We are always happy to sell our products or services and receive payment, but what happens if the client later contests the charge and refuses to pay? Or what if the person using the card isn't supposed to be using it? You could be stuck with a huge bad debt that would take a number of healthy sales to correct. Here are a few things you can do to minimize the chance of those situations occurring.

The following information is taken from the December 1992 issue of the Agency Inc. Newsletter*, Volume 3, Number 12. This publication is dedicated to servicing the SABRE-related travel agencies and is available for subscription by calling Source Publications at 1-918-491-9088.*

Table 13.2 Credit Card Sales Protection Procedures

When Someone Charges Something in Person	Actions and Reasons
Check the expiration date on the card and make sure it is still valid.	Look at the Valid From and Good Through dates on the card and check that it is embossed, not printed.

When Someone Charges Something in Person	Actions and Reasons
Look for a hologram or other security mark.	These emblems are difficult to duplicate. If you can't find one, you may be holding a fake card.
Disclose the terms of the sale and get a signature, if possible.	The more that's in writing and signed by the customer, the harder it is for him to contest the charge. Make sure terms and conditions are easily spelled out on the receipt.
Run the card through an imprint machine (the little box you use to imprint the person's name and card number onto the sales slip), fill out the sales draft completely, and get a signature. Make sure the proper date of sale is displayed on your imprint machine.	Take the customer's card and run it through an imprint machine using the proper sales receipt. Make sure it is legible and completed with all pertinent information included. Verify that the signature on the card matches that provided by the customer on the sales form.
Get an authorization number for each transaction.	Run the card, amount, and expiration date through the electronic terminal to receive a sales authorization from the service company. Write the authorization number on the sales draft.

If you plan to take orders over the telephone without seeing the person and getting his signature, you can still take a few steps to better protect yourself. Since the chances of getting burned over the phone or by mail are much higher than in person, the credit cards will probably charge you a higher discount rate for this type of business transaction.

When processing a telephone transaction:

1. Get all credit card information and repeat all numbers, dates, and names.
2. Verify that the person making the purchase is the person to whom the card was issued.
3. Always get an authorization number and write it on the sales receipt.

4. Verify the person's billing address before he hangs up.
5. Try to get him to come by to pick up the merchandise. Have him sign the sales form at that time.

If you are processing a credit card sale by phone, if at all possible, fax the customer a copy of the invoice including all credit card information. Request that he sign the invoice and return it to you by fax for a rough "signature on file" agreement. A signature on file agreement means the customer agrees to pay you for all future charges against that credit card by the same customer. A formal signature on a file card includes the agreement duration of effectiveness, the names and sample signatures of all persons authorized to charge against this credit card, an imprint of the credit card, credit card expiration date, termination stipulations, and change-related conditions.

Trying to avoid hassles by not going electronic will probably cost you money. Everyone is better protected with electronic processing because you lessen the chances of mistakes and omissions, and you should probably just take the electronic plunge from the start or expect to pay higher discount and transaction fees.

The main difference between electronic and manual processing is that with a manual, you have to physically call in and request authorization by voice, rather than have the credit card machine dial in automatically by modem.

What to Do If a Charge Is Contested

Unfortunately, even if you have a credit card payment approved, you can still run into problems. There is a lot of credit card fraud floating around out there, and certain people will take advantage of situations if presented with the chance. Your established customers are not usually the problem. New customers or those you will never see again can leave you with a bad bill or a contested charge that can cost you money.

Taking the steps outlined here may seem like a hassle, but you will have a fighting chance with the credit card company should the charge ever be contested or disputed by the customer. If the customer signed the sales draft, saw the terms and conditions, and clearly knew what was being purchased and for the proper amount, you have an excellent case in your favor. The more of the transaction that was handled in writing, the better the chance you have of keeping the money. Caution and procedures are the solution to this possible trouble area. Define credit terms, stick with them, and fight for your money when the time comes.

The Least You Need to Know

You will probably have to accept credit cards in one form or another or risk losing customers, especially if you run a restaurant or retail store. Taking the proper steps and understanding the process helps speed up the installation process and protect your collection rights at a later date should problems arise.

- Electronic processing is the least expensive, easiest way to process credit card transactions. The credit card companies will push you in this direction, and with good reason.
- The various credit card companies charge between 2 and 5 percent of the transaction amount in exchange for their guarantee of payment. This can be very expensive when applied across the board to all transactions, so you may want to limit situations in which you will accept credit cards.
- Treat each sale like a legal agreement. Get signatures and transaction details to back up any fraudulent claims made by the customer at a later date.
- Telephone and mail-order credit card sales are more expensive due to their higher likelihood of fraud. You are billed higher fees for the increased risk.
- Get an authorization number from the credit card company for each transaction. Period.

Chapter 14

What to Do If They Don't Pay

In This Chapter

- The value of customer relations when requesting payment
- How overdue customer payments impact your business
- Recommended credit and collection policies
- A review of your legal options

"What do you mean we are out of cash?" shouted Judy. "Our books clearly show sales of about $60,000 for last month, so how can we be out of cash?"

"We have this problem with a few of our major accounts that make up around $35,000 of our monthly sales. They have recently started paying us in 60 days instead of 30, which affects our cash flow," remarked Judy's controller. "We didn't authorize the change and also didn't notice customers were taking longer to pay before it was too late."

"Where do we stand in the cash department?" asked Judy.

"We owe payroll and our vendors, and our annual licensing fees are due. Those total around $45,000, and we only have $30,000 on hand. How are we going to make up the $15,000 shortage?"

"I guess I will give the company a short-term loan of $15,000 and not take a salary for this month," answered Judy. "Remember, I can't keep doing this, or I will be out of business and we all will be out of jobs. Get those receivables on track, and get me involved personally should this not start to improve immediately."

Unfortunately, Collection Problems Come with the Territory

It is an unfortunate fact of business life that some people will not pay their bills on time. For the most part, they are not trying to avoid their obligations but simply think that spending the money on something else is more important than paying you.

This doesn't do you much good and provides no consolation when you are writing checks from your own checking account to cover their delayed payment.

Even worse, there are people who simply are deceitful and intended from the beginning to use your products or services without paying. These people can cost you a lot of time and money in trying to recover the agreed-upon payments. In addition, you rarely get the total amount due since collection fees, court fees, and a lot of your time are often required to make it happen.

The major problem with delayed payments is the impact it has on your cash situation. You have to pay your employees and vendors on time, which means that you need to collect payments from customers, or you are quickly out of business. This means that you are writing checks to cover the *float* provided to your customers, which is the time lag between when you have to pay *your* bills and when your customers pay their bills. Repeatedly being forced to pay your own bills on time while everyone else takes more time can lead to serious financial problems. And if you're growing quickly, you may be affected even more by slow-paying customers.

> WHAT? **Float** The time period during which you have to cover expenses that should have been paid out of money received from customers. During this time, you are essentially lending money to your customers.

Plan from the start to have an effective credit and collections policy, and stick to it. Prevention is the best protection from collection problems. Not handling credit and collection properly can put you out of business, even though your sales exceed expectations.

Avoidance Is the Best Remedy

Just as avoiding saturated fats is a great way to minimize the likelihood of a heart attack from clogged arteries, avoiding deadbeat clients is the best way to avoid business problems from depleted cash reserves.

Implement policies from the beginning that address the need for credit. Ensure that you stick to the policy, that your employees understand the policy, and that you do not make exceptions to the policy without good reason to back it up. Every time you extend credit, you are giving someone a loan. Make sure they are worthy of the trust you are giving them. Avoid giving credit to new customers without first having them complete a credit report. Many times, you can get a customer to pay for the order with a credit card if the amounts are relatively small (under $1,000). Over that, you can always ship products Cash On Delivery (COD) or only after you receive a check or money order.

One way to try to avoid payment problems with customers is by maintaining close contact to be sure that they were happy with what you provided them, whether it was a service of some kind or a product you sold. Don't just deliver the goods and send out the invoice. Follow up with a phone call to let your customers know that you care they were happy with their purchase. This way, if you find out there was some problem or they are not satisfied with whatever they bought from you, you have the chance to fix the problem. Once your customer is happy, your chances of being paid have risen significantly.

Another important step is timely follow up after you've sent out the invoice. Be friendly but firm as soon as the payment is due. You don't want to ruin your relationship with your customer by screaming and shouting at them for a late payment if there is a reasonable explanation. Always give customers the benefit of the doubt if they have a history of purchases from you and have paid promptly in the past. Also be firm in asking for a date when you can expect payment, and follow up on that date.

By being friendly with customers but getting across the point that payment is expected, you increase the chances of keeping that customer, rather than losing him over some angry words. However, if you've spoken with a customer two or three times and a promised payment has not arrived, it's time to get tougher.

You do not want to provide a service or sell a product to a customer only to find out they cannot pay. If you run the financial numbers, you will find you must sell *three* of what you originally sold in order to recover the profits you would have received from the deadbeat order. However, you can never really make up for a sale a customer never pays for.

> If your business is growing quickly, your expenses are also growing quickly, giving you even more reasons to pay closer attention to your collections. If you aren't receiving customer payments in a timely fashion, you may soon be bankrupt.

For example, at a 50 percent profit margin, a $20 sale costs $10 to produce; you make a $10 profit on the sale. When that client does not pay, you lose not only the profit but also the initial cost of the product, or $20. To recover that $20, you must sell two more items that make you $10 each in profit to recover the initially lost $20 sale. Add to this cost the collection fees, court costs, employee expenses, and interest expense on the loan you took out to cover the delinquency, and you can easily see that nonpaying clients are an expensive

Sunk cost
Money already spent that cannot be recov-ered. Does not take into ac-count opportunity cost or how else the money could have been spent.

problem you need to avoid. The moral of the story is that no matter how hard you work, you can't make up for lost profits or cost of goods sold.

Some people treat the first deadbeat sale as a *sunk cost* and only look at recovering the $10 cost to produce the product as what they need to break even. I prefer to consider the cost of the entire lost opportunity, which makes me more respectful of the value of good customers and more leery of offering credit to companies or people I don't know.

The Law Treats Services and Products Differently

In no way would I want to jeopardize your friendships by turning you into a lawyer, but a few legal issues are nice to understand before you start offering products or services to your customers.

All product sales transactions are covered by the Uniform Commercial Code (UCC), which are laws developed in the 1940s to ensure uniform sale transaction laws across the country. Although UCC rules are complicated, let me try to simplify them for you here.

A thorough understanding of contract law is critical to understanding business, since you are really selling an agreement, or contract, to perform a service or sell a product. The contract only comes into play when something has gone wrong and the parties involved cannot work out their differences among themselves.

The UCC only covers the sale of products ("goods" in UCC terms) and does not cover the sale of services. According to the Statute of Frauds section of the UCC, if you are selling goods with a sale price of $500 or more, then you must have a written contract before you can go after someone for a breach of contract. Under $500, a verbal agreement is enforceable, but it is still a good idea to get it in writing. After all, if a customer is afraid to commit to the sale in writing, what makes you think that they won't hedge on paying you later? If a client is serious, he will sign an agreement that outlines what is to be provided. If you think about it, the agreement protects both sides and helps prevent the possibility of a misunderstanding.

To have an enforceable agreement or contract, you must at least have:

1. The seller and buyer specifics, such as name, address, and phone number.
2. The specifics regarding the products in question, such as quantity, price, and description.
3. Specific delivery and payment terms.

This may sound like a lot, but if you think about it, you couldn't really provide the product unless you knew this information anyway. Most importantly, both parties must sign the agreement.

If you plan to provide services, then you should have some type of written agreement between the client and you that outlines the services to be provided, the amount of up-front expense involved, the total amount of the service contract, when services are to be performed, and when payment is expected. Once again, if a customer hedges on signing a simple agreement with this basic information, then he will probably hassle you when it comes time to pay.

Getting some type of nonrefundable deposit up front (somewhere between 25 and 50 percent) is also a good idea as an indication of the client's seriousness and may help minimize the possibility of his changing his mind after you have already started the project.

Accept Cash, Then Checks, Then Credit Cards, Then Credit Terms

Possession is nine-tenths of the law, and this is particularly true when it comes to cash. Whoever has the cash is in the catbird seat, and more cash is almost always better than lots of receivables from customers who can choose to pay at their discretion.

There are various ways to receive cash instead of dealing with credit of any kind. Cash comes in its standard green form (which is almost never used in nonretail businesses), personal or company check, bank draft, cashier's check, or letter of credit (which is typically used when dealing with international shipments).

Bank drafts and cashier checks are like cash since the issuing financial institution took money from the customer or an account before issuing the draft or check. There is a warm fuzzy feeling that you get deep in your pocketbook when you get a check that you know will go into default only if the issuing bank goes out of business.

When accepting a personal check, make sure it is signed by the person giving you the check and that the signatures match, and get two forms of identification, such as a driver's license (for identity) and a major credit card (which indicates acceptable credit). Make sure it is not postdated or written in two different colors of ink. Start some type of a list that shows the bad checks received and from whom. Some companies post the bad checks for public display. This is not necessarily legal, but peer pressure is often a strong motivator.

When shipping products, you can request COD terms, usually provided by United Parcel Service (UPS), which means that the customer must write a check to the delivering driver before the product is left. There is a COD processing fee of around $4.50 for the service. UPS then sends you the customer's check for you to cash.

Letters of credit are used frequently for international transactions. The customer's bank issues the letter of credit, which ensures that the funds in question are available for transfer once the company receives the desired products or services it ordered. The funds are then transferred from the issuing bank to your bank, and everyone is happy.

Credit cards come in all shapes, colors, and sizes. The most common are VISA, MasterCard, American Express, and Discover. Make sure the name on the card matches the name of the person making the purchase transaction and that the signatures match between the card and the credit receipt, and then run the card through the approval process. At that point, the funds should be transferred to your bank account and only lost if the charge is disputed by the customer. (See Chapter 13 for more information about credit card sales.)

There is some disagreement on whether you should prefer credit card or check transactions. A check is a legal binding agreement between the issuing company (person) and your company. If the check is bad, you have a strong case for collecting on the check through the courts. Credit card sales that have been approved will be credited immediately to your account but can still be contested by the customer later. In those cases, you end up arguing with VISA or MasterCard about the charge. If there is a question about how you processed the sale, you could find yourself on the losing end of that battle.

Selling products or services using credit terms is at the bottom of the credit ladder. Most larger transactions are handled on a credit basis, meaning the customer has a specified time frame within which he can pay, which is usually 30 days. After 30 days, the account is considered delinquent, and collection procedures are started. See "Your Legal Rights When It Comes to Collections" later in this chapter for more about collecting from delinquent accounts.

As politicians and economists say, it is better to take credit than to give.

You will probably have to offer credit terms to your standard customers, just as you will want credit terms from your regular vendors. It is just a part of doing business that most people accept as a standard requirement. Set an amount above which you require a credit application and credit background check before extending the credit. Do the background check before you issue the credit or risk being disappointed later. Customers understand your need to protect yourself.

Some of the bigger credit information agencies include TRW Business Credit Report, Equifax Credit Information Services, and Trans Union Credit. The report costs a few dollars but can save thousands if it keeps you from making a poor credit extension decision. Sample credit applications are available at most office supply stores. Make sure that you ask for at least three credit references as part of the application, and then call the references to verify the prospective customer's credit standing.

D&B Reports and Their Limitations

The industry standard for business information reporting is Dun and Bradstreet (D&B). A D&B report on a company contains payment history, business officer names, addresses, phone numbers, revenues, number of employees, high and low credit balances, payment histories, and other pertinent financial information.

To receive these reports, you need to be a regular subscriber to the service, which involves a yearly contract fee along with a per-report cost. The overall cost is often too high for a small business to justify, since you may only need a few reports each year.

A new possibility is to run a credit check through some of the available online services such as CompuServe or America Online. For a fee of around $60 or $70, you can request a credit report on a single company without paying for an annual contract. Of course, that fee is much higher than what you would pay if you subscribed to the credit check service on an annual basis, but if you just need to run a check once in a while, using an online service may save you some money and give you some valuable information without a long-term commitment.

Of course, as you're reviewing some of the credit reports, keep in mind that a lot of the data is self-reported, so don't use any one report as your sole source of information. You may also want to make some phone calls to colleagues to see what they know about your new customer or scan some newspaper clippings on the company (your local library probably collects them). Using additional information sources will help improve your knowledge of your prospect so you can make a better informed decision about giving credit.

No credit reporting agency or technique is perfect, and you want to take as many precautions as are reasonable before lending money to a new client. After all, extending credit to a company is the equivalent of lending them money.

Net 30 Days? Send the Collection Letter on Day 31!

Okay. You've decided that offering credit to your customers is a good thing. What can you do to best ensure they pay as agreed?

First, make sure your clients understand the credit policy when they are initiating the transaction. Do not hide the specifics because this will only contribute to later misunderstandings. You are extending the credit, so you get to specify the terms you can live with. They can either accept the terms or not.

Second, give them an incentive to pay early. Offer a small discount (2–5 percent) for payment within 10 days. This gets the cash into your hands more quickly and provides them with a financial incentive to pay earlier instead of later.

Third, call them 3–5 days before the 30-day point to verify billing information and to remind them the payment is due in a few days. It is also a good idea to ask if there will be any problems with timely payment. If they say yes, this gives you a chance to be informed earlier so you can take proper actions.

Finally, once the account goes past the payment due date, then it is time to begin the collection process. Your customer has broken his agreement and should be handled as a delinquent account. If you are prompt with the follow up, he will probably pay more promptly in the future to avoid the embarrassment.

Send a card to your customers' accounts payable department once or twice a year thanking them for prompt payment. Acknowledgment works well on all types of people, even accounting types.

A standard accounting report, called an *Accounts Receivable Aging Report*, shows you the customers who currently have credit, the total amount they owe you, and the number of days (hopefully not months) the account is past due. Most computerized accounting packages can easily provide an aging report that you can use as your trigger for focusing on trouble accounts. Run the aging report at least every two weeks, and make sure the collection follow-up is prompt, consistent, and professional, yet firm. Collecting outstanding debts is an interesting balancing act as you try to keep your customers on track with their payments without offending them.

If you are not currently using a computer software package to handle your accounting, you should seriously consider it. You'll find it much faster and easier to print out reports regarding your customers' payment records. Refer to Chapter 18 for more information on automating your business.

What Percent Will Not Pay, As a General Rule

Each industry has its own standard *bad-debt ratio*. This information is generally provided by Standard Industrial Code (SIC) and is available from Dun and Bradstreet or through the Almanac of Business and Industrial Financial Ratios (Prentice Hall, 1995). In general, your bad-debt ratio should be under 1 percent of your sales, but certain industries may see bad debts as high as 2.5 percent. Mail-order businesses can have bad-debt ratios that are much higher than businesses that deal with the customer directly. Companies with high bad-debt ratios must take this into account each year or they will be in for a rude awakening when the bills come due and they are out of cash.

You need to create a policy that dictates when an account is treated as a bad debt. Talk with your accountant to determine when this should happen. No matter what your situation, track your bad debts and develop a tracking ratio that allows you to monitor changes in the situation closely.

> **Bad-debt ratio**
> The ratio of the uncollectable funds divided by total sales, expressed as a percent.
>
> WHAT?

Everything outlined so far can be handled by in-house personnel. However, there may come a point where you need the assistance of a dedicated group of professionals who know how to get people to pay. See the later section that covers dealing with collection agencies.

Your Legal Rights When It Comes to Collections

The unfortunate has happened and a person is clearly not going to pay you. This should not happen very often, but when it does, you need to decide if pursuing the deadbeat customer is worth the time and effort. Make every effort to resolve the disputed amount before pushing things into court. Once the legal gavel falls, the conversation becomes stilted and often nonproductive. Try to get all agreements in writing to help build your case if you ever have to take legal actions.

Small claims court is provided for resolving smaller dollar disputes in the $500 to $5,000 range, depending on the state you're in. Small claims court is designed for nonlawyer types, and the rules are a lot less strict than seen on Perry Mason. Larger dollar disputes are handled in other courts and usually require the assistance of an attorney.

You will need two trips, minimum, to file a small claim: one to file the claim and the other to appear in court. You have to file in the county where the events occurred or where the deadbeat is resident. If you are suing a company, you'll need to file suit in the county in which the company is doing business. The filing fee is minimal, ranging from $5–$100. So, if you are trying to sue for under a few hundred dollars, the small claims process may not be worth it to you. The reason is that, it is much easier to win a judgment in small claims court than it is to collect the money.

Just because you won, doesn't mean that you will be paid! It is your responsibility to collect the money involved, not the court's. Your basic collection options are:

- Wage garnishment, where the employer is instructed to remove a specific amount of money from the deadbeat's paycheck.
- Nonwage garnishments, where the money involved is deducted from a company bank account.

- Property attachments, in which physical stuff is confiscated to pay the debt.
- If you are suing a business and know the company's bank account number, which you have if you've ever accepted a check from them, you can try to collect your judgment by "attaching" the bank account, which means the company has to pay you first before paying any other bills.

Of course, none of these are options unless and until you have a judgment in your hands.

You can also file a lien against property owned by the nonpaying party. This lien is recorded at the courthouse and secures the debt with the prescribed property. The property cannot be sold until all liens are removed.

There are numerous books on the market that deal with the detailed intricacies of collections in general and the small claims process in particular. The best medicine for bad debts is to avoid them if at all possible using some of the techniques covered earlier in the chapter.

Working with Collection Agencies

When all else fails, and you still want to pursue the deadbeat customer, then you should consider a collection agency. Whether the agency will be national or local in coverage depends on your specific situation. Both are listed in the Yellow Pages of your phone book.

A collection agency will charge a fee for their service, usually between 25–33 percent of the amount they collect for you. Higher fees may be charged for specialty accounts that require more extensive involvement by the agency.

Get a written contract from the agency and check their references before proceeding. They could do you more harm than good by threatening customers in an inappropriate way or by getting your initial money and alienating customers through the use of threatening practices. The contract should have specific performance objectives on the part of the agency, and if those objectives are not met, you should be able to terminate the contract. The collection agency should provide reports on a regular, mutually agreed to, basis for you to evaluate their performance.

In addition, make sure they conform to collection procedures outlined in the Fair Debt Collection Practices Act. These practices were designed to regulate collection agency activities, but companies performing their own collections should consider adhering to the same principles.

In general, the act states that: 1) threats to property, persons, or reputations are not allowed; 2) obscene language and telephone badgering is not allowed; 3) publicly humiliating the person by a printed list or other public statements is not allowed; and 4) sending documents on misleading letterhead or threatening legal actions are not permitted, along with numerous other practices.

Collections is a tough business and one full of frustration. As a collection agency manager friend of mine in Chicago puts it, "I don't like to talk on the phone. I think it comes from all those years of being lied to over the telephone."

The Tax Man Never Rests

Beware of the tax man when assessing the impact of bad debts. If you are using an accrual basis of accounting, then you will be taxed on the outstanding receivables until they are declared as bad debts. This is because the receivable was recorded as income when the work or sale was completed. Consequently, you could be paying taxes on bad debts. Unfortunately, you have the burden of proving the debt is uncollectable, or bad, should the IRS call you on the expense deduction. Discuss your bad debts with your accountant before taking the deduction.

If you are on a cash basis of accounting, then the tax man only appears when the cash is received. Since you only record a sale as income when you actually get paid, there is no such thing as "bad debt" from the IRS' perspective. Of course, you'll want to pursue the money that's owed to you, but you'll only pay taxes on the sale when you actually receive the money.

The Least You Need to Know

If you are a small business owner who pays his employees and vendors out of his own reserves, while not paying himself because of slow paying customers, you know the meaning of true courage and faith.

- Customer credit should be earned, not treated as a right. Make the customer prove he can repay the debts he plans to incur.

- You have to sell multiples of your product to make up for the lost cost and profit associated with the one not paid for. Make sure you get paid the first time.
- Avoid credit problems by using a credit application and evaluation procedure before extending credit to ensure you will receive the payment when agreed.
- Just because you win a small claims court judgment doesn't mean you will collect. You still have to go after the customer for the funds.
- Treat people who allow their account to become past-due, who have repeatedly told you they will pay and don't, like people who are stealing from you. They are!

Part 5
Additional Topics of Importance

You're probably wondering how to deal with a business that's quickly growing. Everyone thinks about that: What am I going to do if there are too many orders for my product today? Trust me, few of us have that problem, but eventually, you will probably find that you need to hire employees to help keep the business going.

The majority of businesses in the U.S. are one-person shops with no employees. If you hire someone, you're bigger than most businesses. So congratulate yourself when you get to that point.

Learn how to find employees, calculate how much in taxes to take out of their paycheck, and use other automated systems to make your life much easier. Then when you get really, really successful, the last chapter of the book will help keep your feet on the ground.

Chapter 15

Complicating Life by Adding Employees

In This Chapter

- Why adding people to your organization is a good thing
- The value, and risk, of a personnel manual
- Effective and legal interviewing procedures
- When a contractor is really an employee
- Dealing with employee benefits

"Tell me this again," said Julie. "Didn't you smell it when you went by her desk?"

"Sure I did," said Bill, the company lawyer. "But so what? There's nothing in your company procedures manual that covers drinking on the job."

"Because of that, I can't fire her?" asked Julie. "She carries a bottle in her purse. She takes a nip in the bathroom on a regular basis. I have even accidentally picked up one of her coffee cups to find that she was drinking Irish coffee. She's drunk on the job, and I want her gone!"

"That is understandable but not legal. Has her drinking affected her job performance in any way? Have you lost business you can definitely point to because of her drinking? Has it disrupted the normal flow of business in such a way that has cost the company money?"

"I know that it must have happened, but I can't point to a specific instance," said Julie. "So, you're telling me that I'm stuck with her because firing her would open us up to a wrongful termination suit based on our not having a no-drinking policy in our manual."

"Pretty much. You'll need to watch her closely and look for signs of poor performance that can then be documented. Then, you can let her go for poor performance. In the interim, you should never mention the drinking problem to her and act as though nothing is wrong. Otherwise, you play right into her attorney's hands when you finally let her go. Sorry."

When You Are Successful, You'll Need Help

That's right! If you follow all of the great advice I'm giving you, you will probably become so successful you just won't be able to do it all alone for long. At that point, you will need to add employees to your organization. It may only be a clerical person who handles billing and answers the telephone, or a complete staff of people who handle all those new projects you just brought in as a result of your incredible marketing skills.

In either case, you need to address the new challenges associated with running an organization that now has staff members. There are lots of ways to find employees, but before we jump into how to find the right employees, how to manage them, and all of that detailed stuff, let me present a few bigger issues for you to consider.

1. You have been on your own, and possibly working alone, since you started your company. Make sure that you actually need an employee for functional reasons, not simply because you want someone around the office for business companionship. Have you gotten to the point that you are losing business because you don't have enough help?
2. Employees cost money and must pay for themselves either today or in the very near future. Once you hire an employee, you assume the responsibility for paying him regularly, no matter what the business' financial condition is. Even if you have a really poor month, you still have to sign those paychecks to your employees. Are you ready to absorb that expense or would it be smarter to push yourself a little more for a short while and build up a nest egg?
3. When you add people to your organization, you inherit a responsibility for their financial support. If you aren't making enough money to support yourself, you probably can't afford to support someone else.
4. You become the last employee to be paid if the company has cash flow problems. Are you ready to accept not getting a paycheck for a week or two (or three or four) without resenting the other employees who have gotten paychecks?
5. Employees take up space, use telephones, and make decisions; you must expand your business operations to include them. They'll need to take responsibilities from you in order to help the company grow. Are you ready to let go enough to use them effectively?

6. Have you ever managed people before? Are you familiar with the challenges of encouraging and leading employees? Do you need to take some classes in effective supervision before taking the plunge? Even if you have managed workers before, a refresher is probably a good idea.
7. Know that a small business is different from a large corporation in that one employee out of a total of two makes up 50 percent of the personnel. If that person has troubles, 50 percent of the company operations are in trouble. Be aware of the large effect one person can have on your business, your customers, and your earnings.
8. If you are in a service business, make sure that your employees reflect the proper attitude and image you have worked hard to establish. A few weeks of poor telephone attitude toward your customers can unravel years of consistent service on your part. If you are really lucky, one of your established clients will tell you about the problem first, but few customers ever complain, they just leave! Teach your employees early about the level of service they are expected to provide.
9. Your customers will need to adapt to working with someone on your staff. Make sure that the new employee maintains the same level of concern and dedication to customer satisfaction. The best thing that could happen for your business would be for your customers to like working with your employee as much or *more* than they liked working with you. Now you can focus on other business issues besides customer satisfaction.
10. Don't forget that employees can always (and probably eventually will) find another job. This is your business and you will be around long after they are gone, unless you are very lucky and find the right long-term fit.

I have had both excellent employees and poor employees work with me over the years and have found that poor performers have a much bigger impact in smaller companies than they do in huge corporations. Larger companies can afford the luxury of one or two poor performers, smaller companies cannot. If you find a problem employee, one that can't seem to do the work right, or at a reasonable pace, let them go quickly, before they do serious damage to your business. Unfortunately, the tendency in small businesses is to take care of employees as if they were members of your family. Keep in mind that the best thing you can do for a problem employee is to get him off your payroll and out looking right away for his perfect job—obviously, the one you had to offer wasn't it, so why hold him up?

You may be tempted to hire a friend or relative so you'll have someone on your staff whom you can trust; be sure he is qualified for the job. Don't let trust be the primary reason you hire him or your company will suffer. Go over with him the details of what you really know about him, compared to what you have simply assumed or heard since you first met. The last thing you want is a surprise that causes you to fire a friend or relative, which disrupts the business, can end a friendship, and makes holidays even more stressful than they already are.

If the company only makes money when you are there, then a vacation becomes much more costly than the trip itself. You're really paying for: the actual vacation expenses, lost company revenues as a result of not being at work, and the time needed to get back up to speed once you return to the office and find you are very behind in your work.

Don't ever forget that you started this business. It is yours, not your employees'. Try to let go of the daily decisions so that they can carve a place for themselves in the operation of the business, or you will wind up with morale problems down the road. But remember, you sign the checks and ultimately make the big decisions. They may also need to be reminded of this, as you give them increasing responsibilities.

Once employees take on more responsibility for the company's activities, you may wonder how you ever did everything yourself. There isn't a more satisfying business experience than to find a series of orders, invoices, projects, and bank deposits that your employees created without your involvement. To call in from a well-deserved vacation and find thousands of dollars worth of revenues and profits coming into the company while you are gone is the essence of small business success. Your business needs to be able to create revenue without your involvement or it will never grow beyond your own abilities. That can only happen when employees get involved and are given the freedom to act on their own, within certain guidelines you set.

Keep an eye on your strategic goals (check out Chapter 3 for more on this). Do you want the company to become bigger than you or simply support you and your family? If you want to keep it small, then you may never need another employee, other than an occasional relative or temporary helper to handle clerical stuff. If you want to grow so the company works on a relatively independent basis, then you need employees. Accept that as a reality and plan for it in advance. That way, you can be on the lookout for the right person and snatch her up when the timing is right.

Sources of Help

Depending on your personnel needs, there are a few avenues you can take when you begin seriously looking for employees. First, you can try out potential employees through a part-time employment arrangement before making a full-time hiring commitment. Or hire candidates for a specific project, as *independent contractors*, and see how they work out. Finally, temporary help agencies can serve as excellent sources of candidates who have already been screened for your particular job opening.

Other sources include college and university co-op programs where students learn on the job through structured programs that help them apply what they've learned in their course work, as well as high school programs that match interested students with part-time employers. Many colleges and high schools also encourage students to apply for "internships" during summer and winter vacations, where they work for an employer full-time during those breaks from school. Although internships are generally shorter term than co-op programs, you can generally have a student help out on some important projects during a summer vacation. All are an excellent way to give students a chance to gain real-world experience while benefiting from their efforts at your company.

Temporary Agencies—Use 'Em Only When Needed

Temporary agencies provide a wide array of personnel talents, from clerical (secretarial or typist) to industrial (heavy lifting or construction) to professional (CPAs or consultants). Turn to an employment agency if you need someone on relatively little notice or for a short period of time. These people are also great for seasonal work such as during the holiday rush or for periodic work such as end-of-month inventory taking.

There is rarely any long-term commitment for a specific temporary person, so when you decide to stop using him, make a phone call and the person is gone. You can bring in temporary help almost on a moment's notice and use her services only for the amount of time you need them, but you do pay a price for this convenience.

Expect to pay at least $12 per hour for a worker through a temporary agency with minimal computer and clerical skills. The price goes up from there and varies based on geography. You do not pay that person's payroll taxes, medical, or other benefits, and she is never an employee of your business; she is employed by the temporary agency.

The level of professionalism associated with temporary agencies has improved significantly over the years. You tell the agency the skill set you need and they give you an hourly rate that they will charge for that person. It is then their job to find the person who meets your criteria. Most agencies have a satisfaction guaranteed policy, where you must be satisfied with the person's work or they will either replace the person or not bill you for their time. The more specific you are about the skills you need, the better they can fit your needs.

The downside of working with temporary agencies is that you can waste a lot of time in interviewing and evaluating different candidates sent over by temporary agencies for your consideration. If you aren't clear upfront about the skills you need, you may also find yourself training new people on a regular basis.

The upside is you can evaluate different job candidates quickly through a temporary agency, which handles a lot of the first-round screening and qualifying for you, and then hire the "temp" as a permanent employee later, if she works out. Typically, temporary agencies make you sign an agreement to pay them a fee if you hire one of their employees during a set time period (such as three or four months), but in most cases, it won't break the bank. And just think about how much easier the agency made your life by providing this employee. Don't they deserve that fee?

Independent Contractors—Pay for the Expertise

Independent contractors come in all shapes and sizes (literally). As with temporary agencies, you hire a contractor for a particular job or length of time and you let her go when you are done. Contractors expect to be let go at some point, so the parting is rarely with hard feelings. Typically, the length of a project is specified in a contract when a contractor is brought in, so there are no surprises about what happens when the work is done (she leaves unless you want to hire her to work on a different project).

Generally, these folks have an area of expertise such as an accounting background, computer graphics training, or specific business skills you know your company needs. You must qualify a contractor on your own and decide whether that person is the best for your specific project. The working relationship is between your company and the contractor directly, but she works as a consultant to your firm, not as an employee. You have no ongoing obligations to the contractor.

One of the major differences between working with a contract employee and a temporary employee is the contractor has been hired directly by your company to do a specific task but a temporary employee is actually an employee of the temporary agency that is "renting" her to you for a fee. With independent contractors, you would spell out upfront exactly how long they are being asked to work, on what project, to do what specific types of activities, and at what cost.

Temporary employees, on the other hand, really don't have any part in setting the terms of their work with you; their employer discusses those with you and then provides the individual best suited to help you out. In many cases, temporary employment contracts are open-ended, too, so you can end it whenever you want. With an independent contractor, you work out the specific end-date of their project upfront.

Expect to pay more for the contractor than a temporary. One reason is that the contractor is operating as a business owner, too, and must cover all of his business costs with each project. Typical price ranges for writing services start at $15–20 per hour, document layout and design contractor fees range between $20–45 per hour, and professional services such as attorneys range from $65–150 per hour. The beauty of working with a contractor is that the person comes in with well-developed skills that are immediately applied to your problem with little or no training needed. You get the desired results quickly and efficiently.

I generally learn a lot from working with a professional independent contractor. The good ones know their stuff and put it to work quickly. Finding a good one is a lot like finding a prince: you have to kiss a number of toads before finding the right one. When you find the right one, he appreciates working for you on a regular basis, and you are relieved to have someone you trust.

Fellow business owners are a tremendous referral source for specific contractors who do their jobs well. Start asking for referrals even before you have a need to use their services, so when the need arises you have a list of qualified contractors from which to choose. You will probably need these people when some type of emergency arises, so it helps to have the relationships already established before the crisis.

When hiring an independent contractor, remember that the IRS has specific criteria that determine whether a person is a contractor or an employee. If you hire someone as an independent contractor but the IRS decides later that she was really an employee of your company, you may be liable for past payroll taxes, social security payments, and benefits. Be clear upfront about how the IRS would characterize your relationship before taking chances with an independent contractor. See the "When an Employee Is Really an Employee" section in this chapter for a detailed listing of criteria.

Professional Experience at a Discount Rate

Here is an idea for you: tap into the huge reservoir of people who have professional experience but who no longer work outside the home. This includes housewives and househusbands who now take care of their children during the day. It also includes retired men and women who are healthy and may want to earn some extra money. Frequently, these workers bring substantial expertise to their work and present few personnel headaches.

In exchange for these talents, they require that you be pretty flexible on their work hours. People taking care of their kids need to work around school schedules, and the retired don't want work to cut too deeply into their free time. I have found these groups easy to work with and a great personnel financial investment as part-time workers. Check with the local PTA for people who are active with the schools and ask around. You might just be surprised who you find.

Test Drive the Employee First

Just as you can date for a while before deciding to get married, you can test out potential job candidates before making a long-term commitment. There are several intermediate steps you can try before taking the plunge.

Since everyone is always on their best behavior during job interviews, it is very difficult to determine whether a person is a good fit for your company in that kind of a setting. You need to observe the job candidate in other situations before deciding whether to hire him.

Part-time employment is a great "try-and-buy" approach where you get to test the water with the prospective employee. Use them 20–30 hours per week, and see how you work together. If it works, you have someone who comes on full time with a lot of background that would otherwise need training at full-time rates. If it doesn't work, you can count your blessings and let him go.

Similarly, you can "try before you buy" with temporary employees. Why not leave the hassles of advertising for employees, interviewing them, and qualifying them to temporary employment agencies who specialize in that kind of thing? Then you just tell them what kinds of skills you need and they send over their best candidates for you to check out. After you select a temp and work with them for awhile, you can decide whether to try a new employee when their initial contract is up or you can hire the temp permanently, which generally means simply paying the temp agency a small fee for all its work.

Checking out college and high school students through co-op programs where the student works for you a set number of hours per week for a semester or during a summer vacation is another option for testing out potential full-time employees. After working with a student for several months, you can decide whether to offer him a full-time job when he graduates.

At a minimum, you should establish a 90-day probationary period that every new employee must endure. A probationary period is a time for both you and your new employee to decide whether this is the best job for him. After the 90 days is up, you can make him a full-fledged employee, which means he is now entitled to any of the benefits you give your other employees, or you can let him go.

There's no reason to rush right into hiring full-time employees if you would feel more comfortable taking it slowly. Try some of these approaches to checking your potential employees out before making a big commitment to them.

When an Employee Is Really an Employee

It is incredible how complicated it becomes to determine whether a person is an independent contractor or an employee. The same person performing the same work under slightly different circumstances can be considered an employee, costing you much more financially than an independent contractor.

A person is an employee unless he is held responsible for results only and the methods, hours of work, and tools used are under his control and not dictated by you. The IRS tends to lean on the side of finding workers as employees, not independent contractors, because it means they get more in employment taxes from you, the employer. So be sure you're clear on whether you have an employee or independent contractor working for you.

The basic test to determine whether someone is an employee or not is whether you control the person's activities or whether she make those decisions. Does the person perform services for more than one company? Is she responsible for her own profit and loss and is she used for specific expertise applied to specific projects instead of for just showing up during specific time frames? The more restrictions that you apply to a contractor relationship, the more likely that contractor is to be considered an employee.

The IRS has a set of 20 criteria they consider when defining an employee's status. Use these criteria to substantiate your claim that a person is a contractor instead of an employee. Make sure you have a written subcontractor agreement with the person that clearly spells out the separate liability relationship. This is your best protection should the subcontractor status be questioned. These subcontractor agreements are a standard part of software packages (such as It's Legal) and are available from fellow business owners and from the library. Make sure that the contractor provides his own liability insurance and worker compensation insurance or you may find yourself the recipient of a nasty legal suit if the contractor gets hurt on the job.

> REALLY!?
>
> Call the IRS office in your city and request their publication 937 on independent contractors to determine whether you have employees or contractors.

The More Employees You Have, the More Restrictions

All companies are not created equal. Depending on the state in which you are doing business and how many employees you have, you will be affected by very different rules and regulations. One way to deal with these various state and federal government regulations is to develop a *company policy manual*, or employee manual, for everyone's reference.

A company policy manual spells out what the company expects of its employees and what they can expect in terms of benefits. New employees are given a copy of the policy manual and are responsible for adhering to these policies. A well-defined policy manual clears up employee confusion, because everyone is given the same information.

It also helps specify who should be contacted with follow-up questions. For smaller companies, the policy manual becomes the personnel policy manual. Know the laws of your individual state and create the proper policy manual to address those state laws.

A few personnel issues apply to all companies, independent of the number of employees. You should clearly spell out the number of company holidays provided to employees each year and the amount of vacation and sick time a person is eligible to take during the year. If you have other company policies that employees need to be aware of, state them in the policy manual.

Drafting your own handbook is cheaper than having an attorney write it, but a legal review is essential to make sure you haven't made significant errors.

If you write a policy manual, make sure that you comply with the written policies. It is a good idea to leave out statements regarding policies that don't apply to your company yet, because of its size. Whatever you state as a policy, you must be prepared to follow.

State and federal laws kick in at different company-size levels:

- ➤ If you have fewer than four employees (depend ing upon the state), you are the master of your domain and can hire, fire, and reward pretty much as you see fit.
- ➤ If you have fewer than 15 employees, you still have a lot of personal discretion on how you work with your employees. For example, race and sex discrimination laws do not apply to businesses of fewer than 15 employees, except as defined by specific states. However, some state employment laws do kick in, based on the state in which you do business.
- ➤ If you have between 15 and 49 employees, you have to worry about a wide array of federal laws that address discrimination and other important personnel-related issues.
- ➤ If you have 50 or more employees, you need the same level of policy manual as IBM or General Motors. It must include policies on family and medical leave, harassment, drug-related policies, discrimination and virtually any other workplace-related issue such as smoking.

Medical Insurance Plans and Benefits

Wasn't life grand? As the business owner, you have always had your medical insurance paid by the company. Now you have an employee. Does this person get company-paid insurance just like you? What is the law?

To start with, the law covering medical and life insurance benefits is the Employee Retirement Income Security Act (ERISA) that was passed by Congress in 1974. This act does not require employers to provide medical, retirement, or any other benefits of any kind. It only regulates how these benefits must be handled if they are provided. Employers typically offer benefits as a way to attract employees to their company and as a way of improving everyone's own quality of life.

> **REALLY!?**
>
> Smaller companies are exempt from many employment laws. For example, hiring of relatives or friends over others is, by definition, discriminatory. This would make most small businesses in violation of federal and state laws. Call your local Department of Labor or your local Chamber of Commerce for guidelines when you begin preparing your policy manual.

The snag comes in when you offer benefits to certain employees (such as you and members of your family) and don't offer the same benefits to other employees. In general, it is better for business and morale to offer the same benefits to everyone or to no one. The safest way to avoid this situation is to verify benefit offerings with an attorney or a benefits specialist.

The policy manual helps keep misunderstandings regarding employment benefits to a minimum, which will help you avoid possible litigation later due to unfulfilled expectations on the part of employees.

Sexual Harassment Issues

Picture this: Your company is being sued for sexual harassment. You clearly know nothing happened, but you are in front of the judge who asks about your internal policy regarding sexual harassment. He wants to see it in writing. *Oops.* It has been verbally expressed to all employees but never in writing. He and the jury decide in favor of the person filing the suit on the grounds that if you really meant it, you would have put it in writing. If you did not specifically state sexual harassment was prohibited, then the opposite must be true—you must condone sexual harassment.

If you do not put such important policies in writing, you are in potential trouble. If you are a small company not currently bound by the sexual harassment laws because of your size and you have a statement in writing, then it can also be used against you. You have to play the game to your own best advantage which means that a lawyer is required. Be safe, rather than sorry, and discuss the information provided in your handbook with an attorney to be sure you are not opening a can of worms with certain statements. It's always a good idea to discuss your sexual harassment policy with your attorney as a preventive measure.

Is there a lighter side to all of this? I have looked for it and can't find it. It is unfortunate that working with employees has become so dangerous, but it appears to be the nature of the beast. The best prevention for a nasty lawsuit situation is to avoid it in the first place. Treat all employees as people who perform a function for you. Mentally neuter them when they come in the door and treat them as company assets who perform a function. Nothing more.

Avoid the temptation to become friends with your employees. Keep the proper amount of professional distance between them and you while never being unfriendly. They work for you. You sign their checks. No matter what, you are never going to be one of the guys, or girls. It just comes with the territory. It will become difficult to handle personnel situations with authority if you spend every evening socializing with your employees.

The Limitations of Noncompete and Solicitation Clauses

How could these former employees do this? You spent three years building up that account and they stole it away within 90 days of their leaving your company. Their overhead isn't as high as yours so they undercut your price, by 30 percent. What could you have done to prevent this? A noncompete clause could have been one way to go.

While noncompete clauses are treated differently from state to state, you should definitely look into them as one way to protect yourself and your company from ex-employees stealing your ideas and opening up shop across town. When an employee signs a noncompete agreement, essentially he is agreeing not to compete with you in a specific geographic area (such as in a particular city or region of the country) for a specified period of time (such as one to two years) by performing the same function for another company as he did for you. So, for instance, your director of sales couldn't quit and go work for your competitor right away in a sales-related position. Depending on how your agreement is worded, it might be possible for him to take a job as a janitor at a competing firm, but he couldn't have anything to do with sales.

Some states treat signed noncompete agreements very seriously and will prevent a former employee from taking a job at a competing company if you file suit to that effect. Other states take the view that noncompete agreements limit where a person can work and don't uphold them. Check with an attorney who specializes in employment law to find out whether your state supports noncompete agreements. If it does, work with an attorney to write up an agreement that protects you rather than try to do it on your own. You might just create more headaches for yourself down the road if you try and handle this stuff yourself.

You cannot keep someone from making a living in his home town. A *noncompete clause* signed as part of the employment process with your company essentially says that a person cannot earn a living in the same town as your business since he agreed to not compete with your company when he joined on, but few courts in the country will uphold a company's rights to keep a person from making a living.

They will, however, uphold a company's rights to retain its customers without worrying about a former employee stealing those customers away. This is called a *nonsolicitation clause*, which says that the employee agrees to not pursue your existing customers for business that is related to your company. This agreement lasts for a specific period of time, usually 1–2 years. Former employees are restricted from using the customer contacts acquired while working with your company to aid another company, including their own.

The best way for you to cover yourself in this situation is to have the employee sign a noncompete agreement as part of his employment. This is particularly true for an employee who has regular customer contact.

Okay. It makes you seem a little paranoid, but it may also save thousands of dollars of business from walking out your front door. When a customer starts to wave cash in front of a former employee, her loyalty to you will be severely tested. Without the noncompete agreement, you may end up with a personal disappointment and a financial loss without legal recourse.

Effective, and Legal, Interviewing Techniques

There are some questions that should never be asked of anyone because they are either inappropriate, illegal, or both. You would probably never ask your best friend why she ever married that louse of a husband, or you'll risk losing a friend. Similarly, you should never ask certain taboo questions when interviewing people for a job.

Why? Simple. If you ask an illegal question and the person you were interviewing does not get the job, he can use the fact that you asked the question as grounds for a discrimination suit. Even if the question was asked purely as a conversation starter, such as "Did your children enjoy the Christmas holidays?" or, "How old are they now?" The problem is the topic should never have come up, and now you will need to show that you don't have discriminatory hiring practices.

You should also avoid using secondary questions to determine prejudicial information. The purpose of an interview is to determine the employee's ability to do the job—nothing else. Don't trifle with potentially discriminatory questions—nothing the interviewee reveals is worth the cost of defending an employment discrimination lawsuit!

Start any job search with a clear definition of what you want in the ideal person for the job. Create a job description that includes areas of knowledge the person must have to perform the job. Education and former experience must be clearly defined; develop objective criteria by which candidates can be screened. The more clearly you know what job you want them to perform and the kind of expertise you need, the more likely you are to find the right person to fill the open position.

> WHAT? **Job description**
> A detailed listing of the duties to be performed by the person filling the job, also including the required skills, education and certification levels, and other criteria directly related to the job.

In reality, and in the eyes of the law, you are trying to find the right person for the job, regardless of race, sex, marital status, or other criteria. The suggested interview procedures help to ensure that you find the information you need without jeopardizing your company in the process.

Never bring up the following topics while conducting the interview:

- Marital status
- Veteran status
- Race
- Religion
- Children's information
- The interviewee's age
- Sex and sexual orientation

You will need to know answers to many of these questions after the person is hired since emergency and medical information may pertain to children and spouses, but do not include them as part of the interview. In addition, make sure that you provide no verbal agreements about the length of employment or reasons for future possible dismissal. These may later be construed as commitments by the person being hired. These verbal commitments might be used against you later should problems arise with this person's performance which cause you to let them go.

You might be able to determine information from secondary questions. For example, asking why a person moved to your city may indicate that they came with a spouse who was transferred. Asking if working on Sundays is a problem may raise information about the person's religious activities.

Here are several "do's" as taken from *The Personnel Policy Handbook for Growing Companies*:

- Give the applicant a copy of the job description and ask if there are problems performing any of the stated functions.
- Make written notes about the interviewee and how this person meets the criteria outlined in the job description.
- Get the applicant to discuss recent, prior work situations.
- Outline the positive and negative sides of your company.
- Explain the company policy on smoking and such.
- Tell the applicant all of the great things about the company.
- Don't ask the applicant about their personal situation, such as marital status, parental status, religion, sexual orientation, race, or disabilities.
- Don't make notes on the application or résumé about irrelevant information that could be construed as discriminatory such as hair color, weight, height, and clothing.
- Don't tell the applicant that you are looking for people with limited experience.
- Don't tell some applicants the positive parts of the job while telling others the negative aspects. Be consistent in how you describe the position.
- Don't ask about child care arrangements.
- Don't lie about or cover up any bad news about the company.

Present the most positive aspects of the company in the most consistent manner. Your final intent is to find the best person to fill the job opening. Period. If you mislead them about company-related problems, you can find an employee making a substantial career change under false pretense which can only lead to management troubles and a possible lawsuit.

The Least You Need to Know

- No man, or woman, is an island when it comes to succeeding in business. You must have the assistance of others if you want the company to grow beyond your capabilities. Lay the groundwork for growth; create an environment where employees can grow professionally and financially. Allow them to feel like a part of the process, and you will reap the rewards associated with having a successful business that operates without you.
- Give potential employees a tryout before making a permanent commitment. Use probationary periods or temporary assignments to find out how they fit in with your operations.
- An ineffective employee in a large organization can be disruptive, but in a small company, he can be disastrous because of the effect he has on others and on customers.
- State and federal laws kick in at different company-size levels, based on the number of employees.

Chapter 16

Demystifying the Payroll Tax

In This Chapter

- An overview of payroll procedures
- Deposit and reporting deadlines
- When to consider an outside payroll service
- Unemployment tax payment and reporting deadlines

I'm a professional engineer, thought Kevin. I should be able to understand something as basic as payroll taxes. After 15 years of working and receiving paychecks, it was hard for him to imagine that it could be this complicated.

Okay. Deductions are made from the employee's paycheck based on earnings and several tax types. What is this FICA thing? And then there's unemployment. This is for both the state and federal taxes. I can handle that. The deposits are made quarterly for the state and annually for the federal. Or was that the reporting procedures?

Forget about that for now. Let's get this company portion of the payroll deductions under control. Hey. Wait a minute. These numbers are exactly the same as the employee ones. Did I make a mistake, or are they supposed to be equal? Maybe the company pays it all? No, that can't be.

Wow. Now I know what a dog feels like when it chases its tail. Time to take Jill up on her offer to explain this stuff to me. It's clear that it's really unclear, and I just don't have the time to figure it out on my own.

"Hi, Jill? This is Kevin. Have I got a deal for you. What are you doing for lunch today and were you serious about explaining payroll tax procedures to me?"

Payroll Taxes: You Can't Avoid Them So You Might As Well Learn How to Deal with Them

Unless you intend to be a sole practitioner all your life, at some point, you will have employees. And with employees come payroll taxes. No one I know thinks payroll taxes are fun or interesting, but as the business owner, you need to have a basic grasp of the legal requirements. Otherwise, you can get tangled up in bureaucratic red tape and headaches that make asking for a loan sound pleasant by comparison. You don't have to be a rocket scientist to calculate payroll taxes, but you do have to pay attention to the details.

As you read through this chapter the first time, you may feel kind of overwhelmed. Don't worry. Over time, this feeling will pass as you become more familiar with all the rules. Eventually, it will make perfect sense.

Here's one of my favorite business secrets: Just because you have employees doesn't mean that *you* have to do the accounting for your payroll. That's what staff (and service bureaus, and accounting software) is for! So read on for an introduction to the regimented, deadline-filled world of payroll tax accounting—so that at least, you can find out what you'll be delegating to someone else.

Payroll Tax Overview

Ever talk to someone from the IRS? To picture a typical payroll tax auditor, imagine that IRS representative without a sense of humor, and you're likely to be pretty close to the mark. So, the first thing you need to know is that all taxing jurisdictions (federal, state, local) have their own requirements and filing deadlines that they take very seriously indeed. If you file all the right forms on time, most likely you won't have many problems.

Which leads to the next question: How do you figure out which forms to file and when to file them? There are three basic types of payroll taxes: income taxes (which you withhold from wages), social security and Medicare (you pay half, the employee pays half), and unemployment (the employer pays it all). States and some cities have income taxes, as does the federal government, so you need to consult both the federal guidelines and relevant state and local guidelines to determine how much to withhold and when to pay it over to the taxing authority. Social security and Medicare are easier to figure out, since they are federal taxes and subject only to the federal rules. Unemployment is subject to both state and federal rules, with potentially complex interactions between the rules requiring even more detailed record keeping.

To find the federal rules, contact the Internal Revenue Service (IRS), which has a package of tax rules and guidelines for businesses, including Publication 937, *Employment Taxes and Information Returns*, and Publication 15 (also known as Circular E), *Employer's Tax Guide*. Not the most fascinating reading in the world I'll admit, but something you need to know about if you have employees and handle your own payroll tax accounting. For the state rules that apply to you, contact your state Department of Revenue (for income tax withholding information), Department of Labor (for unemployment tax information), or Secretary of State (in case you can't find the right bureau to answer your question). Look in the blue pages (governmental section) of your phone book under Federal or State government to find out where to get the information.

Your employees will give you information about their tax status, number of dependents, and withholding allowances on a federal form W-4, and you can use that information to look up the right withholding amount in the tax tables or apply the right percentages for your state's formula. However, just because you figure it out once, don't think you're done for the year. If your employee's pay changes, the withholding amounts will most likely change, and you also have to be aware of the relevant ceilings for social security taxes and unemployment taxes. Detailed, repetitive calculations are what payroll tax reporting is all about, together with weekly, monthly, quarterly, and annual reporting requirements.

So, you've filled out the forms and followed the instructions—now you just drop them in the mail and relax, right? *Wrong!* Federal taxes and some state taxes are subject to depository requirements, and you can't just mail a check with your return. In essence, you deposit the taxes at your local bank using a payroll tax coupon with your employer identification number (EIN) on it. The depository schedule may not be the same as the reporting schedule (this depends on a whole bunch of factors), so read the regulations carefully.

Tax Type	Employee Portion	Company Portion	Total	Threshold
Federal Income Tax	As determined from the W-4 form.	None.	15%, 28%, or 31% depending on salary level.	Depends on filing status.
State Income Tax	As determined from the W-4 form.	None.	Determined on a state by state basis.	Depends on filing status.
Social Security	6.2%	6.2%	12.4%	$60,600
Medicare	1.45%	1.45%	2.9%	Unlimited
Federal Unemployment	0%	6.2%	6.2% less the state percent payment.	$7,000
State Unemployment	0%	Depends on the state.	Depends on the state.	Depends on the state.

Fudge on these taxes, and you will pay big time and without mercy. It is one thing to be late on a payment to a creditor. It is another to be late on payroll deposit payments to the IRS, since you are essentially playing with the employee income deductions. It is the IRS's money that you are administering for them. The IRS will eat you alive in late payment fees and interest if you delay, so make sure that you read the next section and file on time.

Filing and Paying Payroll Taxes

You have performed the calculations, made the payroll deductions, and paid the employees their well-earned paychecks, but there is still more for you to do. You now need to report the deductions to the IRS and make a bank deposit to ensure that the IRS gets the money you've so carefully deducted from everyone's paycheck.

IRS Form 941, Employer's Quarterly Federal Tax Return

You report all the deductions you've taken from the payroll to the IRS for a given calendar quarter on **IRS Form 941, Employer's Quarterly Federal Tax Return**. This is for payroll tax-related information only. The form must be in the mail, and postmarked, by the last business day of the month following each quarter. For example, the first quarter (January–March), you must complete and mail the 941 form by the last business day of April.

Make your payroll tax deposit with a company check at your local bank along with the *Federal Tax Deposit Coupon* that tells the IRS which company is making its deposit. The coupon should have the deposit amount filled in, along with the box associated with the quarter to which the deposit is to be applied and the type of tax based on the particular IRS form number (941, First Quarter). The bank will give you a standard deposit receipt in return.

> WHAT?
>
> **Employer Identification Number (EIN)**
> A number given to any company that has employees. If you have employees, you must have an EIN to ensure all your tax payments are credited to the correct account, which is indicated by your unique EIN. Call the IRS to get your EIN (FREE!) and Federal Tax Deposit Coupon book (IRS Form 8109).

You deposit the federal payroll taxes on either a monthly or semiweekly basis, depending on the size of your payroll. If your total tax deposits exceeded $50,000 in the prior four quarters, then you will probably have to deposit semiweekly. If not, you can deposit on a monthly basis on or before the 15th of the month. The IRS will let you know. In general, you deposit taxes on a monthly basis for your first year.

> REALLY!?
>
> Depository banks don't have to accept checks on other banks for payroll tax deposits, so when you are choosing your business bank, make sure that it can accept payroll tax deposits.

Make sure that you get your payment into the bank before the end of the *banking day*. There is a time difference between the end of the banking day and the time the bank closes. Be sure you know when the banking day ends. For example, the banking day may end at 2:00 p.m. while the bank closes at 4:00 p.m. The deposit must be in the bank by 2:00 p.m. in the above situation.

If no wage payments are made in a month, no deposits are needed. And if the 15th falls on a holiday or weekend, you can deposit on Monday and still be on time.

The semiweekly and monthly deposit designations have nothing to do with when you pay your employees. The IRS expects to receive payroll deposits monthly or semiweekly (depending on the size of your payroll).

Semiweekly depositors must stay on top of things. If you pay your employees on a Wednesday, Thursday, or Friday, then your tax deposit must be made by Wednesday of the following week. If payday falls on Saturday, Sunday, Monday, or Tuesday, then deposits are due at the bank on Friday of that week. There is a special three-day rule that adds a day to the deposit deadline for each day that a holiday falls between the payday and deposit date.

The following table summarizes the payroll filing procedures for you.

Payroll Deductions Made	When Payroll Checks Are Written
Federal bank deposits required.	Either semiweekly or monthly, depending on tax levels. Deposits are made with IRS coupon form 8109.
Payroll deduction form 941 completed and postmarked.	On a quarterly basis on the last day of the month following each quarter.
State unemployment reporting and payment.	Usually quarterly but the last business day of the month following each quarter.
Federal unemployment reporting and payment.	Annually using IRS form 940 and coupon form 8109.

State and Federal Unemployment Taxes

This part gets easier. You have been accruing unemployment payments with each payroll period. The states make you complete a reporting form and deposit the required funds on a quarterly basis by the last day of the month following each quarter. The federal reporting is done on the IRS form 940, which you must complete annually by the end of January of the year following the reporting period and mail along with a check for the proper amount.

The state tells you what rate you must pay for unemployment, based on past unemployment benefits paid to past employees. This unemployment rate indicates their assessment of the amount of risk your company poses to the unemployment fund. If you have a number of employees who leave your company and file for unemployment compensation, you will see your unemployment tax rate increase. Tax rates reflect expected costs for your industry but are adjusted based on your specific experience. If no one leaves your company and files for unemployment, after a few years, your rates may even go down!

REALLY!?

Your unemployment tax rate will fluctuate depending on how many employees have ever filed for unemployment. If former employees file for unemployment benefits, you'll see your unemployment rate increase, unfortunately.

Simple Rules to Live and Save Taxes By

Here are a few rules that I learned the hard way. I relay them here with embarrassment and with the hope that I can save you from the same mistakes.

1. Report your payroll taxes, yes, all of them on all of the nice little forms, when the reports are due. That's right… on time!
2. Make sure that your deposits are accurate and on time. Only an act of God can save you from IRS penalties and fines if they are levied against you and/or your company.
3. Use a payroll software package such as Quick Books with QuickPay to ease the payroll process. You can get the needed numbers from the system relatively painlessly.
4. Find someone who understands the payroll tax calculation and reporting process. Have them show you their completed forms and walk you through the process.
5. Stay on top of things, and always include the additional payroll tax expenses when considering an employee raise. Perhaps you should offer your employee additional benefits, instead of a raise.

The payroll tax reporting and deposit procedures will eventually become second nature to you, but it definitely is confusing when you first start out. I had a tough time finding all of this information in one spot and made some serious blunders that cost me thousands of dollars. Don't make the same mistake. Get the right advice early in the process and follow it. The late fees are tough to swallow.

Using a Payroll Accounting Service: It May Be Worth It

There is always the option of giving this task to someone else to handle. Your accountant will generally do payroll tracking for you as part of a standard service offering. There are also outside payroll services that specialize in nothing but payroll accounting. This may be too much for what you need at this time, but you might ask your fellow business owners about how they handle their own payroll. After all, the payroll tax process is an important concern for all business owners independent of size and age; experience is a good guide in this area.

The Least You Need to Know

Payroll taxes aren't much fun but you *can* survive. Here's what you need to know in order to minimize payroll tax problems:

- Employee-paid payroll taxes include social security, Medicare, and federal and state withholding. The company and the employee pay equal amounts of social security and Medicare. The company pays all the federal and state unemployment tax.
- Payroll tax deposits are made either semiweekly or monthly, depending on the size of your company's payroll.
- Federal payroll taxes are reported on a quarterly basis using the **IRS 941 form**. Similar forms are necessary for state payroll tax reporting.
- Federal unemployment taxes are paid and reported annually using the **IRS 940 form**.
- Don't be late on reporting or deposit deadlines because the penalty fees are huge!

Chapter 17

Working at Home or Away?

In This Chapter

- The benefits and pitfalls of working at home
- IRS considerations for home offices
- Choosing the right location for your business
- When to rent, lease, and buy

"How's it going in your corner office?" Mary called to ask.

"Great! Instead of getting up at 6 a.m. to drag myself downtown by 8:30, now I can leave my bedroom at 8:29 and be at work 30 seconds early," explained Jim.

"Sounds wonderful. What do you do with all your free time now?" she asked.

"I work! One of the drawbacks of having a corner office in the basement is it's just too easy to keep working long after all the downtown workers have left for home. And, while I see more of my children than I used to," Jim said, "they can be a distraction, especially when I'm on the phone."

"So are you ready to come back to work with the big boys?"

"Not on your life!" came the reply. "I can handle the distractions, and running my own business from a convenient location is one of the most rewarding things I've ever done. Why, some days, the only reason I leave my home office is to make a deposit at the bank."

Home Offices: A Great Place to Start

Who hasn't sat in rush hour traffic and fantasized about working from home? What? Give up soot, smog, rude drivers, and several hours of my day to work from a spare room at home? Why do that? Simple: It sounds great. And it can be, if you have the discipline to make it work.

Let's take a look at some of the good and not-so-good points associated with a home-based business.

Table 17.1 The Pros and Cons of a Home Office

Good Points	Discussion
A 30-second commute from the kitchen to the spare bedroom	You save 1–2 hours per day in commuting time, which provides more time for business. You can also work at night, after others have gone to sleep.
Save money	You already pay the rent or mortgage. Save the money you would spend on office space and put it back into your business.
Tax advantages	You should be able to deduct expenses associated with the office section of your house, which otherwise would not be deductible. You may actually make money off the deal. Read about it later in the section.
Family benefits	You are closer to the family, which allows for meals at home. You might be able to rope family members into helping, on occasion.
Risk-free trial run	You can test the water regarding your business idea without incurring a lot of outside financial costs and obligations. If it works, then move to a regular office.

Potential Pitfalls in Paradise	Discussion
Motivational liability	You can get sidetracked into personal stuff such as cleaning the kitchen. Personal phone calls can take up a lot of your day when people know you are at home. After all, "you're not at work" in their mind. You're at home. You will need to set them straight on this one.
No commute	On the days when you don't want to work, the commute helps to separate your home life from business. When you work at home, you might spend that extra hour on the couch that otherwise would have been productive.
Lack of peer contact	You are relatively isolated in your home office, where a regular office provides contact with other business owners. They are not only colleagues, but also sources of leads, business, and guidance.

Starting your business from home is a relatively painless way to begin either a service business (such as consulting, accounting, massage, and so on) or a small product-oriented business such as mail order or light manufacturing. You are already paying for the house and utilities. It makes sense to use these prepaid expenses to your best benefit, but be cautious of the potential pitfalls associated with running a business out of your home.

This section deals with the financial and personal aspects of working from your home. You'll also find a section on determining the right time for moving out and whether you should lease, rent, or buy your office space.

Local zoning, building, or landlord ordinances may keep you from starting a business in your home. If your business requires customer parking, increases street traffic, or causes wear and tear on your property, you may find it difficult to start a home-based business. Check with the city and your landlord for approval before investing too much money and time into working out of your home.

Low Overhead, but It May Not Be Deductible

As we said when I was in the Army: Uncle Sam can't make you do anything. He can only make you really sorry that you didn't! Working out of your home is financially attractive in the early days, but you need to follow the proper steps to ensure that the IRS allows your desired business and personal deductions.

It is tempting, and reasonable, to assume that expenses associated with the business section of your house would be tax deductible as a business expense. And they may be, but you have to be careful how you present it on your taxes and back up the claim with paperwork.

You can deduct the expense of your home office even if you are employed by someone else, but it still must be used solely for work done for your employer and not as a part-time playroom for the kids.

As the judge says, "He who has the most paperwork wins!" Documentation of expenses is critical in making your case for home office business deductions to the IRS.

Here is the key: the business section of your house must be used "regularly and exclusively" for business purposes. This means that your home office must be your principal place of business operation, such as where you actually do your work for clients. Or you must regularly meet with clients, patients, suppliers in your home office as a part of your business operation. These meetings must occur in your home office and not in other locations within the house.

You must really use your home office as an office, not as a shortcut for some desirable tax deductions. The IRS is getting tighter on these restrictions instead of looser, and you must take the proper steps upfront to back up your case for a home office deduction.

This tax avoidance strategy stuff gets complicated very quickly, so see a tax professional before you get too tricky, or you can trick yourself into a lot of hassles and minimal savings, and become a potential IRS audit candidate.

The percentage of your home expenses that are allocated to your office is calculated on either a square-footage or number-of-rooms basis. For example, assume that you have a five-room house of 1,500 square feet. One room comprises one-fifth of your house if all rooms are about the same size. So, take one-fifth of all housing expenses and allocate them to the business as expenses. You just saved money on your personal bills, but gave up one-fifth of your house to the business in the process.

You can also use the square footage approach if the one room is much larger than the others. For example, assume that the room is 500 square feet of the 1,500 square foot house, or one-third. You can still take the one-third deduction but you should make the case that this particular room was the best candidate for the office and is exclusively used for that purpose.

Beware of your home computer. It is not a home and business toy when speaking with the IRS, no matter how you really use it. By the way, you probably need to keep detailed track of usage hours or you might find yourself pushing Uncle Sam uphill, which is a tough one. If you plan to use it for business, then use it for business. You really don't want your kids playing with important business files, anyway. Can you imagine the mayhem that would occur in your house if your 5-year-old son accidentally erased all of your accounting records and you did not have a backup? Keep yourself, your clients, and your family out of this minefield and keep your business and personal computers separate.

> REALLY!?
>
> It may cost more, but it makes life easier to have separate business and personal checking accounts and telephone lines. This allows you to clearly define business and personal expenses along with telephone charges. Otherwise, you really need to log every telephone call made. Ugh!

See IRS publication 587 for details on home office deductions. There are also numerous tax guides available at most bookstores (like the one you bought this great book from) that provide detailed information on setting up your home office from a tax standpoint. The laws are changing on this hot area every year, and timely information is your best trouble-avoidance strategy.

You Can't Beat the Commute, but Watch the Distractions

I mentioned this earlier, but it's worth saying again. When you work at home, you will be tempted to start a little later, quit a little earlier, and maybe hang around at the swimming pool instead of making that business phone call. It's tough to leave the backyard on a beautiful summer day and walk into an office full of paperwork and stuff to do. But, if you don't walk into that office and start working, you will not keep that beautiful backyard for very long, if you know what I mean. It takes a lot of discipline to work at home and keep yourself on a work schedule. Your family also has to support you or you're already behind the eight ball.

It is tough to discuss a complicated $10,000 project with a client when little Jennifer walks into the room wearing a full pint of chocolate ice cream on her face. How do you get her out of the room while closing this client on the project? Get the picture? Put yourself and your family on a schedule and stick with it. Don't take personal calls at home. You probably wouldn't take them at your company office, so why take them at home. Business is business, no matter where you transact it. Otherwise, it's a hobby. You wouldn't have made it this far in the book if you only wanted a new hobby. Stick to business, even if it occurs in the second bedroom of your house. One essential piece of equipment for the home office is a door! Make sure your can close your door to shut out the distractions of home and family life.

Make Your Office a Home

> REALLY!?
>
> Renting furniture is a low-cash way to outfit your office. There are also rent-to-own plans, which allow you to make your furniture rental payments apply toward the purchase price. You may be surprised at how reasonable the prices are.

Now, here is the good news. If it really is a business office, then you should spend the money to make it work. Get a comfortable chair. Get the desk and table combinations you need to be productive. Spend the money needed for telephone and computer equipment. You may even want to pop the cash for a stereo just for the office. You'll be spending a lot of time in your office, so make it work for you. By the way, these all become business deductions since they are related to the business. Make your office into a home within your home to ensure that you want to go there and are productive once you arrive.

When Is It Time to Move Out?

You have been working diligently in your office for a while now, and things appear to be stabilizing. Clients expect you to remain in business and start providing you with repeat business. The delivery people know that your business exists and don't freak out when they deliver a business-related package to a residence. Things appear to be going along well. Why would you consider moving out of the house and into a new location? Simple. To either make your life easier or to make more money… or both.

Typical indicators that it's time to consider a move include some of the following:

- When the office gets too small for the things and number of people you need to run your business.
- When the level of business activity at the house gets so high that it disrupts the daily routine.
- When your clients begin to wonder about your commitment since you don't have a "real" office.
- When your clients appear uncomfortable coming to your home for business meetings, and you start feeling uncomfortable having them walk through your house to get to the office.

> Letterhead, envelopes, business cards, and telephone listings must be changed when you move offices. These hassles and expenses are not trivial, and you may decide to get a separate office from the beginning to avoid the confusion and expense at a later date when you have to move out of the house.

In short, you should move out when you have made it and when the problems associated with the business become operational and not financial. Then it's time to look at moving out into a separate office.

Finding the Right Location for Your "Real" Office

Locating your new office is a lot of fun, but it's time-consuming. Just like buying a house for your family, you are setting up an important part of your lifestyle. A long commute means you are away from home more, but this may place you closer to your clients and prospects. A more expensive space may present the desired image and bring in more money, but with a higher up-front cost on your part. Consider all these factors when moving to an office that is not in your home.

Try these points on for size when looking at a new location:

1. If you provide a service, does it make sense to be centrally located near your clients and prospects? Probably. Is the potentially longer commute worth it on your part?
2. Are you moving to please yourself or to improve business operations? Either is fine, but understand your motivations.

3. Will you make up the commute time by being more productive while in the office, as compared to working out of your home? You may spend extra time with the commute, but find that your day ends earlier since you are more productive while at work without distractions from home.
4. Is there a competitor in the area of your new office? If so, does this hurt you or help you? Sometimes, people want to "shop around" and look for locations where competing companies are easily accessible. This applies to retail and many professional services. Will this competitor cause you to lose existing clients or make it difficult to gain new ones? If so, should you move far enough away from the established competitor so that you have a geographic advantage in your new location?
5. If you have a manufacturing type of business, does the new location make much difference to the operation? Probably not, since you ship to your clients and you can do that from just about anywhere. Once again, move to improve business operations, not to stroke your ego due to your new-found success.
6. Is moving going to cost you customers? People do not like change unless it benefits them. How will this change benefit, or cost, your existing clients?
7. How much more business do you have to create from the new location to justify the additional expense? Not sales revenue, but actual profits after all marginal costs are taken out. Is this number reasonable and can you achieve it within the needed time frame?
8. What if you didn't move? What would happen? Is there an external reason forcing the move that takes the "if" completely out of your hands and turns it into a where, when, and how?

I'm sorry that I can't give you standard answers to these and the myriad of other questions that no doubt will arise. The answers are heavily dependent on your particular situation, but here are a few rules that may help to narrow the field of confusion.

- Manufacturing business locations are chosen most often based on shipping, receiving, parking, space, and other operationally oriented criteria. If you primarily ship, mail, or work over the phone, it really doesn't matter where you locate your office as long as it supports the daily operation.
- Service businesses that require the clients to come to you are heavily location dependent. Why would clients go out of their way to come to your place when your competition is just down the road from their office? Get geographically close to your clients, and they will come.

- A nicer location may present a better image but may not necessarily generate more revenue. Don't confuse appearance with profits; they are not always equal. (Read the opposite argument next.)
- Basing your service business in a well-recognized location or building may increase name recognition with your clients. You are associated with this respected office location, which should reflect well on you and increase trust. Trust is a necessary ingredient for any successful service business. Does the new location instill that trust without placing your company in financial jeopardy?
- Retail requires high visibility frontage. Period. If they can't find you, they will not buy. They may not even know that you exist. Traffic is needed and encouraged in a high visibility location such as a mall, craft and service fairs, downtown areas, and busy streets.

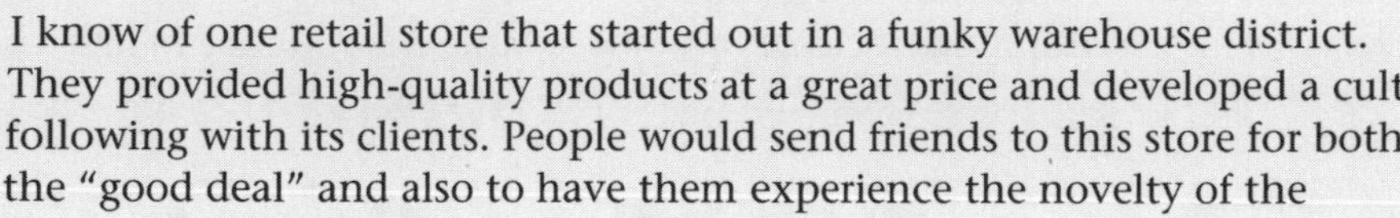

I know of one retail store that started out in a funky warehouse district. They provided high-quality products at a great price and developed a cult following with its clients. People would send friends to this store for both the "good deal" and also to have them experience the novelty of the situation. The store thrived and grew to the point that the owner decided to move to a high-visibility frontage that was substantially more expensive but offered the allure of more traffic.

The store moved and increased their overhead due to the increased rental costs but never saw the anticipated increase in sales. They were no longer funky and the novelty was gone. In addition, a new competitor moved in across the street when they moved. Which caused the decrease in sales? The owners are really not sure; it was probably a combination of both.

A possible moral to the story is to realize what has made you successful in the past, and don't fiddle too much with it. You have to make the tough calls, and this is one of them. By the way, this company is doing just fine and altered their operations to accommodate the new sales and cost situation. Small companies that survive only do so by responding to the changes in the market and their business operation.

Look at what your existing and potentially new competition is doing. Ask your customers about their reactions to your possible move. Get as much information as possible before taking the plunge. It would be a shame to take an operation that is working well from your home with its associated low overhead and place it in jeopardy due to an unnecessary office move.

Here is just a quick reminder to consider things such as lighted and adequate parking for your clients. Our training center's female clients like to use the covered, lighted parking area at night. Make sure that the building is in compliance with the Americans With Disabilities Act (ADA), which requires access to disabled persons. Check for wheelchair ramps, doorways that are wide enough to accommodate a wheelchair, and rest rooms that are designed for wheelchair access. Signs should be posted in Braille for those who are visually impaired.

Ask your potential clients about the things that are important to them; I never expected that rest room design would be as important to our female clients as it turned out to be. I worked with the building management to get our women's rest rooms upgraded before those on other floors or the men's. It paid off, and we got higher evaluation marks for our improved facilities and more business from our female clients. Your clients know best what they are looking for. If you provide it, they will come.

Lease, Rent, or Buy? It Comes Down to the Numbers

Should you lease, rent, or buy? This one is simple, again. Which one works out to be the financially most attractive? Leasing ties you into the same location for a longer period of time but provides you with lease rate stability. Renting provides you with the monthly option of moving elsewhere, but your rent can fluctuate at any time, and the landlord has the option of asking you to vacate. Buying provides tremendous stability, but with a large financial commitment on your part.

I suggest that you consider this progression for a service business:

1. Start out at home until your business warrants moving out.
2. Look into renting space in an executive suite of offices. Here you get the clerical support needed to operate without incurring a huge financial commitment. You can also generate contacts with other suite members.
3. Lease your own space when the restrictions of the executive suite begin to cost you time, money, or both.
4. Buy your own building when you have a successful track record under your belt. Many companies use the SBA for funding of this type of business-related building purchase.

If you have a manufacturing business, try this approach:

1. Work out of your house for as long as possible. You may be able to do this by using production houses for the actual production aspects, while using your home for office-related functions.
2. See if you can partner with another company that already exists. Use their surplus capacity as an interim step.
3. Lease your own space when you're confident about future business, such as when you have ongoing contracts or retainer agreements.
4. Buy when you are ready. Once again, look to the SBA for help in financing the purchase of a building.

The Least You Need to Know

Office location is an important topic for both you and your clients. Consider your business location from your client's perspective; consider the finances from your perspective to find the optimal blend of location and expense.

- Just because you run your business from your home doesn't mean that the expenses are tax deductible. Follow the IRS rules, and win a prize.
- When you work at home, treat it just like a job. Go to work at regular hours and discipline yourself to stay on the job even though you are only in the basement.
- Location is critical to most service and retail operations. Don't overlook this very important aspect of your business.
- Product and manufacturing businesses are less location dependent. Their location can be based on price, space, and access to transportation.
- Minimize your commitments and expenses in the early days. Gradually work your way up to leases and purchases after you have a successful track record.

Chapter 18

Using Automation for Increased Efficiency

In This Chapter

- Using technology for your benefit
- Automating your business
- Applying computer and telephone technology
- Computerized accounting overview
- An introduction to online services

"So why hasn't the newsletter gone out?" asked Frank. "We intend to do this on a regular basis, and it shouldn't be such a big deal."

Todd, the marketing director, looked frustrated at the question and did his best to give a diplomatic answer. "The database of names is in an old format, and we do the mail merge for the labels in our word processing software package. Trying to make the two work with each other is a headache. Why didn't we just stick with the package we started with?"

Frank thought back on it. He had taken all of his customer contact information to a typing service that entered it into a computer program. Then they gave him a disk and told him the name of the software package they used, so he bought it to make things simple. His now ex-brother-in-law had upgraded the database to a "fully relational" one, whatever that meant.

Now, Frank couldn't even print out mailing labels. He wondered if he would ever be able to create a telephone list using the new package. It just shouldn't be this hard.

"I guess the latest and greatest is just not so great for us, is it? Let's call a temporary agency and see if we can get someone in here who understands how all of this stuff works. Maybe we should send one of us to a training class to learn how mail merging operates. One day in a class would certainly pay for itself if we could avoid a situation like this again," said Frank.

"Maybe we can get some training on that fax program, too," said Todd. "We mail out 1,000 pieces per month at around 50 cents each to our local customers. That is $500 per month in postage and printing that would be completely saved by using fax distribution instead of the mail. I know how much you like to save money. What about giving me some time and money to get trained on that, too?"

"Five hundred bucks a month? Not bad! I wonder how else this computer equipment can save us money and time?"

Automate from the Start for Later Success

"If I'd only known that in high school..." or the equivalent thought has popped through most of our minds at one point or another. The fact is that many things are easier once you have some experience with them. You are in luck. Much of the experience you wished you had is already available in the form of computer software programs and other automation equipment.

Automate as much of your office operation as possible from the beginning. Don't wait until later to decide if it's a good idea to automate. Assume that it's a good idea and be on the lookout for equipment and software that solve your problems.

The key is to realize that computers and other pieces of equipment are an essential part of business life. The sooner that you include them in the operation of your business, the easier it will be to grow and make money. One type of equipment you will *definitely* need is a computer, so you might as well start on the right foot.

The reason to invest in a computer right off the bat is that over time, you will set up certain ways of performing office procedures. It's more difficult to change procedures that were originally done manually than it is to improve procedures that were set up on the computer from the start.

Automate the Routine and Savor the Creative

Picture this: You are moving a little screw from the left side of your desk to the right side of your desk, and then back again. Repeat. Now, repeat again. Again. Again. Get the picture? Boring!

If you like this type of work, you are probably not cut out for the crazy world of entrepreneurship. Most entrepreneurs I know hate routine stuff such as paperwork, filling out expense reports, doing the bookkeeping, and completing tax forms. For this reason, paperwork, expense reports, bookkeeping, and tax forms are often late or not done at all. It's a big problem that doesn't have to occur.

Computer programs already exist that can handle most of this boring stuff for you, and many of them cost under $200! Cheap, once you own a computer.

You can find a software package to automate most routine tasks in the office such as word processing, payroll and tax deductions, spreadsheets, customer contact information, and more. As mentioned in previous chapters, you can buy software to set up your company's corporation articles and bylaws and even create a policy manual. Check out the handy table at the end of this chapter that summarizes all these software packages—this should save you some legwork.

>
>
> **Routine tasks**
> Things you do that are pretty much the same as the last time you did them, except for minor variations. Printing out monthly invoices or counting inventory are two routine tasks that don't take much brain power, but that have to be done.

The weeks (yes, weeks!) you would have spent setting up these operations on your own are instantly eliminated for a small investment! Play your cards right and automate from the beginning.

Typical Automation Strategies

Everyone has his own opinion about automation, computer systems, and software and firmly believes that he is right. Here is my opinion on using automation in your business. It may turn out later that it's not perfect for your particular situation, but it should work well enough to get you started on solid footing.

1. Look for the routine areas of your business operation that don't require any creativity but simply require doing the same type of operation over and over again. Typical areas include, but are not limited to, generating invoices, sending mass mailings to

clients, generating proposals, pricing calculations, tracking customers, sorting employee performance evaluations, and handling payroll tax-related clerical tasks, accounting, and bookkeeping.

2. Ask other business owners how they handle these areas for themselves. Guess what? They have the same problem. Why not learn from their experience?

3. To handle tasks such as invoicing, bookkeeping, financial report generation, payroll check generation, and tax reporting, look at accounting and payroll packages like QuickBooks, QuickPay, M.Y.O.B, and DacEasy that are *compatible* with each other and with other software packages you put on your computer.

4. Pick a "suite" of computer software packages that all work with each other to provide word processing, spreadsheet, database, and presentations capabilities. A suite package combines several different software packages in one, rather than having you buy them separately, which typically costs much more. The most popular suite product being sold today is Microsoft Office Professional, which includes Word for Windows (word processing), Excel (spreadsheet), Access (database), and PowerPoint (presentation graphics).

5. Take a training class on the software packages. Every day you spend in class will probably save you 2–5 days of working on your own. Trust me on this one; I see it all the time. The only exception applies to people who already know the packages in question; they stand a chance of making it work without class.

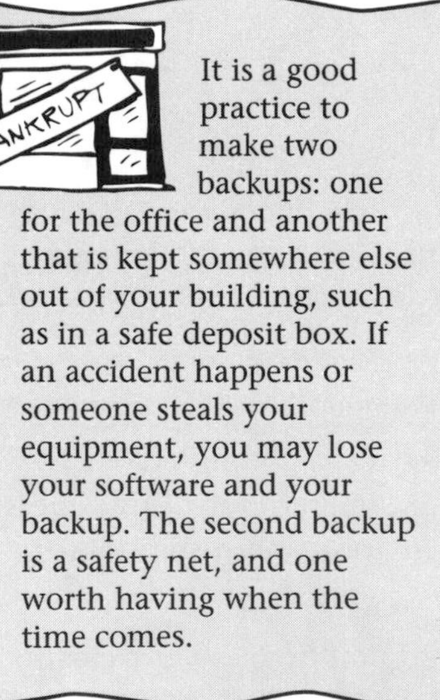

It is a good practice to make two backups: one for the office and another that is kept somewhere else out of your building, such as in a safe deposit box. If an accident happens or someone steals your equipment, you may lose your software and your backup. The second backup is a safety net, and one worth having when the time comes.

6. Organize the various working files you create on the computer into meaningful directories, and use meaningful file names to identify them, just as you would organize information in a filing cabinet. If you are not the person who creates and maintains this information, make sure you understand the "filing system" your assistant has created on the computer. Avoid embarrassing situations because your right-hand person has called in sick or decided to quit without notice.

7. Make a *backup* of that data on a daily basis, if possible. Computer hard disk drives fail! Period! When they do, you lose your data or pay a lot of money to someone who will probably only recover a small portion of it. Look into a backup program that will handle this for you automatically. They're not expensive and will help safeguard all your valuable files.

8. Keep it simple, Simon is the "KISS" principle. Okay. So it wasn't Simon the last time you heard this one. You caught me! Anyway, keeping it simple is a good thing. You don't want to become a computer "geek," spending hours and hours on your computer. You simply want to get your invoices and letters out as easily as possible. Create form letters, standard invoices and credit letters. Try not to customize everything, and you'll save a lot of time with standard letters and packages.
9. Resist the temptation to apply new technology before someone else has tried it out first. Keep away from the leading (or "bleeding") edge of technology unless you specifically have the expertise to know what you are getting yourself into. A simple technology snafu can cost you tons of time, money, and aggravation. Let someone else work out the technical bugs.
10. Always invest in printers or copy machines that create high-quality results. The printed page is what your customers will see and is the impression you leave. A laser printer is almost a mandatory investment in today's business world.

Computers, Telephones, and Bears, Oh My!

Marketing and sales will make or break your business. Sales efforts involve customer information, telephones, and the mail. The more people you contact in a professional, timely manner, the more likely you are to increase your sales and the closer you are to retiring early. Computers and telephones are part of doing business, and you should take steps to utilize them to their full capacity.

First, a Look at the Computer Side of Things

I am going to make this simple. Buy a computer! Take the plunge. You will need a computer. Period. Over 75 percent of the computers in use today are Intel-based, IBM PC-compatible types such as IBM, Compaq, Dell, AST, Gateway, and others. Another popular kind of computers are the Apple Macintosh types, which are very popular for graphic arts, layout, design, and multimedia. You can use most software programs for either IBM or Macintosh computers; you just need to get the right version for the type of computer you're using.

If you don't have thousands of bucks to invest in a new computer right now, then maybe you should consider leasing some computer equipment. Many companies offer leases, which means that you pay a regular monthly fee for the use of a computer for a particular period of time, and at the end, you give the computer back or buy it for a small fee. Computer leases work a lot like car leases, actually.

In addition to getting around spending a big chunk of cash all at once, leases also give you time to check out different computers to help decide which is best for you and your business. Of course, this is really only an advantage if you get a relatively short lease in order to test run the computer. If you sign up for a lease of many months, or years, you're effectively locking yourself in to using that type of computer. You'll still be able to switch to something else at the end of the lease, but several months down the road, you'll have all your files set up and know a lot of the programs for that kind of computer. At that point, you're probably not going to want to start over from scratch.

So my suggestion is this: Try both a Macintosh and an IBM/PC version for a couple of days each to see which is easier for you to use and understand. Then, after trying both kinds, decide which one you want to own long term. Signing up for a lease is one way to finance that big investment.

My personal preference is an IBM PC or *clone* (the computer works exactly the same as the IBM model; it just is manufactured by a different company). Make it at least a 486DX2/50 type with 16 megabytes of RAM and a 300 megabyte hard disk drive. Also consider getting a high-density 3.5-inch disk drive, CD-ROM drive, mouse, modem, and graphics capabilities. If these numbers mean absolutely nothing to you, just bring this book to a computer store and have them show you the different models that meet these criteria.

Don't expect your computer fax card to replace a fax machine. You will have paper documents to send, such as those requiring a signature or that were corrected with a pen. You will need a regular fax machine in these cases.

With the computer, you should also consider buying a high-quality monitor (super VGA card and monitor), because you will spend a lot of time staring at it, and a fax/modem, which allows you to communicate through the telephone lines.

Now go buy a fancy mouse pad, a computer work-station, and a comfortable chair. You will spend a lot of time using this beast. You might as well save the wear-and-tear on your body from the beginning and get the right stuff to make the boss comfortable. It is easier on you and everyone else!

Reach Out and Touch Someone by Phone

As for telephones, you can try to use your personal line for business calls, but you'll quickly discover this approach is inconvenient for your customers, your family, and your business. Naturally, your local telephone company will charge you for the privilege of adding a telephone line, so economics will play a part in how many separate phone lines you can afford.

It makes sense to have a separate business phone line set up right away. One reason is so that customers can find you in the Yellow Pages or through directory assistance. If you have a company name but use only a personal phone line, people will not be able to find you. Another reason for a separate line is so you can separate your business and personal life. If you have young children, it is *imperative* that they not speak with customers. You will appear very unprofessional if your children answer calls or can be heard screaming in the background. So have a separate line installed.

You will find that one and two line phones are common and inexpensive. Make the first line your primary telephone line that is listed in the phone book and have it "roll over" to the second line when the first is busy. This means that calls to the first line ring on line one if the line is free, but ring on line two if line one is busy with a call. You may also want to consider having a separate phone line installed to handle your faxes. You will need to send and receive faxes at all hours, and you save yourself hassles by simply having a separate line.

When you need more than two incoming lines, you'll need special wiring and have to shell out some money. The capabilities are greater, but the added expense can be substantial if you are not careful.

Voice mail is pretty common and pretty much a mandatory business tool. There is a raging debate about whether a live person answering the phone is better than electronic voice mail. I lean toward the electronic approach because the messages are usually more accurate and the cost is less. However, many people just hate talking to a machine and will hang up, although they would leave a message with a person.

> BANKRUPT
>
> Do not put call waiting on line one if you plan to have line one roll over to line two. The telephone company gets real confused, and it just doesn't work very well.

I suggest that you start with a live person answering your main phone line and monitor the messages left against the number of calls you receive during the course of the business day. If you normally receive 30 calls, and only find 5 messages left on the machine on the days you are out of the office then you are losing 25 caller contacts during those times. That usually means lost revenue. Experimentation is the key.

To ensure that you rarely lose any calls, consider getting a cellular phone with voice mail as one of the calling features. Forward your business line to your cellular phone when you are not in the office. When your cellular phone is on, you will receive calls without the caller knowing the difference. When your cellular phone is off, callers will be forwarded to your voice mail system where they can leave you a message. Use today's technology to keep in touch with your clients and suppliers. Cellular technology is so developed now that you can have calls automatically forwarded to you even if you are in another city. The advantage is freedom, but the disadvantage is that it is getting harder and harder to get away from clients.

Each new phone line and feature costs money, but the telephone is not a place to skimp financially. One lost call could mean a lost customer. How much is one sale worth to your company? How many new customers are needed to pay for this investment in technology? If the number is small (one or two in a month) then it is probably a good investment. If it is too large, then look for another solution.

Electronic Mail and Faxing

In the past, electronic mail (e-mail) was used solely by major corporations with internal computer networks. However, the electronic world has expanded, and e-mail is now available to just about everyone, at very little expense.

You can also install electronic mail as a part of the computer network at your company. Assume that you have a few computers in your offices. You can connect them to each other using some type of local area network (LAN) product, and your employees can share printers and files. This is an improvement on the "sneaker-net" system that many companies have, in which you copy the file to a disk and run down the hall in your sneakers to print it out on another person's machine. However, if you have just a handful of employees, electronic mail may be overdoing it a bit. It may be easier just to yell over the partition.

Electronic mail allows you to send a message (like an electronic letter) to another person on the same computer network. You can also send whole files from computer to computer. In this way, you can share information with others without using paper or overnight delivery services. The process is much faster and often less expensive.

> WHAT? **Cyberspace** The electronic world of online services. You can work from home, your hotel, or a cabin in the woods with equal effectiveness. Does this present incredible possibilities, or what?

There are commercial services, such as CompuServe, PRODIGY, and America Online, that provide you with an electronic mail you can use to contact people on their service (if you know their Internet address). More on online services later in this chapter.

A great way to maintain contact with your clients and save money is through effective use of *facsimile*, or *fax*, technology. It costs you at least 32 cents, plus printing costs, to mail something via the U.S. Postal Service to your local clients. It costs you nothing, zero, zip, to fax to them, assuming you have unlimited local phone service. The only cost is for the fax paper, which they pay for. Instead of 100 customer contacts costing you $32, it is now *free*! This is one of my favorite words.

When choosing to lease or purchase a fax machine, consider the convenience versus cost factors carefully. You want to be able to *read* what comes through the fax. Make sure that the machine you choose has a paper cutter and takes a long (98 foot) length paper roll, or you will drive yourself, or someone else, crazy cutting the fax pages and changing paper.

There are software packages on the market such as WinFax Pro and Procomm that automate the fax procedures. You create the documents that you want to fax and decide who should receive it. Start the program up and go home while the documents are faxed to everyone. The fax program will also send documents out overnight while you sleep. The following morning, your clients have received this new information from your company and you got a good night's sleep… for free! Yes, this is definitely worth investigating.

Of course, you should definitely check out your state's "junk" fax laws before deciding to send out unsolicited information by fax. There are laws in place that prohibit you from sending information by fax that someone has not requested. Although companies can send junk mail through the U.S. Postal Service, they generally can't do the same by fax.

Avoid fax overload. Your clients are happy to hear from you when you have something to say, but don't annoy them by wasting their time and paper. Use fax technology properly, and you can save money while maintaining better contact.

Automating Your Sales Contact Procedures

Contact management software is to sales management what the word processor was to the typewriter. You can completely automate your sales contact procedures using one of the many contact management software packages currently on the market. Two popular packages are ACT! from Symantec and Lotus Organizer. Both are available at almost any computer software store.

These packages allow you to keep a complete record of customer addresses, telephone numbers, and fax numbers. In addition, you can keep all contact information in one file. For example, you note when you last talked with the person, what you talked about, and when you are supposed to make your next contact. This is all done automatically once you enter the information. Keeping such detailed notes helps you stay on top of valuable customer relationships.

My marketing manager came to me the other day with an ACT! success story. She had received a return call from a lady and couldn't remember why she had called her in the first place. She entered the lady's name quickly into ACT!, saw the reason for the call, and closed a sale that otherwise might have been lost. For $150, this program has already paid for itself.

Automating the Payroll Process Using Quickbooks and QuickPay

Don't even think about trying to become a payroll specialist. You don't have the time and probably don't have the expertise to do all of the bookkeeping properly. Computer programs already exist that can do this for you in a simple and accurate way. Automated accounting is the way to go if you don't plan to have an outside company perform this service.

When evaluating bookkeeping, payroll tax, and accounting packages, be sure they include, as a minimum, the following features:

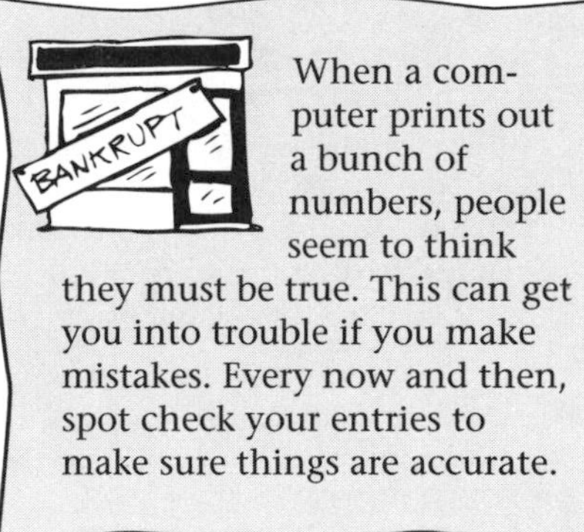

When a computer prints out a bunch of numbers, people seem to think they must be true. This can get you into trouble if you make mistakes. Every now and then, spot check your entries to make sure things are accurate.

- A flexible Chart of Accounts that you can set up and modify at a later date to fit your business requirements.
- Easy-to-use reporting features (income statement and balance sheet preparation are bare minimums). You may benefit from budget versus actual reporting, or cash flow reports, so don't choose a software package that limits your reporting options too much.
- Options that meet your business needs. If you manage payroll or inventory accounting, for example, you need software that can handle those requirements.

This stuff is easy and painless, once the initial social security, unemployment, and state tax rates are set. Get help in the beginning to set up your accounts properly, and then use this program to track your financial success. You can also run financial statements from these financial packages, so there is no reason for you not to know the state of your company finances.

Other Useful Business Software Packages

As I mentioned earlier in Chapter 6, there are software packages available to help you create legal, corporate documents, such as employee policy manuals, corporation articles, and bylaws that you will need when starting your business. I mention a couple here that I'm familiar with, but there are other packages out there. As always, be sure that the documentation you generate has been reviewed by professionals from a legal standpoint.

- You can use It's Legal (Parson Technology) for generating your corporation articles and bylaws. It's Legal also provides a standard subcontractor agreement, along with tons of other legal forms.
- Try Employee Manual Maker (Jian Tools) for generating employee policy manuals and business planning documentation.

Planning for Technical Obsolescence

Technology is great stuff. That is the good news. It is also expensive and constantly changing. That is the bad news. Whatever you buy today will probably be a boat anchor in three years. That's right! Three years.

For example, I bought a laptop computer from a factory outlet store in 1991 for $2,200. The same computer had been sold for $4,300 just 90 days earlier. The buyer changed his mind and I got it for 50 percent off the retail price since it was considered "used" equipment. I sold that same laptop in July of 1994, just three years later, for $650—$1,550 less than what I paid for it. As computer equipment improves and changes, older equipment drops in value very quickly.

This situation is not unusual when dealing with computer equipment. You will typically see a major technological advancement happen every three years and software upgrades happening every 18 months, which means that you may find yourself constantly investing in newer, better equipment just to keep up.

Buy what you need for today because you need it now. Accept that it will decrease in value and get the most use out of it today. Never buy cutting-edge technology unless you need it. Use the old stuff until it slows down your business's efficiency and bottom line. Then upgrade. You can't guess what new features will be available even months from now; computer technology just changes too fast.

Online Services Are Effective Tools

You were in a restaurant the other day and overheard two women in their sixties talking about surfing. Surfing the electronic networks, that is. Pull out your computer keyboard and get ready to "hang ten."

CompuServe, PRODIGY, and America Online are services that used to exist only for those who spoke in technical tongues. Computer geeks connected through these networks for hours at a time and shared a world that few knew existed... until now.

The most commercially available network is probably CompuServe, which has over three million members and has been around for a long time. CompuServe provides you with a software package that you use with your modem to send e-mail, participate in discussions with people from around the world, and research business topics. CompuServe is geared primarily for the business owner, while other services are set up for families and individuals.

The Internet is an even wider network of communications activities than the commercial online services can offer, and you can gain access to the Internet through CompuServe, America Online, and PRODIGY.

The main point is that you cannot exist any more as an isolated information island. There is an electronic world out there that is becoming a part of everyday life for both you and your customers. There are business opportunities opening up in cyberspace that you don't want to miss out on.

CompuServe Is a Mainstay

How's this for being an entrepreneur? It is 1972. You and your dad are sitting around the house and come up with an idea. People cannot afford their own mainframe (computer-ese for huge) computers but still need to process information. What if you offered a service that allowed them access to a mainframe, but on a sharing basis? If you got enough people to sign up, you could divide the cost of operation over a bunch of people and pay for the equipment and make some money. Well, someone and his dad did this, and it worked better than expected.

In 1972, this father and son team decided to tap into the massive amounts of processing power available on mainframes that were not being used in the evening and on weekends. Most businesses shut down during those times, but their computers were left running. They sold the processing time for around $5 per connection hour and charged a small connection fee for the service. The rest is history. What started out as MicroNet is now *CompuServe* and has three million subscribers.

CompuServe has tons of special interest groups (SIGs) called *forums*. These are great places to find out information from other people who may be in a similar technical, personal, or business situation. Simply double-click on the **Forums** icon on your computer screen and follow your nose to your desired forum.

A CompuServe subscription costs $9.95 per month and allows unlimited use of basic services, including up to 60 e-mail messages per month and a number of general information services. Access to additional services costs $4.80 per hour for 2400 baud modems (modem talk for slow speed) and $9.60 per hour for 9600 bps (the higher the baud number, the faster the modem is). There are a number of rate plans, and you can get the details by calling 1-800-848-8990.

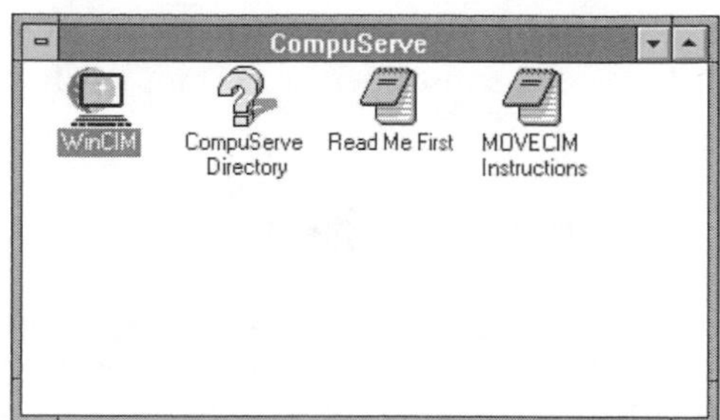

The CompuServe Information Manager (CIM) screen.

Also, look in the mail for special CompuServe enrollment offers that include free startup and a few months of free basic services. Everyone is vying for new subscribers, so look for some great deals that are offered just to get consumers to try a service.

I believe that CompuServe is the mainstay of the online community. Every major technical company has some type of CompuServe-related service. Don't reinvent the wheel when first starting out. Join CompuServe to get your feet wet, and graduate to the other services as you grow.

The Internet Is Rapidly Becoming the New Interstate

Internet-this, Internet-that. Everyone's talking about the Internet, but does anyone really know what the heck this thing is? Well, it's like a huge version of some of the commercial online services such as America Online and CompuServe. You can send messages to anyone else in the world who also has an Internet address, and you can do research and participate in discussions on just about any topic imaginable.

The Internet has become such a hot spot that virtually all the other commercial online service I've talked about here now also give you access to the Internet. So you only have to join one online service now and you can check out all that's happening out in cyberspace.

> REALLY!?
>
> You can access CompuServe from just about anywhere in the country. I often travel and pick up my CompuServe mail by just making a local call or dialing an 800 number to access the CompuServe network. After that, the operation is identical to my connection in Austin. Call 800-848-4480 for 2400 bps connections and 800-331-7166 for 9600 bps connections from anywhere in the nation.

You may find it less frustrating to start with a commercial service that tries to make things as simple as possible for its subscribers and then graduate to the Internet down the road.

America Online Is Playing Catch-Up

Here is an excellent place to begin your online adventures. *America Online* has been around since 1985 and has created one of the friendliest systems on the market. However, its range of services does not compare with CompuServe and the price is around the same. For $9.95 you get 5 hours of connection time, and you pay $2.95 for each hour of connection time after that.

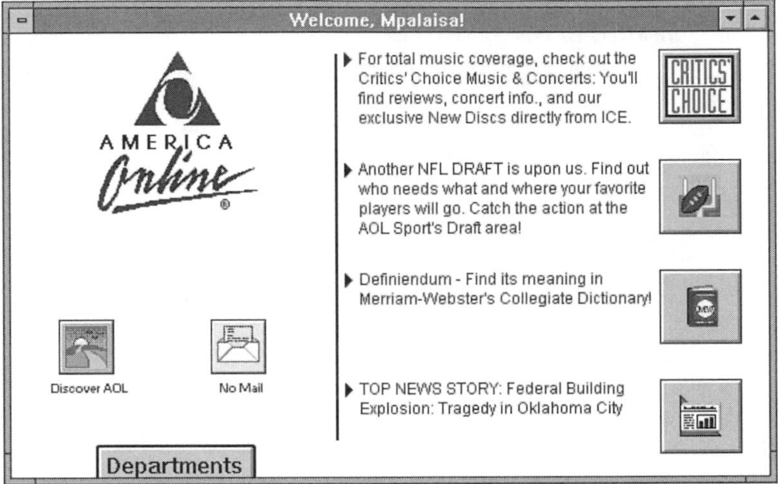

America Online.

You can find a subscription to America Online in just about any magazine, new computer purchase information packet, or mail promotion. They are trying to rapidly build the number of subscribers to their system and are sending out free trial offers to everyone and his brother. Or you can call 800-827-6364 to sign up. If you are not ready for CompuServe, give America Online a call. It's a great place to start.

In a Nutshell

Just to keep all this software information in one place for you, I've created a handy table that summarizes all the packages we've talked about and provided some phone numbers and price ranges to get your automation investigation on the right track.

Product	Company	Cost	What It Does	Phone
Act!	Symantec	$79	Business contacts	800-824-4355
America Online	America Online	$9.95/mo	Online service	800-827-6364
Biz Plan Builder 5.0	Jian tools	$129	Business planning	800-346-5426
CompuServe	CompuServe	$9.95/mo	Online service	800-848-8990
DAC Easy Accounting 2.0	DacEasy, Inc.	$149	Double entry accounting	800-322-3279 214-248-0205
Employee Manual Maker	Jian tools	$139	Personnel manuals	800-346-5426
Internet	Local service provider required	Varies	Online service	800-723-2763 800-444-4345 415-859-5318
It's Legal	Parson Technology	$26	Corporation articles and bylaws, subcontractor agreements	800-223-6925 319-395-7300
Lotus Organizer	Lotus	$102	Personal information manager	617-253-9151
M.Y.O.B. 5.0	Bestware	$119/$209 w/payroll	Double entry accounting	800-322-6962 201-586-2200 xt. 300
Microsoft Office	Microsoft Corp.	$599	Wordprocessing, spreadsheet, database, presentation	800-227-4679
MultiMedia MBA (Small Business Edition)	SoftKey, Intl.	$99.95	Small business information resource with strategies and planning included	800-228-5609 617-494-1200
ProComm	Data Storm	$99	Fax/communication software	314-474-8461
QuickBook	Intuit	$99	Payroll/accounting	415-322-0573
QuickPay	Intuit	$51	Payroll/accounting	415-322-0573
WinFax Pro	Delrina	$79	Fax software	800-268-6082

The Least You Need to Know

Which would you rather listen to: the hum of a computer fan running in the night or the complaints of an employee who is overworked? Effective use of technology can keep you from having to hire that extra person. Automation can make you more efficient, keep the number of employees to a minimum, and make the ones you have more effective.

- ➤ Automate from the start.
- ➤ Only use technology that is proven. Don't invest big bucks in the latest and greatest untested product.
- ➤ Automated accounting makes bookkeeping relatively easy to perform, as long as your accounts and procedures are set up properly from the beginning.
- ➤ Expect that your computer technology purchases will become obsolete in three years, which means you'll need to upgrade your current computer or buy a new one.
- ➤ Sign up for one of the online services, such as CompuServe or America Online, in order to gain access to a world of business contacts.

Chapter 19

Dealing with Success

In This Chapter

- The personal aspects of success
- Financial pitfalls of success
- Separating reality from public image
- When to pass the baton

"He does seem a little disoriented lately," said Emily to her husband. She started working for Rick five years ago and had never seen him like this. "It's weird. He shows up late for meetings, signs checks weeks after they are written by the accountant, and just doesn't seem to care. I hope that he's okay."

Jack, her husband, shook his head. "He just sounds bored to me."

"How could he be bored?" cried Emily. "We're doing more business than ever. Our clients are happier than ever, and we just can't seem to do anything wrong. The word around town is that our rocket is the right one to be affiliated with, and Rick made all of this happen. How could he be bored?"

"I'm sure that Rick likes all the activity and the money," said Jack. "I'm talking about the daily routine. He has never struck me as a 9–5 sort of person, and now he has to show up to

make sure things get done. Sometimes, he even has to wear a tie; you know how he feels about them! He has essentially become an administrator. That's like putting a racehorse in a petting zoo. Maybe Rick needs to run again."

"What do you suggest?" asked Emily. She felt Jack was onto something here, but she was too close to the situation to clearly see the next step.

"Take him out for a cup of coffee and tell him what you think. He might be waiting for you to come forward as his replacement," said Jack. "You are the natural successor, and I'd be amazed if Rick was against giving you even more decision-making power at this point. Maybe he just needs you to give him a nudge, to let him know you are ready to take on more authority."

Emily smiled. She remembered Rick's energy during the early years of the company, as they succeeded in growing 200 percent a year. She wanted to see that energy and enthusiasm return. Maybe Rick could focus on the new publishing side of the business, while leaving her to manage the training side that had become the company's bread and butter. That would be a win for all concerned. But how would Rick react?

Dealing with the Personal Aspects of Success

Your fears and joys have found you. You are still in business and exceeding your wildest expectations. In short, you and your business are a success. Too cool!

Find a quiet, peaceful place and ask yourself this question: "If I don't go out of business, then what will I do?" Watch the flood of insight that occurs when you stop focusing on just making it. Where should you head next?

You have undoubtedly put in long hours, suffered through numerous trials, and dug deeper into your soul than you ever thought possible. Otherwise, you would not be where you are now. As a business owner, you recognize all the hard work and commitment it takes to keep a business going. Business life is different for you now, and your new insight is well-earned.

Bask in the glory of your personal situation, but know that success has its own sets of traps that can undo all your hard work and achievements. This chapter is designed to introduce you to life after success and to help you decide what comes next in your business venture.

They All Love You When You Are Successful

Who helped you when you first started out? Think about it. Were there many colleagues and advisers or just a few? Were they old friends or new acquaintances who saw that what you were trying to achieve had merit? The people who know you today did not know you back when things were tough.

Nothing breeds business interest faster than the smell of money. Your business success makes you a very desirable business partner, dinner date, speaker, and financial planning client. You will soon appear on everybody's mailing list. You will be invited to parties and other social functions. You may even be the guest of honor. (Can you believe it?) These acknowledgments are well-deserved, and I encourage you to enjoy them while they last. I also encourage you to remember that you could become an unknown again as quickly as you became a success.

People who helped you along the way may need help themselves from time to time. Supporting competent people who stood by you in the past almost always pays positive dividends. Remember: Unless you are extremely lucky, you and your business will have a wide array of ups and downs. Business, family, and personal friends are the people who will get you through the dark times and allow you to prosper when it is again light.

Success breeds success, but it also brings out opportunists who will try to benefit from all of your hard work and offer nothing in return. Try to determine early on in your business relationships whether someone is trying to offer help, take help, or use you—and respond accordingly.

Watch Your Ego and Pocketbook

Have you ever known someone whose emotional state was linked to his credit cards? The better the mood, the more money he spent. Now multiply that effect several times over and you have the potentially dangerous situation of a successful business owner whose ego is linked with the financial success of the company.

I have seen people, including myself, start to pay for events, dinners, and other nonessential items simply as a way of expressing their business ego. I was essentially saying that the business was doing so well that I didn't need to worry about petty little things like a few hundred dollars for dinner. In reality, frivolously spending that money drove me nuts, but I still did it. I just needed to stroke my ego with my charge card. Very dangerous.

> BANKRUPT
>
> You can also look at your company's profits as a means for you to enjoy yourself. This is also a scary situation. Ask yourself this before you spend, "If this were other people's money and I was the president of their company, would I still spend the money this way?"

Once the business gets to a certain point, you will be tempted to dip into the till and spend for personal gratification instead of for business. Sure it is your business; nobody doubts that. The issue revolves around your need to spend company resources for personal gratification. Several thousand dollars is a lot to an individual, but a nominal amount to a business. Beware when you start to spend the business money for items the business doesn't really need.

You could spend your company right out of business if you're not careful and put yourself, the company, and the employees in the same spot they were in a few years ago when first starting up. You owe them and yourself more than that.

Pat yourself on your back for your successes, but leave the business checkbook at home. Even the constitution has a separation of powers. You should do the same, even if only in your mind. Don't treat your business as your personal checkbook.

Instinct Is Good, but Planning Makes It Work

If your business is structured as a corporation, the money that comes into the business cannot be spent for your personal use unless you take it as income. It belongs to the company separately. However, if you run a sole proprietorship, taking money out of the business is fine from a tax standpoint, because you and the business are really one entity. However, you shouldn't be spending company funds on yourself.

Thinking on your feet is a great characteristic for boxers and business people. Here is the potential problem: How do you maintain the quick decision-making techniques that got you through the early times while still moving in a smart direction that applies to today? I have seen successful business people violate their own plans because they thought this new direction was better than the one previously evaluated. Don't move too quickly to change company direction or switch strategy just for the sake of change.

Now that the company is really doing well, avoid the tendency to think that you are always right. Your instincts obviously are good, but rely on input from your staff regularly to ensure you don't miss opportunities. In many cases, your employees may have excellent suggestions and strategies to propose that could be better than your initial plans. Don't leave them out of the decision-making process. Get others involved so that the company can grow and prosper.

Even When It's Going Great, You Still Feel Like Throwing Up!

Old habits die hard, and this is one of those tough situations for people who survive hard times. When you become used to difficult times, it is hard to adjust to good times. It may become so stressful that you wonder, "When will the situation go back to normal—back to those hard times?"

I don't think you ever let go of the fear that things can go back to how they were in the slow, old days. I remember days in a row when my phone did not ring. I would walk into my training lab and it often felt more like a tomb than a thriving business. In the very early days of the company, during the late 80s, economic times in Austin were tough, few people knew who we were and our product mix was untested. Marketing efforts were under way, but it just took time for them to work. Things were slow. When I thought we might go under, I was physically ill.

Things are better today. Much better! (Whew!) But, I still have this nagging fear that activity will suddenly drop off for no reason and we will be back where we were. I use this fear to keep me moving forward with new ideas, marketing approaches, and business concepts.

Know that slow times happen as part of the start-up phase, and don't let them get you down. Use these times to invest in more marketing, in developing new products and services, in training to improve your skills, and in planning for the future. Once things get rolling you probably will have less time for these activities.

Reality Checks Are a Good Thing

Keep people around who can act as a sounding board. There are times when you will need to make important decisions and your employees cannot give you the feedback you need. In many cases, you'll need to consider whether to invest more of your personal funds to grow the company, or how to improve your personal life without damaging the business. Only you can make some of these decisions, and other business owners are often the best advisers to consult for those issues.

For example, one of my employees wants me to invest in another training lab. She contends that we are losing money by not having the additional space and wants me to make the investment. For her, it is a matter of where she spends her time. For me, it is a three-year commitment to making that lab work. She can get another job, but I can't think of working for someone else unless the company goes under and I'm forced to.

I gave her the three estimates for the additional training lab (all were over $100,000) and asked her if she knew enough about the business opportunity to happily invest at least $100,000 of her own money. She looked serious for a moment as she realized the decision that I had been faced with. She is now working on a financial and capacity utilization report to try to justify the additional expense.

You invest your own money in a way that promotes the company's success and your own personal goals. You have to invest; just do it wisely.

I have a team of fellow business people who know me, know my business, and bring tremendous business expertise to the table. They act as my reality check when I make major decisions. I encourage you to keep a sharp eye out for people such as these so you can form your own personal network of business advisors. They are invaluable resources as rapid growth and its associated opportunities arise. Setting up an informal business advisory or discussion group can be an invaluable way of getting regular feedback from trusted colleagues.

Dealing with the Financial Aspects of Success

It eventually comes down to money. You must be making money or you would be out of business. Congratulations! Now that you have all that cash floating around, let's take a look at some potential pitfalls associated with the financial aspects of success.

All the "Small" Expenses Turn into Big Bucks

I have several coffee cans at my house that are filled with pennies, nickels, dimes, and quarters. A friend recently came by and noted that there was probably a lot of money in those cans. Funny how all of those little coins add up to some major savings.

Spending $200 here, $300 there, and another $700 on this new piece of equipment adds up to $1,200. Would you have spent $1,200 on that particular combination of items? If so, the money was well spent. If not, then you need to start considering all expenses above a certain dollar amount in terms of their total impact on the company and not as separate, unrelated purchases.

Likewise, in your business, little expenses here and there can add up to be big cash drains. This becomes particularly true when you allow your employees to order products, inventory, and office supplies without your approval. You have to let go of many tasks in order for the company to grow, which includes some purchasing functions. However, a surprise bill for thousands of dollars is never fun. Set up procedures for tracking or approving expenses over a certain threshold (for example, $200). Review your accounting on a monthly basis and always review your financial statements to ensure that your expenses aren't way out of line. It is your job to keep the company financially healthy. If you can't do that job, you should find someone such as an accountant or bookkeeper who can.

Watch the Overhead and Stay Nimble

Overhead is a revenue-eating shark. Every month it requires the same, if not more, cash feeding than the month before. This is the nature of overhead items. They occur every month, and you must pay them or you are out of business. Generally, these include office rent, utilities, phones, and employees. If sales drop off, you still have to pay these. It is scary to have to write checks for each of these expenses during months when sales are low. If the situation continues very long, you'll need to take steps to correct it, which often means reducing overhead through layoffs and downsizing of the operation. Tough decisions for any business manager.

Avoid this situation by only adding to overhead when absolutely necessary. Avoid spontaneously adding people, space, or equipment unless you know that the expense is justified for the longer term. (See my lab expansion example in the prior section.)

By keeping your overhead low and your relationships with contractors and temporary agencies in good standing, you have the ability to provide your clients with the services they need. That is your secret weapon when competing against the big guys; you are nimble enough to adapt to a client's particular situation and can charge less because of lower overhead expenses. The big guys have a lot of inertia and overhead, which can seriously get in the way of change. By the time they realize that they should change, you have already won all of their customers.

Handing Over the Checkbook

Afraid to hand over the checkbook to your most trusted assistant? You should be! It is a big deal and you should treat it as such. Once you turn it over, it will be tough to take it back without hard feelings.

You can stall the passing of the checkbook by taking a few steps to get you out of daily activities while still maintaining some control.

1. Set up credit accounts with your suppliers and let your assistant be the one who approves purchases, while running them past you at the end of the month.
2. Start to involve your assistant in your financially related business decisions. Show him how you analyze different purchases and situations so he knows how you would handle a situation. This doesn't mean he must give up his own perspective, but he must understand it is your money he is spending.
3. Be sure this is the right time to let go; you may be going through a semipersonal crisis that will pass. If so, you may be back to normal in a short period of time. If not, and you are ready to remove yourself from the day-to-day operation of the business, then it's time to pick a successor and begin the training program.

Reporting and budgeting becomes critical when you hand over the checkbook. Set up the financial reports and budgeting process so you can closely track the company's overall financial performance on at least a monthly basis. Otherwise, things can get out of hand without your knowledge. Look at all the celebrities who lost their shirts when they turned over their financial dealings to another person. You are right to be cautious in this regard. Don't rush this decision, but make it if you think it's the right move for the company.

Don't Believe Your Own Advertising

Here is a quick note for your consideration. You really have three faces when your company is small: the face your company presents to the outside world of prospects and customers, the face you present to your staff and other company personnel, and the face you present to confidants and family. The one you present to the outside world is essentially your "advertising" face and should not be confused with reality.

You would never advertise that your company is struggling with a particular issue or problem. This doesn't mean the problem doesn't exist, just that you are dealing with it quietly and internally. You may advertise that your services are the best in town, but if customer feedback indicates satisfaction problems, you need to address them or you are out of business. If you believe your advertising, you may think things are fine when they are really in trouble.

Keep your ego out of the way and monitor company performance with a keen eye on reality. Make your external promotions as positive, upbeat, and benefit-oriented as possible, but don't deceive yourself or your staff in the process. There are always internal struggles that you must deal with in order for your company to continue to be successful.

When Is It Time for You to Step Aside?

Here is a tough one. When is it time to let go and turn the reins over to someone else? Every situation is different, but here are a few points to consider.

1. Are you doing what you want to do? Just because you started the business doesn't mean that you must still like it. Would you rather be doing something else on a daily basis?
2. Would you serve the company better in another capacity? Perhaps the temperament that served the company in start-up mode no longer applies to a maturing business. Should you turn over the day-to-day operations to your more consistent associate who likes the daily grind?

3. Should you merge the company with another, so the joint skills and marketing capabilities together can be more powerful than the two separately? The president of the other company could become president of the new company. This takes care of your people, clients, and you.
4. Do your employees want to own the company? Perhaps you should sell the company to them, freeing you up for other entrepreneurial ventures.

You will know when the time is right to get out of the way. If you have a corporation with a board of directors, they will probably let you know when you become more of a liability to the company than an asset. This isn't a personal insult, just recognition that different skills may now be needed to grow the company. Your business is now at the point where professional management needs to take over and the entrepreneur needs to look for new business and growth opportunities.

Instead of treating opportunities for change and transition as a negative, I encourage you to view it as an opportunity and look for the right combination of talents and positions. You were successful before, and you will be successful again. Sharing that success is a treat rarely experienced; consider yourself lucky to have the opportunity.

The Least You Need to Know

I have bad news for you. This entrepreneurial stuff is addictive, and once you get a taste of small business success, it is tough to not want more. I guess maybe this is the good news.

Do you remember in the beginning I promised you one of the most exciting rides of your life? Well, here you are, and I hope that our work on this book has contributed to your successful journey. Keep your professional perspective while basking in your success. You earned it!

- Beware of turning over the company checkbook to others without safeguards in place.
- Don't always believe what other people say about you. Don't pretend that there aren't any problems when there really are; just deal with them quietly.
- Don't mix your personal interests with those of the company. Your decisions must make good business sense for the company, or you can cause more harm than good.
- Step aside when the time is right. Treat your obsolescence as a sign of your success instead of as a threat to your survival. You may be able to better serve the company in other ways while letting other managers deal with the routine, daily issues.

The Kwik Chek Auto Evaluation Business Plan

June 1995

Bob Smith
Kwik Chek
222 Carson Drive
Austin, TX 12345

Table of Contents

Executive Summary

Kwik Chek Auto Evaluation Service is a comprehensive inspection and evaluation service designed for individuals considering buying a used car in the Austin, Texas area. The inspection is performed at the car's location, eliminating the need to drive the car somewhere else for an evaluation; a complete report of the car's mechanical and electrical condition is provided to the customer. Based on that information, the customer is in a much better position to make a purchase decision regarding a particular used car.

Market Demand

The potential demand for such a service is huge, considering the recent trend away from the purchase of a new automobile and toward the purchase of a less expensive used car, or the trend to maintain an existing car to ensure a longer useful life. With the increased interest in used cars, Kwik Chek has a large potential market for its services. Industry reports indicate that over 81,190 used cars will be purchased in Austin this year alone.

Potential Revenue

Using Kwik Chek's standard price of $49.95, the potential annual revenue would be over $4 million. While it cannot be assumed the company would capture 100 percent of the market, even considering a 20 percent market share, the revenue base would still be over $1 million per year in Austin alone.

Staffing

Bob Smith, a veteran automotive mechanic and business owner, is the president of Kwik Chek. Smith has hired an experienced financial manager to assist in the startup and management of Kwik Chek. Additional technicians and mechanics will be hired to perform the actual services.

Marketing

Advertising, direct mail, and publicity will be used to aggressively promote Kwik Chek's services to the local Austin market.

Financing Needs

In order to establish Kwik Chek and adequately capitalize the company for growth, a $100,000 equity investment is needed. Bob Smith, the president, is personally investing $20,000.

Market Analysis

The Automotive Industry

The recession and general economic downturn of the late '80s and early '90s has had a significant effect on the automotive industry. Consumers who had been purchasing new cars on a regular basis decided instead to maintain and repair their existing cars in order to make them last longer. In addition, consumers who were purchasing cars opted instead for used cars, which retain more of their resale value than new cars.

Used Car Purchases

Evidence of this shift away from new car purchases to used car purchases and increased maintenance is seen in the *Motor Vehicle Manufacturers Association Facts and Figures* from 1988. Between 1980 and 1988, the number of cars on the road increased by 30 million nationwide and the average age of those cars increased from 6.6 years to 7.6 years; obviously, owners are holding onto their cars for longer periods of time before making another purchase.

Seasonality

Car purchases are seasonal in nature, with the peak buying season from March to August. The end of the year and beginning of the year are relatively slow.

Market Size

In Austin, approximately 14 percent of all adults are planning to purchase a used car in a given year, according to the *Scarborough Report on Austin Automobile Purchases*. With an adult population of 569,000, that equates to a total potential market of 81,190 purchases of used cars each year. At a price of $49.95, the total potential revenue for the Austin area would be $4,055,441 annually.

Competition

There are currently two established competitors in the Austin market: Auto Critic and Lemon Busters. Both plan to franchise nationally and offer essentially similar services.

Auto Critic charges $49.50 for its services and checks 90 points on the car. The company has invested heavily in marketing since starting up almost one year ago.

Lemon Busters entered the market only a month ago and charges $59.50 for its services, claiming to check 120 points on the car. This is misleading, however, since they inflate the number of inspection points by counting each individual element (for instance, checking four tires is counted as four points rather than one, two windshield wipers are counted as two, and so on).

Pricing

Five hundred prospective Kwik Chek customers in Austin were sent a one-page mail survey designed to gauge their interest level in such a service. One hundred ten people responded, indicating strong potential demand for Kwik Chek. 70 percent stated they would use the service "at any price," while the remainder found the service to be priced right in the $40–$60 range, with $49 "about right."

Information from the Credit Union National Association (CUNA) also supported pricing of the service in the $40 range in its *Guide to Buying and Selling a Used Car*. In its publication, CUNA advocates hiring a mechanic or car care center to evaluate a car before making a purchase and states the cost for this service should be "$40 or less."

Business Description

Kwik Chek Auto Evaluation provides potential used car buyers with a comprehensive report at a cost of $49.95 on the condition of a car they are considering purchasing. With Kwik Chek, an experienced mechanic performs a careful inspection of over 90 points on the car, reporting any problem areas or defects to the customer. Armed with substantial information about the mechanical and electrical condition of the car, the customers can decide for themselves whether the car is worth the purchase price.

Because used cars are purchased "as-is," the purchaser is generally unaware of any potential mechanical defects that would affect the cost of repairs and maintenance. With Kwik Chek, individuals considering purchasing a used car can have a complete inspection and evaluation performed to identify potential trouble spots in the car.

The evaluation can be performed at the car's location, whether it is a dealer's lot or an individual's home, eliminating the need for the customer to pick up the car and drive it somewhere else for the inspection.

For $49.95, Kwik Chek performs a series of tests in each of the following areas:

- Engine diagnostics
- Suspension and steering
- Brakes

- Accessories
- Transmission
- Lights
- Fluid levels and condition
- Electrical
- Body

A major benefit of using Kwik Chek over the existing method of inspection, which is bringing the car to a mechanic, is the convenience of having the car inspected on the spot.

Competitive Advantage

Despite the fact there are two existing competitors in the Austin area, Kwik Chek has several key advantages. They include:

- Bob Smith is a long-time resident of Austin, having established and managed two previously successful entrepreneurial ventures.
- Our well-developed marketing plan will immediately increase awareness of Kwik Chek and its services. Existing competitors have run ineffective marketing campaigns to-date.
- Kwik Chek is headquartered in downtown Austin, operating from a central hub that will dramatically reduce travel time to customers.
- Pricing is less than one competitor and in line with the other competitor.

Marketing Strategy

Kwik Chek will rely heavily on advertising, direct mail, and publicity to alert potential customers to the company's services. Marketing campaigns developed by existing competitors have heightened awareness of the service but caused confusion regarding how customers can use the service. Kwik Chek intends to build on this increased awareness and improve visibility and knowledge of its services.

Advertising

To focus on residents of Austin, Kwik Chek intends to place small display ads in the local paper for the first six weeks of operation. This exposure will help to quickly build traffic in the shop. The cost of advertising is $4,000.

Direct Mail

Information on Kwik Chek's services will be sent to all residents within a 10-mile radius of the facility, offering a special discount to those who come in by a specific date. A mailing list of local residents will be purchased from a mailing-list broker and a simple color postcard will be designed and distributed to encourage first-time customers to visit Kwik Chek.

Publicity

In order to better explain all the services Kwik Chek has to offer, as well as explain the benefits of using Kwik Chek, press releases will be sent to all local papers. In addition, new hire announcements will be issued as employees are brought on board.

Trade Shows

To make contact with residents who are considering purchasing a car, Kwik Chek will have an exhibit at the local auto show. The audience attending this event is Kwik Chek's target audience, providing valuable exposure at a reasonable price.

The combination of media exposure, direct mail announcements, and regular advertising will help Austin residents quickly become familiar with Kwik Chek and its service offerings.

Operational Plan

In order to service the Austin market, two vans will be purchased for use by mechanics and technicians to travel to customer sites. The vans will be furnished with all necessary analytical and testing equipment.

Customers will call the office to schedule an inspection. A dispatcher will contact mechanics on-duty and send them out to customers.

Mechanics and service technicians will travel by van to customer locations, generally at used car dealer lots, to perform the inspection. Reports will be generated from the van immediately following the inspection by the mechanic, who will also be outfitted with a portable computer and printer. Customers will pay the mechanic by cash or credit card.

Expansion

Once volume reaches the point that customers cannot have a car evaluated within 48 hours, a new van will be purchased and additional mechanics hired to staff it.

Management and Staffing

President

Bob Smith brings his 25 years in the automotive business to Kwik Chek, where he will assume the role of president, overseeing all daily operations of the Austin facility. An experienced mechanic and entrepreneur, Smith intends to quickly expand Kwik Chek into a local chain of evaluation services.

Vice President

Marjorie Jones, an experienced accountant and controller, will handle all the financial aspects of Kwik Chek's operations. Jones joins Kwik Chek after 15 years at a Big Six accounting firm. Her knowledge of financial reporting and cost control will be invaluable to Kwik Chek.

Mechanics

Experienced technicians and mechanics will be hired gradually, as business increases, in order to service customer vehicles. Two will be hired at the start, with approximately eight being added during the first year.

Future Personnel Additions

During the third year, a marketing specialist will be hired to handle all marketing activities for the company.

Funds Needed and Their Uses

To establish Kwik Chek, purchase the vans necessary to operate the service, and invest in marketing methods to quickly build the business, $100,000 is required. Those funds, combined with an investment of $20,000 by the owner, will be used for the following:

Sources	
Investment	$100,000
Equity from owner	$20,000
Total	**$120,000**

Uses	
Purchase of vans	$60,000
Equipment	$15,000
Marketing	$25,000
Office equipment	$10,000
Working capital	$10,000
Total	**$120,000**

Financial Statements

Assumptions

Number of inspection hours per day	11
Number of days per week	7
Inspection hours per week	77
Inspection hours per year	4,004
Maximum inspections per van/month	272
Number of vans needed initially	1.9

Appendix

Résumés of management team

Sample marketing materials

Kwik Chek
PROJECTED CASH FLOW

	January	February	March	April	May	June	July	August	September	October	November	December	1995
Cash On Hand	$10,000	$63,505	$58,187	$52,869	$48,728	$44,587	$41,623	$38,659	$36,872	$36,262	$36,829	$38,573	
Investment	60,000												
REVENUES	$1,177	$2,354	$2,354	$3,531	$3,531	$4,708	$4,708	$5,885	$7,062	$8,239	$9,416	$10,593	$63,558
Total Inflows	$71,177	$65,859	$60,541	$56,400	$52,259	$49,295	$46,331	$44,544	$43,934	$44,501	$46,245	$49,166	
EXPENSES													
Rent	$450	$450	$450	$450	$450	$450	$450	$450	$450	$450	$450	$450	$5,400
Postage	$150	$150	$150	$150	$150	$150	$150	$150	$150	$150	$150	$150	$1,800
Marketing	$1,500	$1,500	$1,500	$1,500	$1,500	$1,500	$1,500	$1,500	$1,500	$1,500	$1,500	$1,500	$18,000
Telephone	$140	$140	$140	$140	$140	$140	$140	$140	$140	$140	$140	$140	$1,680
Answering service	$750	$750	$750	$750	$750	$750	$750	$750	$750	$750	$750	$750	$9,000
Office equipment lease	$336	$336	$336	$336	$336	$336	$336	$336	$336	$336	$336	$336	$4,032
Salaries	$4,000	$4,000	$4,000	$4,000	$4,000	$4,000	$4,000	$4,000	$4,000	$4,000	$4,000	$4,000	$48,000
Paging service	$25	$25	$25	$25	$25	$25	$25	$25	$25	$25	$25	$25	$300
Insurance	$220	$220	$220	$220	$220	$220	$220	$220	$220	$220	$220	$220	$2,640
Maintenance	$101	$101	$101	$101	$101	$101	$101	$101	$101	$101	$101	$101	$1,212
Total Expenses	$7,672	$7,672	$7,672	$7,672	$7,672	$7,672	$7,672	$7,672	$7,672	$7,672	$7,672	$7,672	$92,064
Total Outflow	$7,672	$7,672	$7,672	$7,672	$7,672	$7,672	$7,672	$7,672	$7,672	$7,672	$7,672	$7,672	$92,064
Cash at End of Period	$63,505	$58,187	$52,869	$48,728	$44,587	$41,623	$38,659	$36,872	$36,262	$36,829	$38,573	$41,494	

Kwik Chek

PROJECTED CASH FLOW

	January	February	March	April	May	June	July	August	September	October	November	December	1996
Cash On Hand	$41,494	$34,802	$29,640	$24,479	$20,847	$17,215	$15,113	$13,012	$12,440	$13,399	$15,888	$19,907	
Owner Investment													
REVENUES	$1,530	$3,060	$3,060	$4,590	$4,590	$6,120	$6,120	$7,651	$9,181	$10,711	$12,241	$13,771	$82,625
Total Inflows	$43,024	$37,862	$32,701	$29,069	$25,437	$23,336	$21,234	$20,662	$21,621	$24,110	$28,129	$33,677	
EXPENSES													
Rent	$450	$450	$450	$450	$450	$450	$450	$450	$450	$450	$450	$450	$5,400
Postage	$150	$150	$150	$150	$150	$150	$150	$150	$150	$150	$150	$150	$1,800
Marketing	$1,800	$1,800	$1,800	$1,800	$1,800	$1,800	$1,800	$1,800	$1,800	$1,800	$1,800	$1,800	$21,600
Telephone	$140	$140	$140	$140	$140	$140	$140	$140	$140	$140	$140	$140	$1,680
Answering service	$800	$800	$800	$800	$800	$800	$800	$800	$800	$800	$800	$800	$9,600
Office equipment lease	$336	$336	$336	$336	$336	$336	$336	$336	$336	$336	$336	$336	$4,032
Salaries	$4,200	$4,200	$4,200	$4,200	$4,200	$4,200	$4,200	$4,200	$4,200	$4,200	$4,200	$4,200	$50,400
Paging service	$25	$25	$25	$25	$25	$25	$25	$25	$25	$25	$25	$25	$300
Insurance	$220	$220	$220	$220	$220	$220	$220	$220	$220	$220	$220	$220	$2,640
Maintenance	$101	$101	$101	$101	$101	$101	$101	$101	$101	$101	$101	$101	$1,212
Total Expenses	$8,222	$8,222	$8,222	$8,222	$8,222	$8,222	$8,222	$8,222	$8,222	$8,222	$8,222	$8,222	$98,664
Total Outflow	$8,222	$8,222	$8,222	$8,222	$8,222	$8,222	$8,222	$8,222	$8,222	$8,222	$8,222	$8,222	$98,664
Cash at End of Period	$34,802	$29,640	$24,479	$20,847	$17,215	$15,113	$13,012	$12,440	$13,399	$15,888	$19,907	$25,455	

Kwik Chek
PROJECTED CASH FLOW

	January	February	March	April	May	June	July	August	September	October	November	December	1997
Cash On Hand	$25,455	$18,773	$14,079	$9,385	$6,680	$3,976	$3,260	$2,545	$3,819	$7,081	$12,333	$19,574	
Owner Investment													
REVENUES	$1,989	$3,978	$3,978	$5,967	$5,967	$7,957	$7,957	$9,946	$11,935	$13,924	$15,913	$17,902	$107,413
Total Inflows	$27,445	$22,751	$18,057	$15,352	$12,648	$11,932	$11,217	$12,491	$15,753	$21,005	$28,246	$37,476	
EXPENSES													
Rent	$450	$450	$450	$450	$450	$450	$450	$450	$450	$450	$450	$450	$5,400
Postage	$150	$150	$150	$150	$150	$150	$150	$150	$150	$150	$150	$150	$1,800
Marketing	$2,000	$2,000	$2,000	$2,000	$2,000	$2,000	$2,000	$2,000	$2,000	$2,000	$2,000	$2,000	$24,000
Telephone	$140	$140	$140	$140	$140	$140	$140	$140	$140	$140	$140	$140	$1,680
Answering service	$850	$850	$850	$850	$850	$850	$850	$850	$850	$850	$850	$850	$10,200
Office equipment lease	$336	$336	$336	$336	$336	$336	$336	$336	$336	$336	$336	$336	$4,032
Salaries	$4,400	$4,400	$4,400	$4,400	$4,400	$4,400	$4,400	$4,400	$4,400	$4,400	$4,400	$4,400	$52,800
Paging service	$25	$25	$25	$25	$25	$25	$25	$25	$25	$25	$25	$25	$300
Insurance	$220	$220	$220	$220	$220	$220	$220	$220	$220	$220	$220	$220	$2,640
Maintenance	$101	$101	$101	$101	$101	$101	$101	$101	$101	$101	$101	$101	$1,212
Total Expenses	$8,672	$8,672	$8,672	$8,672	$8,672	$8,672	$8,672	$8,672	$8,672	$8,672	$8,672	$8,672	$104,064
Total Outflow	$8,672	$8,672	$8,672	$8,672	$8,672	$8,672	$8,672	$8,672	$8,672	$8,672	$8,672	$8,672	$104,064
Cash at End of Period	$18,773	$14,079	$9,385	$6,680	$3,976	$3,260	$2,545	$3,819	$7,081	$12,333	$19,574	$28,804	

Kwik Chek
PROJECTED INCOME STATEMENT

	1995	1996	1997
REVENUE	**$63,558**	**$82,625**	**$107,413**
OPERATING EXPENSES			
Rent	$5,400	$5,400	$5,400
Postage	$1,800	$1,800	$1,800
Marketing	$18,000	$21,600	$24,000
Telephone	$1,680	$1,680	$1,680
Answering service	$9,000	$9,600	$10,200
Office equipment lease	$4,032	$4,032	$4,032
Salaries	$48,000	$50,400	$52,800
Paging service	$300	$300	$300
Insurance	$2,640	$2,640	$2,640
Maintenance	$1,212	$1,212	$1,212
TOTAL EXPENSES	$92,064	$98,664	$104,064
NET PROFIT BEFORE TAXES	($28,506)	($16,039)	$3,349
TAXES	$0	$0	$1,172
NET INCOME	**($28,506)**	**($16,039)**	**$2,177**

Kwik Chek PROJECTED BALANCE SHEET	**1995**	**1996**	**1997**
ASSETS			
Current Assets			
Cash	9,000	12,000	18,000
Total Current Assets	**9,000**	**12,000**	**18,000**
Property and Equipment			
Vehicle	60,000	78,000	60,000
Equipment	15,000	19,500	15,000
Less:			
Accumulated Depreciation	15,000	19,500	15,000
Total Property and Equipment	**60,000**	**78,000**	**60,000**
TOTAL ASSETS	**$69,000**	**$90,000**	**$78,000**
LIABILITIES			
Current Liabilities			
Accounts Payable	2,000	2,400	2,900
Total Current Liabilities	2,000	2,400	2,900
Long-Term Debt	0	0	0
Equity	67,000	87,600	75,100
TOTAL LIABILITIES AND EQUITY	**$69,000**	**$90,000**	**$78,000**

Sources

Almanac of Business and Industrial Financial Ratios. Prentice Hall, 1992 Edition, ISBN: 0-13-038282-5.

The Best Home Businesses for the '90s. Paul and Sarah Edwards. Jeremy P. Tarcher/ Putnam Books, 1994 Edition, ISBN: 0-87477-784-4.

The Complete Communications Handbook. Ed Paulson. Wordware Publishing, 1992, ISBN: 1-55622-238-6.

Creating the Successful Business Plan for New Ventures. LaRue Hosmer. McGraw-Hill, 1985, ISBN: 0-07-030452-1.

The Essence of Small Business. Colin Barrow. Prentice Hall, 1993, ISBN: 013285-362-0.

Getting Paid In Full. W. Kelsea Wilber. Sourcebooks Inc., 1994, ISBN: 0-942061-68-3.

The Internet Roadmap. Bennett Falk. Sybex, 1994, ISBN: 0-7821-1365-6.

Job and Career Building. Richard Germann and Peter Arnold. 10 Speed Press, 1980, ISBN: 0-89815-048-5.

"A Liability Shield for Entrepreneurs." Ripley Hotch. *Nation's Business*, August, 1994.

The Little Online Book. Alfred Glossbrenner. Peachpit Press, 1995, ISBN: 1-566609-130-6.

Nobody Gets Rich Working for Somebody Else: An Entrepreneur's Guide. Roger Fritz. Dodd, Mead & Company, Inc., 1987, ISBN: 0-39608877-5.

The Personnel Policy Handbook for Growing Companies. Darien McWhirter. Bob Adams, Inc., 1994, ISBN: 1-55850-430-3.

Small Claims Court Without a Lawyer. W. Kelsea Wilber. Sourcebooks Inc., ISBN: 0-942061-32-2.

Additional Reading

The 7 Habits of Highly Effective People. Covey. Fireside/Simon & Schuster, 1989, ISBN: 0-671-70863-5.

1000 Things You Never Learned in Business School. Yeomans. Mentor, 1985, ISBN: 0-451-62810-1.

Beyond Entrepreneurship. Collins and Lazier. Prentice Hall, 1992, ISBN: 0-13-085366-6.

Business Owner's Guide to Accounting and Bookkeeping. Placencia, Welge, and Oliver. Oasis Press, 1991, ISBN: 1-55571-156-1.

The CompuServe Yellow Pages. Tidrow. New Riders Publishing, 1994, ISBN: 1-56205-396-5.

Essentials of Media Plannning. Barban, Cristol, and Kopec. NTC Business Books, 1989, ISBN: 0-8442-3018-9.

Financing the Small Business. Tuller. Prentice Hall, 1991, ISBN: 0-13-322116-4.

Free Money for Small Businesses and Entrepreneurs. Blum. John Wiley, 1992, ISBN: 0-471-58122-4.

Home Based Mail Order. Bond. Liberty Press, 1990, ISBN: 0-8306-3045-7.

How to Advertise and Promote Your Small Business. McClung and Siegel. Wiley Press, 1978, ISBN: 0-471-04032-0.

How to Start a Service Business. Chant and Morgan. Avon, 1994, ISBN: 0-380-77-77-6.

How to Think Like an Entrepreneur. Shane. Bret Publishing, 1994, ISBN: 0-9640346-0-3.

Inc Yourself. McQuown. Harper Business, 1992, ISBN: 0-88730-611-X.

The Internet Business Guide. Resnick and Taylor. Sams, 1994, ISBN: 0-672-30530-5.

One Minute for Myself. Spencer. Avon, 1985, ISBN: 0-380-70308-4.

Start, Run and Profit from Your Own Home-Based Business. Kishel. John Wiley, 1991, ISBN: 0-471-52587-1.

Starting Right in Your New Business. Tetreault and Clements. Addison-Wesley, 1988, ISBN: 0-201-07795-7.

The Strategy Game. Hickman. McGraw-Hill, 1993, ISBN: 0-07-028725-2.

The Successful Business Plan. Abrams. Oasis Press, 1993, ISBN: 1-55571-194-4.

Using CompuServe. Ellsworth. Que, 1994, ISBN: 1-56529-726-1.

West's Business Law. Clarkson, Miller, Jentz, and Cross. West Publishing Company, 1989, ISBN: 0-314-47214-2.

Glossary

advisory board A group of business associates who act as advisors to your company on an informal basis. You can set regular meeting dates and times for the group to come together to discuss business issues, but you do not compensate advisors for their advice. You may want to pay for dinner, though, so they know you appreciate their time.

assets Those items of value the company owns, such as cash in the checking account, accounts receivables, equipment, and property.

authorized shares The total number of shares of stock the corporation is permitted to issue. For instance, if 1,000 shares of stock are authorized at the start of the corporation, only a total of 1,000 shares can ever be sold to shareholders—no more than that.

bad debt ratio The ratio of the amount of money you believe customers will never pay (also called uncollectible funds) divided by total sales, expressed as a percent.

balance sheet One type of financial statement that you (or your accountant) create to show all the company's assets and all the liabilities and equity owned by investors. The value of your assets must equal the value of your liabilities and equity for the statement to balance, which is where the term came from.

banking day The days of the week that banks are open for business. You must make deposits at the bank before a certain time of day, which is usually around 3:00 p.m., in order for the deposit to be credited on that same day. If you make the deposit after the 3:00 p.m. cutoff, the deposit will not be credited to your account until the next banking day, which may be the next day or, if you make a deposit near the end of the week, the next banking day may not be until Monday of the next week.

benefit What the customer gains by using your product or service. For example, the benefits of the drill bit are that it makes holes.

board of accountancy The group of accountants that makes decisions regarding generally accepted accounting principles.

board of directors A group of experienced business leaders who are asked or elected to serve as advisors to a company. In return for assuming responsibility for the long-term growth of the company, directors generally receive either cash compensation or shares of stock. In other cases, the largest shareholders may ask for or require a seat on the board of directors as a means of protecting their large stake in the company.

bookkeeping Involves accurately tracking where your money is coming from and where it is going. You can hire a bookkeeper to manage your record-keeping or invest in a computer program to do much the same thing. Bookkeepers are not necessarily accountants, though they do help organize all your information for use by your accountant.

brutal honesty Saying all of those things to yourself that you would hate someone else to say to you. You will thank yourself later for the candor.

business inertia The inability of a company to change its thinking or ways of doing business. Generally, larger, more bureaucratic companies have more inertia than smaller, leaner businesses that can respond quickly to changes in the marketplace.

business judgment rule Protects members of corporate boards of directors from lawsuits filed by shareholders, customers, or others if the decision that caused the lawsuit was made in the best interests of the corporation.

C corporation The business structure used primarily by major corporations so they can sell shares of stock to the public. Other forms of a corporation have restrictions on the number of shareholders that can exist, while a C corporation does not.

cash flow analysis A financial statement that shows how much money the company had at the beginning of the month, how much money came in through sales and payments, how much went out in the form of payments, and what was left at the end of the month. Successful entrepreneurs watch the amount of money coming in and going out of a company (cash flow) very carefully so the business doesn't run out of cash.

Chart of Accounts A list of all the categories a business uses to organize its financial expenditures and sales.

clipping services Companies such as Bacon's and Luce Clipping Services read thousands of newspapers and magazines on the lookout for articles about or references to specific companies that have hired them to do this. Many businesses hire clipping services to watch for articles about their company and the competition. Unless you have the time to read virtually every major business magazine and newspaper, you may want to hire some professionals to do it for you.

close A request by the salesperson for a specific action on the customer's part. Asking for the order is the ultimate close, but there are smaller closes that occur at each stage of the selling process to gradually move the customer closer to the sale.

close corporation Owners or shareholders are active in the daily management of the corporation, which has no public investors.

commodities Products that have no distinguishing features or benefits, such as flour, salt, and pork bellies, so that there is little or no difference in pricing between competitive products.

consideration Something of value, such as money or a right to do something, that is given usually at the signing of a contract.

corporation A type of corporation such as the Subchapter S and Subchapter C used by professionals such as attorneys and accountants. Such corporations have "P.C." after the company name to indicate the company is a professional corporation.

cost of sales The costs directly linked to the production or sale of a product or service, also called the Cost of Goods Sold (COGS). These generally include the cost of raw materials, the cost of labor to run the machine that produced the widget you sold, and other expenses that were required in order to sell the product or service.

cost plus pricing Calculating your price using the cost to the company plus your desired profit margin. So a widget that costs $1 to produce with a desired 50 percent profit margin would sell for $1/.5 = $2.

current assets Company assets that are liquid or can be converted to cash in less than one year.

debt financing A means of securing funding to start or expand your business by way of a loan of some sort. The business takes on debt, instead of investors, as a way of getting the money it needs now.

demographic profile Usually refers to a specific set of demographic characteristics used by sales and marketing to target likely sales prospects. Sometimes called an "ideal customer profile."

demographics A set of objective characteristics that describe a group of people. Includes characteristics such as age, home ownership, number of children, marital status, residence location, job function, and other criteria.

depreciation Since nothing lasts forever, accountants assume everything you own decreases in value over time. So every year, a portion of an item's value is subtracted based on how long it is expected to last. Computers, for instance, are expected to last just three to five years. So every year for three years, one-third of the value of the computer is taken as an expense on the balance sheet. Buildings, which have a much longer useful life, have a much smaller percentage subtracted each year.

direct competitor Anyone who can, and will, eat your lunch today if you let them. (These are companies that sell the same product or service your company does, going after the same customers.)

distribution channel However your product or service gets from your facilities into the hands of customers. Different ways of distributing your product include direct sales, using employees to sell your offerings, retail stores, mail order, and independent sales representatives or manufacturers' representatives.

dividends Money paid to shareholders out of the corporation's net income (after taxes are taken out). This is a form of compensation to the shareholders for having made the investment in the corporation by purchasing shares.

Doing Business As (DBA) When you start a sole proprietorship that is named something other than your given name, you must complete some forms to officially use that name. The form you complete is a Doing Business As, or DBA, form. For instance, Jane Smith & Associates would need to file a DBA form at the county clerk's office because it's something other than just Jane Smith.

double taxation Where the business pays tax on its annual profits and then passes the income to you, the majority shareholder, who again gets taxed at the personal level; thus, the same dollar has been taxed twice.

employee manual A document prepared by the company and issued to all employees indicating the company's policies and procedures.

equity financing When someone gives you money in return for ownership of a portion of your company. You are giving up equity in the business in return for capital, which is *equity financing*. The other kind of financing is *debt financing*, which is when you get a loan that is paid back later. Equity financing does not get paid back. Investors get their money back by selling their shares to someone else.

factoring The process of receiving money now for payments your customers are expected to make to you in the next few weeks. There is a cost to having that money now though, which is paid in the form of a percentage fee to the factoring company or factor.

feature The different characteristics of a product or service. For example, the features of a drill bit might include its size, length, and the type of material it is made of.

federal tax deposit coupon Coupons issued by the IRS for collection of withholding taxes on a regular basis. Your Employee ID Number (EIN) and amount due for the tax period are printed on the coupon. The coupon then accompanies your check made payable for the amount due.

fictitious name statement See *Doing Business As*.

fixed expenses Business expenses that do not vary each month based on the amount of sales, such as rent, equipment leases, and salaries. Payments for these expenses are essentially the same each month, whether you achieve $1 million or $1 in sales.

float The time period during which you have to cover expenses that should have been paid out of money received from customers. During this time, you are essentially lending money to your customers.

franchisor A company that has created a successful business operation and concept that offers to sell the rights to the operation and idea on a limited geographic or market basis. The buyer of the franchise rights is called the *franchisee*.

free-lancer An individual who works for several different companies at once, helping out on specific projects. Free-lancers are like consultants and are paid a set rate for their services, no benefits, no sick pay, no vacation allowance. The advantage is that free-lancers can usually set their own hours, earn a higher hourly rate than they would get from full-time employment, and work with more than one company at a time.

gross profit The amount of money left after you cover the cost of sales. Out of gross profit, you pay your operational expenses. Gross profit = revenue – cost of sales.

income statement A type of financial statement that reflects all the income and expenses for a particular period of time, which is generally a year.

independent contractor Another word for a free-lancer that the IRS frequently uses. It means that the company you're doing work for is not your employer. You have the freedom to decide when, where, and how you will get the work done that your client has given you. You pay your own taxes and benefits but you can also deduct expenses associated with getting your work done, such as for a business phone line, travel, and supplies.

industrial espionage The practice of collecting information about competitors through devious methods. Using public information sources that everyone has access to isn't considered espionage, but rummaging through corporate waste paper baskets after hours would be.

inertia Indisposition to motion, exertion, or change; resistance to change.

interests Things that you enjoy doing, including the parts of your current job that you like the most, as well as what you do for fun in your spare time.

job description A detailed listing of the duties to be performed by the person filling the job in question; a listing of the required skills, education, certification levels, and other criteria directly related to the job.

liabilities Amounts that you owe. Typical liabilities include loans, credit cards, taxes owed, and other people to whom you owe money. Short-term liabilities, which are paid back within 12 months, are also called accounts payable. Long-term liabilities include mortgages and equipment loans.

life cycle A product or service goes through four distinct phases between being introduced to the market and being discontinued or taken off the market. From embryonic, to growth, to maturity, to decline, all products or services eventually progress.

Limited Liability Company (LLC) A new type of business structure available in almost every state that has many of the advantages of a partnership or Subchapter S corporation but fewer of its disadvantages.

limited partnership A special form of partnership in which a partner invests money and does not participate in the daily operation of the business. This partner is also only liable for the amount of money he has invested, and no more.

liquid assets Anything the company owns that can be quickly sold and turned into cash, such as accounts receivables, computer equipment, or stocks and bonds. Assets such as buildings or huge machinery would not be considered "liquid" because selling them would take a considerable amount of time.

logistics The set of activities that deal with making the daily routine effective. The daily grind of answering the phone, mailing letters, and dealing with customers takes time. You will probably need clerical help once you become successful to offload the daily routine paperwork so you can have time for other activities.

maintenance temperament Someone who enjoys keeping established systems running like a well-oiled machine.

managerial accountants Help you use your financial information to make business decisions. Generally, these accountants are on staff at a company and are responsible for recordkeeping and reporting.

manipulation When customers feel that they are not in control of the sales process—that they will be encouraged and persuaded to purchase something they don't really need. Underlying this activity is the sense the salesperson really doesn't have the customer's needs and interests at heart.

market niche A segment of the market that has an existing need for a product or service that nobody currently offers.

market positioning Creating a positive image in the minds of potential and existing customers. The purpose of market positioning is to have potential customers perceive your product or service in a particular way that makes them more likely to want to buy from you.

market segmentation Dividing the total available market (everyone who may ever buy) into smaller groups, or segments, by specific attributes such as age, sex, location, interests, industry, or other pertinent criteria.

market value The value of a product or service as determined by what the market will pay for it. The market value of a used computer is much less than what a business probably paid for it because computer values decline quickly.

market-based pricing Where offerings are priced at a level set by what everyone else is charging, rather than by costs. With this strategy, you can generally make more money assuming your competition is charging reasonable rates and you can keep your costs down.

marketing Involves selecting the right product, pricing strategy, promotional program, and distribution outlets for your particular audience or market.

marketing theme The overall thought that pops into people's minds when they think of your company and its offerings. For example, Pepsi's theme is "youth." Their soda is the drink for people who feel, or really are, young—the "new" generation.

markup The amount of money over and above the cost of producing a product or service that is added to pay for overhead expenses and profit.

merchant number A number given to your company that is used to identify which account should be credited when a customer makes a purchase. It also verifies that you're allowed to accept credit cards in payment.

mind share The portion of a person's thinking processes that includes perceptions of your company's offerings. One hundred percent mindshare means that any time he needs your type of offering, he thinks of your company.

net income Money left over after all company expenses have been paid out of revenues. Net income can be either positive or negative, depending on how good a year you had, but it can't stay negative for long or you'll be bankrupt.

noncompete clause An agreement employees or suppliers sign indicating they won't steal your ideas or business methods and go to work for a competitor or become competitors by starting their own firm. Generally, noncompete clauses are one section in a larger employment agreement.

nuisance Someone who takes up a lot of your time but really poses no threat to your lunch plans. (A weak competitor who has no clue.)

officers Senior members of a management team or board of directors elected to serve as secretary, treasurer, president, and vice president of the corporation or board.

operational expenses Those expenses associated with just running your business. No matter how much you sell this month, you will still have these expenses. These include your salary, your rent payment, the cost of the electricity in your office, and other similar costs of operating the company.

opportunity cost The profit that would have been gained by pursuing another investment instead of the one currently in process. For example, if you go out on a date with one person, you lose the potentially good time you could have had with someone else. Sound familiar? That is opportunity cost.

outsourcing Corporate-speak for hiring outside consultants, free-lancers, or companies to provide services that in the past have been provided by employees.

owner's equity What is left over when the liabilities are subtracted from the assets. Take what you have, subtract what you owe, and you are left with owner's equity. This is the number that you want to maximize since it reflects the value of your company. The initial value of your company stock and retained earnings are added together to calculate owner's equity.

partnership When you and one or more people form a business marriage; your debts and assets are legally linked from the start. Any partner can make a commitment for the business, which also commits the other partners.

perceived value The overall value the customer places on a particular product or service. This includes much more than price and considers other features such as delivery lead time, quality of salesmanship, service, style, and other less tangible items than the price. Essentially, a perceived value pricing strategy means determining what people are willing to pay and charging that amount, assuming you can still cover all your costs.

percentage markup The amount of money a business adds into a product's price, over and above the cost of the product, expressed as a percent. So a piece of candy costing $.05 to produce that has a markup of $.10 (meaning that the price to the consumer is $.15) has a percentage markup of 200 percent. This is calculated by taking the original cost and dividing it into the amount of markup, and then multiplying the result times 100.

personal attributes Things like being patient, working with other people, taking initiative, and other intrinsic personality-related traits.

pretax profit The amount of money left over after all the business expenses and costs of goods sold are subtracted from total sales, but before taxes have been subtracted and paid.

price erosion When competitive sales present enough alternate product selections to your customers that you must drop your price to keep their business. This erodes both price and profit margins.

price war When all competitors compete based on price and keep undercutting their competitors to get sales. As each company lowers its own price, others drop their prices to compete, resulting in profit margins in the industry as a whole falling to critically low levels.

product positioning A conscious attempt on the part of your company to differentiate between your offering and those of your competitors. You "position" your product in people's minds by creating a perception of your product or service so that potential customers think of your products or services when they have a need.

prospectus A formal legal document a company prepares before being able to sell shares of stock to the public. The prospectus details all the pros and cons of investing in that company, so the potential purchaser of the company's stock is fully informed of the potential risks upfront.

proxy statement A form distributed to shareholders who will not be attending the company's annual meeting so their votes regarding the election of the board of directors, or other issues, can be counted. If a shareholder cannot attend the company's annual meeting but wants to vote, he can submit a signed proxy statement turning over the right to vote a certain way to the board.

pull and push marketing strategy A *pull strategy* convinces your potential customers to request your offering through their suppliers. In essence, the end user pulls your offering through the distribution channel by putting pressure on suppliers to carry it in their inventory. A *push strategy* sells your product to distributors, who then promote it to their customers. A pull strategy is driven by customers. A push strategy is driven by distributors.

registered agent The official contact point for all legal matters. The registered agent is located at the registered office, which is the official address for corporate business.

retained earnings Earnings from the company that are reinvested in operating the business. An item usually found on a company's balance sheet.

revenue Money you receive from customers as payment for your services or the sale of your product. Some people also call it sales.

routine tasks Things you do that are pretty much the same as the last time you did them, except for minor variations. Printing out monthly invoices or counting inventory are two routine tasks that don't take much brain power but that have to be done.

sales Begins where marketing leaves off and involves all the steps you take to get the customer to buy your product or service.

sales revenue targets The sales goals you set that affect all the other financial figures.

scattergun marketing A scattergun sends buckshot in a wide pattern in the hopes of hitting something. Scattergun marketing sends marketing information everywhere in the hopes that someone will hear it and buy—the opposite of target marketing.

secured line of credit A line of credit that has some form of asset as collateral.

shareholders Any individual or organization that owns shares of stock in a company.

short-term loan A loan that is to be paid off within one year.

skills Acquired skills such as typing, speaking a foreign language, playing golf, and so on.

sole proprietorship You transact business without the legal "safety net" associated with a corporation. You are personally responsible for all the business' obligations, such as debt.

startup temperament Someone who thrives on new and exciting projects and challenges.

strategy A careful plan or method; the art of devising or employing plans toward a goal.

Subchapter S corporation A type of corporation that has a limited number of shareholders, and the profits are passed directly through to the owner.

sunk cost Money already spent that you cannot recover. Does not take into account opportunity cost or how else you could have spent the money.

tactical Relating to small-scale actions serving a larger purpose, such as a strategy.

target marketing A marketing approach involving focusing your marketing efforts on those groups—those potential customers—most likely to buy your products or services.

tax accounting A type of accounting concerned solely with how much money you will have to pay in taxes. Tax accountants can help you take steps to minimize your tax bill.

underwriter A company responsible for marketing and selling shares of stock in a company to outside investors.

unqualified prospect An individual who says he needs your product or service but who has not yet confirmed he is able to make the purchase decision. To be sure you are dealing with someone who can buy from you, work through the four qualification criteria.

unsecured line of credit A line of credit such as a credit card that a company can turn to for cash and that is not backed by some form of collateral. Secured lines of credit are usually backed by some form of deposit, accounts receivable statement, or other company asset that the bank can use to pay off the debt if the company can't pay off the line of credit.

variable expenses Those costs that vary according to how much of a product or service is produced. Just as things usually cost less when you buy them in bulk, producing a product in large quantities works the same way. The more you produce, generally the lower the cost per product. So the cost of sales varies according to how much is produced.

wealth Consistently having money left over after all your bills are paid.

Index

A

B

C

D

E

F

G-H

I

J-K

L

M

Q-R

S

T

U-V

W-Z